Praise for *Blood, Bones & Butter*

"Luminous . . . [Readers will] marvel at Hamilton's masterly facility with language."

—*The Washington Post*

"Magnificent. Simply the best memoir by a chef. *Ever.*"
—ANTHONY BOURDAIN

"It's a story of hungers specific and vague, conquered and unappeasable . . . There are rhapsodic passages aplenty about eating and cooking, and while such reveries can easily seem forced or trite, [Gabrielle Hamilton's] ring sweetly true. She's recounting actual rapture, not contriving its facsimile on cue. You can feel her amazement as her father roasts whole lambs on a spit and her awe at the dexterity with which the chef André Soltner pulls off a perfect omelet, using only a fork."
—FRANK BRUNI, *The New York Times Book Review*

"The best chef book since Anthony Bourdain's *Kitchen Confidential* . . . the book makes Hamilton as real to us as someone we've known all our lives and captures the essence of contemporary cool on the plate."
—JOSH OZERSKY, *Time*

"This book is every bit as rich and satisfying as the marrow bones the author roasts at Prune."
—MICHAEL RUHLMAN, *The Wall Street Journal*

"At its core, *Blood, Bones & Butter* is about falling in love with food, every day, over the course of a lifetime. It's a romance. Hamilton's writing about food is so vivid it could make you half-crazed with hunger, leaving you in front of the open fridge with a cold chicken leg in one hand and the book in the other."

—*The Boston Globe*

"A searing, sometimes painful, always engaging account of a life that revolves around food as Earth does its sun."

—DIANNA MARDER, *The Philadelphia Inquirer*

"*Blood, Bones & Butter* fits squarely in the tradition of triumph-over-screwed-up-childhood memoirs by Tobias Wolff or Mary Karr. It's just plain great. Hamilton's writing is as vigorous, evocative and un-adorned as her cooking."

—*Newsday*

"A memoir that flings open the kitchen door to expose the back-breaking toil and passionate obsession of a world-class chef."

—*O: The Oprah Magazine*

"Move over, celebrity cupcake bakers, molecular gastronomists, loca-vores, and other assorted foodies: a new food writing hero is here. Gabrielle Hamilton might hate that title just as much as she despises being called a 'female chef,' but she deserves it—and goes beyond it. Her memoir transcends food writing and is just plain good writing. Is there room on the shelves for another food memoir? Yes. Especially if that memoir is Gabrielle Hamilton's *Blood, Bones & Butter*."

—LYNN ANDRIANI, *Publishers Weekly*

"Like Prune, which starts as a restaurant but ultimately resonates as a feeling, *Blood, Bones & Butter* uses the edible, subtly and skillfully, to initiate and announce the exploration of bigger things."

—*Elle*

Blood, Bones & Butter

Blood Asparagus
11" x 11"
human blood on paper towel
2000
Gabrielle Hamilton

Blood, Bones & Butter

The Inadvertent Education
of a Reluctant Chef

Gabrielle Hamilton

RANDOM HOUSE TRADE PAPERBACKS | NEW YORK

Originally published in hardcover and in slightly different form in the United
States by Random House, an imprint of The Random House Publishing Group,
a division of Random House, Inc., in 2011.

Portions of this work were originally published in different form in
Food & Wine and *The New Yorker.*
The essay by Gabrielle Hamilton contained within the Reader's Guide
was originally published in different form in *Bon Appetit* as
"Blood, Bones & Baked Eggplant" (January 2011).

Grateful acknowledgment is made to the following for permission
to reprint previously published material:
The New York Times: "The Summer Cook: Ode to Joy: A Trip to Alda's Kitchen"
by Gabrielle Hamilton, *The New York Times,* 17 Aug. 2005: F1, copyright © 2005
by *The New York Times.* All rights reserved. Used by permission and protected by
the Copyright Laws of the United States. The printing, copying, redistribution or
retransmission of the Material without express written permission is prohibited.

Trustees of Hampshire College: "The Pantry Game" by Gabrielle Hamilton,
copyright © 1984 by Gabrielle Hamilton. Originally appeared in *Norwottuck,*
Fall 1984. Reprinted courtesy of the Trustees of Hampshire College.

Library of Congress Cataloging-in-Publication Data
Hamilton, Gabrielle.
Blood, bones & butter / Gabrielle Hamilton.
p. cm.
ISBN 978-0-8129-8088-2
eBook ISBN 978-1-58836-931-4
1. Hamilton, Gabrielle. 2. Chefs—New York (State)—New York—Biography.
3. Restaurateurs—New York (State)—New York—Biography. I. Title.
TX649.H345A3 2011
641.5092—dc22
[B]
2010017518

Printed in the United States of America

www.randomhousereaderscircle.com

4 6 8 9 7 5

Book design by Susan Turner

This book is dedicated to all of my families—the one I come from, the one I married into, the one I am making with my own children, and the one I cook with every day at the restaurant. You are my blood, my bones, and, for sure, my sweet butter.

Blood, Bones & Butter

Blood

1

We threw a party. The same party, every year, when I was a kid. It was a spring lamb roast, and we roasted four or five whole little guys who each weighed only about forty pounds over an open fire and invited more than a hundred people. Our house was in a rural part of Pennsylvania and was not really a house at all but a wild castle built into the burnt-out ruins of a nineteenth-century silk mill, and our backyard was not a regular yard but a meandering meadow, with a creek running through it and wild geese living in it and a Death Slide cable that ran from high on an oak to the bank of the stream and deposited you, shrieking, into the shallow water. Our town shared a border so closely with New Jersey that we could and did walk back and forth between the two states several times in a day by crossing the Delaware River. On weekend mornings we had breakfast at Smutzie's in Lambertville, on the Jersey side, but then we got gas for the car at Sam Williams's Mobil on the New Hope side. In the afternoons after school on the Pennsylvania side, I walked over to the Jersey side and got guitar lessons at Les Parson's guitar shop.

That part of the world, heavily touristed as it was, was an important location of many events in the American Revolutionary War.

George Washington crossed the Delaware here, to victory at the Battle of Trenton, trudging through the snowy woods and surprising the British in spite of some of his troops missing proper shoes, their feet instead wrapped in newspaper and burlap. But now my hometown has become, mostly, a sprawl of developments and subdivisions, gated communities of small mansions that look somewhat like movie sets that will be taken down at the end of the shoot. Each housing development has a "country" name—Squirrel Valley, Pine Ridge, Eagle Crossing, Deer Path—which has an unkind way of invoking and recalling the very things demolished when building them. There is now a McDonald's and a Kmart—but when I was growing up, you had to ride your bike about a mile down a very dark country road thick with night insects stinging your face to even find a plugged-in Coke machine where you could buy a vended soda for thirty-five cents. Outside Cal's Collision Repair in the middle of the night that machine glowed like something almost religious. You can now buy a Coke twenty-four hours a day at half a dozen places.

But when I was young, where I lived was mostly farmland, rolling fields, rushing creeks when it rained, thick woods, and hundred-year-old stone barns. It was a beautiful, rough, but lush setting for the backyard party my parents threw with jug wine and spit-roasted lambs and glow-in-the-dark Frisbees. The creek dividing the meadow meandered and, at its deepest bend, was lined with small weeping willows that grew as we grew and bent their long, willowy, tearful branches down over the water. We would braid a bunch of the branches together to make a Tarzan kind of vine rope that we could swing on, out over the stream in our laceless sneakers and bathing suits, and land in the creek. That is where we chilled all of the wines and beers and sodas for the party.

We were five kids in my family, and I am the youngest. We ran in a pack—to school, home from school, and after dinner at dusk—like wild dogs. If the Mellman kids were allowed out and the Bentley boys, the Drevers, and the Shanks across the street as well, our pack numbered fifteen. We spent all of our time out of doors in mud suits, snowsuits, or bare feet, depending on the weather. Even in "nature," running around in the benign woods and hedges and streams, diving in and out of tall grasses and brambles, playing a nighttime game that involved dodging the oncoming headlights of an approaching occasional car, bombing the red shale rocks down into the stream from the narrow bridge near our driveway to watch them shatter—we found rough and not innocent pastimes. We trespassed, drag raced, smoked, burgled, and vandalized. We got ringworm, broken bones, tetanus, concussions, stitches, and ivy poisoning.

My parents seemed incredibly special and outrageously handsome to me then. I could not have boasted of them more or said my name, first and last together, more proudly, to show how it directly linked me to them. I loved that our mother was French and that she had given me that heritage in my very name. I loved telling people that she had been a ballet dancer at the Met in New York City when she married my father. I loved being able to spell her long French name, M-A-D-E-L-E-I-N-E, which had exactly as many letters in it as my own. My mother wore the sexy black cat-eye eyeliner of the era, like Audrey Hepburn and Sophia Loren, and I remember the smell of the sulphur every morning as she lit a match to warm the tip of her black wax pencil. She pinned her dark hair back into a tight, neat twist every morning and then spent the day in a good skirt, high heels, and an apron that I have never seen her without in forty years. She lived in our kitchen, ruled the house with an oily wooden spoon in her hand, and forced us all to eat dark, briny, wrinkled olives, small birds we would have liked as pets, and cheeses that looked like they might well bear Legionnaire's Disease.

Her kitchen, over thirty years ago, long before it was common, had a two-bin stainless steel restaurant sink and a six-burner Garland stove. Her burnt orange Le Creuset pots and casseroles, scuffed and blackened, were constantly at work on the back three burners cooking things with tails, claws, and marrow-filled bones—whatever was budgeted from our dad's sporadic and mercurial artist's income—that she was stewing and braising and simmering to feed our family of seven. Our kitchen table was a big round piece of butcher block where we both ate and prepared casual meals.

My mother knew how to get everything comestible from a shin or neck of some animal; how to use a knife, how to cure a cast-iron pan. She taught us to articulate the "s" in salade niçoise and the soup vichyssoise, so that we wouldn't sound like other Americans who didn't know that the vowel "e" after the consonant "s" in French means that you say the "s" out loud.

And yet I remember the lamb roast as my father's party. I recall it was really his gig. With an art degree from Rhode Island School of Design on his office wall, two union cards—stagehands and scenic artists—in his wallet, five able-bodied children, a French wife, and a photograph torn from a magazine of two Yugoslav guys roasting a lamb over a pit, he created a legendary party—a feast that almost two hundred people came to every year from as far away as the town-houses of New York City and as near as our local elementary school.

My dad could not cook at all. He was then a set designer for the-atrical and trade shows and he had a "design and build" studio in Lambertville—the town where he himself had grown up, the town where his own father had been the local country doctor. We kids were forever running into people who'd say, "Your granddaddy deliv-ered all three of my sons!" Or, "Your granddaddy drove a Cadillac! One of the very few cars at the time in Lambertville!"

After growing up in that small rural town, my dad, the youngest son, went away to college and then to art school. He came back with a mustache, a green Mustang, and a charcoal gray suit and installed himself there, in his hometown. In 1964, he bought the old skating rink at the dead end of South Union Street with its enormous domed ceiling and colossal wooden floor. In that building he started his stu-dio, an open work space where scenery as big as the prow of a ship could be built, erected, painted, and then broken down and shipped off to the city for load-in. Every year when he got the job to build the sets for the Ringling Bros. and Barnum and Bailey Circus there, we would go after school and zip around on the dollies, crashing into the legs of the chain-smoking union carpenters and scenic artists who were busy with band saws and canvas and paint. We would run up and down mountains of rolled black and blue velour, laid out like in a carpet store, and dip our hands into oil drums full of glitter. Prying back the lid on a fifty-gallon barrel of silver glitter—the kind of barrel that took two men and a hand truck to wheel into the paint supply room of the shop—and then shoving your hands down into it up to your elbows is an experience that will secure the idea in your heart for the rest of your life that your dad is, himself, the greatest show on earth.

We made our Halloween costumes out of lighting gels, backstage black velour curtaining, scrim, and Mylar. When we went with our father to see the actual circus at Madison Square Garden, we spent almost the whole show backstage where we met Mishu: The Smallest Man in the World, and petted the long velvety trunks of the elephants in jeweled headdresses. We met Gunther, the lion tamer, and marveled at his blond blond hair and his deep deep tan and, giggling like the children we were, his amazing ass—high and round and firm, like two Easter hams—in electric blue tights.

I associate my dad almost exclusively with that lamb roast because he could dream it up and create the scenery of it. My dad has an eye for things. He can look at the stone rubble covered in scaffolding that is the Acropolis, for example, and without effort, complete the picture in its entirety, right down to what people are wearing, doing, and saying. In his mind's eye, out of one crumbling Doric column, he can visualize the entire city, its denizens and smells, the assembly's agenda and the potted shrubs. Where the rest of us saw only the empty overgrown meadow behind our house, riddled with groundhog holes, with a shallow, muddy stream running through it and a splintering wooden wagon that I had almost outgrown, he saw his friends: artists and teachers and butchers, scenic painters and Russian lighting designers, ship captains and hardware merchants all with a glass in hand, their laughter rising high above our heads and then evaporating into the canopy of maple leaves; the weeping willows shedding their leaf tears down the banks of the stream; fireflies and bagpipers arriving through the low clinging humidity of summer; a giant pit with four spring lambs roasting over apple-wood coals; the smell of wood smoke hanging in the moist summer nighttime air. I mean it. He sees it all romantic like that.

He says, about all of his work, "Everybody else does the bones and makes sure the thing doesn't fall down. I do the romance."

It must have been my mother, the cook, who was in the kitchen with the six burners and the two-bin sink making the lima bean salad and the asparagus vinaigrette and the all-butter shortcakes, counting out the stacks of paper plates with the help of my older sister—the two of them doing "the bones" as my father called it. But it was from him—with his cool, long sideburns and aviator sunglasses, his packet of unfiltered Camels, and box of watercolor paints (and artist's paycheck)—from him we learned how to create beauty where none exists, how to be generous beyond our means, how to change a small corner of the world just by making a little dinner for a few friends. From him we learned how to make and give luminous parties.

There was a Russian Winter Ball, I remember, for which my dad got refrigerator-sized cartons of artificial snow shipped in from Texas and a dry ice machine to fog up the rooms and make the setting feel like a scene from *Dr. Zhivago*. And there was a Valentine's Day Lovers' Dinner, at which my father had hundreds of choux paste éclair swans with little pastry wings and necks and slivered almond beaks that, when toasted, became their signature black. He set them out swimming in pairs on a Plexiglas mirror "pond" the size of a king's matrimonial bed with confectioner's sugar snow drifts on the banks.

"Swans," he pointed out, "mate for life."

For a kind of Moroccan-themed party that my parents threw, my dad built low couches from sheets of plywood and covered them with huge fur blankets and orange velour brought home from the studio. By the time the candles were lit and the electric lights extinguished, the whole house looked like a place where the estimable harem of a great pasha might assemble to offer their man pomegranates, pistachios, and maybe more carnal treasures. There were tapestries and kilims stacked as tall as me, where adults stoned on spiced wine and pigeon pies could lounge. By the time that party really got rolling, I remember walking from room to dimly lit room feeling acutely the ethos of the era—the early 1970s—as if it, too, were sprawled out on the "scene shop" couch wearing long hair and a macramé dress, barely noticing how late it was and that I was still up.

But the lamb roast was not a heavily themed and elaborately staged one-off. It was, as parties in our family went, a simple party, thrown every year, produced with just a fire and a sheet of plywood set over sawhorses for the carving of the lambs. We built a fire in our shallow pit, about eight feet long and six feet wide. It's possible that my dad dug it alone, but if there was an available sixteen-year-old around, like his son, my oldest brother Jeffrey, it's very likely that they dug it together. At each end of the pit they set up a short wall of cinder blocks with a heavy wooden plank on top, looking like the head and baseboards of a giant bed, where the long wooden poles onto which the baby lambs had been lashed would rest. The baby lambs, with their little crooked sets of teeth and milky eyes, were slaughtered and dressed up at Maresca's Butchers, then tied onto ten-foot poles made of ash because the branches of an ash tree grow so straight that you can skewer a baby lamb with them easily.

Jeffrey had a driver's license and a 1957 Chevy truck with a wooden bed and a big blue mushroom painted on its heavily Bondoed cab. It had big dangling side-view mirrors and torn upholstery over which we threw a mover's blanket, but it ran. So on this bluish early summer weekend, Jeffrey drove his new jalopy out the winding country roads, past Black's Christmas tree farm, and past the Larue bottle works. I rode in the bed of the truck, in a cotton dress and boy's shoes with no socks, hanging on as tight as I could to the railings and letting the wind blast my face so hard that I could barely keep my eyes open. Even with my eyes closed, I could tell by the wind and the little patches of bracing coolness and the sudden bright sunshine and the smell of manure when we were passing a hay field, a long thick stand of trees, a stretch of clover, or a horse farm. We passed brand-new deer emerging from the woods and standing in herds of forty in the wide open cornfields. Finally we got to Johnson's Apple Orchard where we picked up our wood for the fire.

The orchard and the Christmas tree farm are long gone, the

butcher shop and the dairy farm are still, oddly, in business, hanging on like grave markers in a sunken and overgrown cemetery—historical "by-the-ways" for the tourists on their way to Bowman's Tower and Washington's Crossing. Where there were four separate places for four separate things, now everybody just goes to the Shopping Plaza to get all of them in one big harshly lit store—milk, apples, meat, even the Christmas tree—while the kids wait in the car and eat fries in the backseat.

At Johnson's orchard, in season, they sold yellow peaches and half a dozen kinds of apples in wooden bushel baskets. But at the time of the lamb roast it was still too early in the year to buy fruit. They had pruned all the trees back for the season, and we filled the truck with the trimmings, piling the apple-wood branches high above the truck bed, which we'd extended with two eight-foot sheets of plywood. This green wood would burn longer and hotter, hissing all night long as the sap dripped down into the flames. On the way back home, I sat up in the cab of the truck between my brother who was driving and my dad who had the window rolled all the way down and his elbow hanging out. He said, "That'll burn with the fragrance of its fruit, you see."

The paraphernalia of butchery may be repulsive to some. But to me, hacksaws, cleavers, and band saws all looked manageable and appealing. I loved going to Maresca's, the Italian butcher shop up the road on the Jersey side, and always asked to be taken along on errands if Maresca's was on the list. There was no "artisanal" at this point, no "organic" or "diver-picked" or "free-range" or "heirloom" anything. In 1976, there was no such thing, even, as 2 percent milk. We just had *milk*. And the Marescas were still just butchers, father and sons butchers—Salvatore, Joe, and Emil—working in a shop with sawdust on the floor. The father Salvatore and his son Joe looked exactly like butchers—with girth, flannel shirts under their long jackets and aprons, and greasy, beefy catcher's-mitt hands. Emil, on the other hand, looked like he could have been a chemist in a lab or a home ec teacher—in an apron, always, but with a V-neck sweater vest over his flannel shirt and a pair of nice brown corduroys. He wanted to be a baseball player, I had heard, but ended up in the family business. Emil spent most of his day in the old kitchen open and adjacent to the butcher shop, skewering and marinating cubed meats and making all the shop's sausages and cooking the daily lunch for the family.

All three Marescas knew as much about an animal as anyone could. They could judge how old an animal was when it was slaughtered by touching the cartilage, how often and what it was fed by examining the fat deposits and marbling in the meat. Pointing out a thick streak of fat in a side of beef, Joe said, "Here you can see the lightning bolt where the rancher started to feed him fast and furious at the end to fatten him up, but what you really want is steady feeding so the fat is marbled throughout."

Outside the shop were two huge forsythia bushes, bursting optimistic and sunny yellow branches. Inside, the refrigerated enamel cases were packed with bloody meat, ground meat, tied meat, and birds, whole and in parts. On the long white tile wall behind the cases, where the Marescas did their actual bloody work, was a giant mural in friendly colors, depicting a roly-poly, mustachioed butcher in a clean white apron, frolicking in a round, green curlicue fenced-in pasture, with cottony white sheep with little soft pink ears and porky, bristleless pink piggies, smiling while sniffing the yellow buttercups. The sky overhead was robin's egg blue, the few clouds were pure white, and the birds and the butterflies went about their song-filled business even though the butcher was wielding a giant cleaver in one hand, headed for one of them. To the right of the mural, hanging from pegs were all manner of hacksaws, cleavers, and giant knives.

Besides meat, Maresca's sold canned goods, and in the spring and summer, a few of the vegetables that Mr. Maresca grew in his garden behind the shop. They were always arranged casually, in a plain carton or basket, on the floor by the refrigerated case, with a handwritten sign on the back of a piece of brown paper bag advertising the price: PEAS 20¢/lb.

I spied those fresh peas in a bushel basket at the end of the counter. While my dad and the guys were talking and leisurely loading the four whole dressed lambs onto newspaper in the back of the truck, I snagged a handful of them and hid behind a display case.

I love how you can snap a pea's stem and pull the string and how it leaves a perfect seam that opens easily under your thumbnail. And then you find those sweet, starchy peas in their own canoe of crisp, watery, and almost sugary pod.

When Mr. Maresca found me eating the pilfered peas, instead of scolding me, he grabbed the hem of my dress and pulled it out to make a kind of pouch into which he placed a big handful of them for me to eat, not in hiding but openly, in the sawdust-floored shop. Every time his son Joe opened the heavy wooden cooler door, I caught a good eyeful of carcasses hanging upside down with their tongues flopping out the sides of their bloody mouths and their eyes filmed-over, milky, and bulging, along with disembodied parts—legs, heads, haunches, sides, ribs, looking like something in a Jack London story. I wanted to follow him in there. I wanted to be in with the meat and the knives and to wear the long bloody coat.

That night we slept by the fire in an otherwise pitch-black meadow, five kids vaguely chaperoned by my brother Jeffrey who was well on his way to becoming a teenage anthropologist, hunter-gatherer, and naturalist. He collected the deer and raccoons that had been hit and killed out on the dark country roads and dragged them back to hang from the trees bordering the meadow until they bled out. Then he cleaned the hides, burned off the hair, saved the teeth, and scraped the sinew from the bones and dried it to make thread with which he'd sew his pants, made of deerskin and raccoon fur. I was enthralled by him and his fastidious, artful, freakish habit. And in love with his boarding-school good looks dressed down by the chin length of his hair and new habit of wearing dashikis. I hadn't totally understood, with the eleven years between our ages, that he may have also gotten into the habit of "turning on, tuning in, and dropping out," and that there was likely a psychotropic reason he could go so long without blinking. My parents hadn't totally understood this either, probably, because on that night, the night before the big party, Jeffrey was left in charge of the fire. He worked the stumps and branches into a fierce, burning domed pyre.

My brother Todd was with us but would have preferred being up in his room, with the door closed—you always had to knock to enter—counting his money, or losing himself in his few but in-good-working-condition acquisitions: his brand-new electric guitar, his reel-to-reel tape recorder, his dual cassette deck, his electric amplifier, and his brand-new soldering iron. With coils of solder and copper paper clips, he fashioned quirky little uninspired sculptures of boats and trains and skiers. Todd, the second oldest, lay in his sleeping bag tuning us out, playing air-guitar Led Zeppelin while listening on his headphones, which he bought himself with money earned busking in town for the tourists. A loan of five dollars was never denied; it was breezily granted but came with interest and was entered into Todd's ledger. He hired me to give him leg massages after work with my lucky rabbit fur, a half hour I found uniquely intimate and a responsibility I took very seriously, and he paid me in dollar bills and mixed tapes.

Simon, who was closest to me in age, was having a pretty bad pre-adolescent, very high IQ, low attention span, pissed-at-everybody-and-everything summer vandalism spree. Every cop car he saw was an opportunity for a five-pound bag of white sugar in its gas tank. Glass panes in empty houses gamely blown out with rocks accurately pitched. He was turned on by his badass-ness and was waiting sullenly until we all fell asleep so he could sneak out of his sleeping bag and go relieve his boredom by walking into town and leaving his mark on it overnight.

My sister Melissa, the middle child, was only a teenager but already responsible and professional enough to have a negative white mark on her tanned arm from her wristwatch and a job as a lifeguard. A wristwatch at fourteen! She had the incomprehensible ability to open a whole scrumptious sugary package of chocolate-covered graham cookies, put two of them on a paper towel, reseal the package neatly for another day, and eat only those two crackers. Left to my nine-year-old devices, I would be sick on the whole package within ten minutes. Melissa would be the one in the kitchen with our mother the next day, dutifully shelling lima beans and cutting butter into flour and sugar while I was in the master bedroom rifling the jacket pockets and handbags of all of our guests, helping myself to twenty-dollar bills and quarters that I would later spend on Dr Pepper, Italian meat hoagies with oil and vinegar and hot peppers, and individually wrapped Tastykake iced fruit pies.

While we were all lying around the crackling and sparking pit, wondering how late it was and how late we would stay up, Jeffrey invented a little language and a nomenclature for our family. He started with my dad, "The Bone." This was not his own invention. Some of the carpenters at the scenery shop had started calling my dad "The Bone" behind his back. Playing with words and language as they do, schoolmates had changed Hamilton to Hambone ever since the eighth grade. My father hated being called Hambone and worse, being called Ham, as that is what his own father was called, by his own mother, no less. But someone clever at the skating rink had just cut to the chase and started calling him "The Bone." *Have you seen "The Bone?" Where's "The Bone?" You better make sure "The Bone" signed off on that. "The Bone" is never gonna go for that.*

From "Pa-Pa Boner," the lewdness and double-entendre of which can still to this day put Jeffrey into a breathless laughing fit, it took nothing to get us going, and soon we were dubbed from oldest to youngest, J Jasper Bone, T-Bone, Bonette Major, Sly and the Family Bone, and me, finally, Bonette Minor. Our battered Volvo station wagon became the Bone Chariot. Something authentically, uniquely my dad's—like the dimmer switches in our house never working, or the house almost being auctioned off at the sheriff's sale because he hadn't paid the property taxes in a year—was "bone-afide." Real, expensive Champagne at Christmas in spite of the lien was "bone-issimo." And parties—all of my dad's parties—became "bone-a-thons."

Decades later, when Melissa and I were in our separate homes with our own families, she left me a message about a bone density study that was being done at her local hospital, and all I could hear in the background of the message was Melissa herself, howling and shrieking into the phone "Bone Density! Bwa ha ha ha ha ha bwa ha ha ha ha ha!"

I won't pretend that I was a humorous or clever part of this little word game we were playing out in the dark meadow by the big fire.

Being the youngest, I had to work very hard to understand the joke, or to make like I understood, and as often as not I got caught up in my own mind, my own puzzle, my drifty imagination. I was the one out of the five kids who was always thrown in the car and taken on long errands with my parents because I was purely content to sit in the car and wander around my own mind. Watching the world itself, the people in it, and my whole internal life was more than enough to keep me entertained. My parents had an understanding at this time about disciplining me: Do not send that Scorpio girl to her room for punishment because she loves it there. So whatever it was that had them all cracking up—whatever jokes and jabs and teasing Jeffrey— now JJ Bone—had got going, like referring to my mother as the one who "got Boned"—I wasn't really getting it. I had no idea. I held on to the leash of their banter, which ran like a rowdy sheepdog twice my own weight, but I would not let go.

I quietly thrilled to be packed into my sleeping bag right up next to them. I felt cocooned by the thick crescendoing song of the crickets, that voluptuous blanket of summer night humidity, the smell of wood smoke, the heavy dew of the tall grass around us, the necessary and anchoring voices, giggles, farts, and squeals of disgust of my older siblings. This whole perfect night when everyone is still, pretty much, intact and wholesome, is where I sometimes want the party to stop.

In the morning the sun will come up and the rest of life will resume—where it will become cliché to admire the beauty of the stars, facile to feel transported by the smell of wood smoke, childish to admit to loving your siblings, and weak to be made secure by the idea of your parents still married up in the house—and we will awaken and kick out of our sleeping bags and find in the pit a huge bed of glowing coals, perfect for the slow roasting of the lambs.

But on this last night that we all spend together fireside, being ravaged by mosquitoes and uncomfortably dampened by the dew absorbed by the cotton army-issue sleeping bags—when we have not yet even eaten the lambs—all that yet troubles us is whether, when it rang, you answered the Bone Phone or the Bone Touch Tone.

When we woke up, the mist was burning off as the sun got strong. My dad was throwing huge coils of sweet Italian sausage onto the grill. He split open big loaves of bread to toast over the coals, and for breakfast, instead of Cocoa Puffs and cartoons, we sat up in our sleeping bags, reeking of smoke, and ate these giant delicious, crusty, and charred sweet Italian sausage sandwiches.

Then there were a million chores to do, and my dad needed us to do them. I learned that I could drive, work, haul stone, hammer nails, handle knives, use a chainsaw, and tend fires—anything boys could do—simply because my dad was always so behind, so late, so overextended and ambitious and understaffed on every project that he was always in desperate need of another pair of hands, even if they were only a nine-year-old pair of girl hands. All of us had clocked enough hours with my dad backstage at theaters, watching the scenery go up or come down, that by the time he was throwing this party in our backyard and instructing us to light the paper bag luminarias right at sundown, we understood theater terms like "the fourth wall" and theatrical lighting expressions like "Close the barn doors!" and " Dimmer two segue to three, please!"

We had to roll up our pant legs and walk barefoot into the frigid stream, build a little corral with river rocks, and stock it with jugs of Chablis and cases and cases of Heineken and cream soda and root beer. Having to walk barefoot into the cold stream to get a beer instead of just comfortably reaching into one of those ice-packed bright red coolers that normal people would use was, in our new vernacular, bone-afide. I had to mow the meadow and rake it, and the smell of fresh cut grass was bone-issimo. We had to fill hundreds of brown paper lunch bags with sand and plumber's candles, then set them out all along the stream's edge under the weeping willows and at all the groundhog holes so nobody broke an ankle or fell drunk into the stream later when it got dark. And we had to juice up the glow-in-the-dark Frisbees in the car headlights so we could play later out at the far dark end of the meadow. Those glowing greenish discs arcing through the jet black night, sent and received by the invisible bodies of my older brothers, were bone-ificent.

The lambs were arranged over the coals head to toe to head to toe the way you'd put a bunch of kids having a sleepover into a bed. We kept a heavy metal garden rake next to the pit to arrange the coals as the day passed and the ashes built up, moving the spent coals to the edges and revealing the hot glowing red embers. The lambs roasted so slowly and patiently that their blood dripped down into the coals with a hypnotic and rhythmic hiss, which sounded like the hot tip of a just-blown-out match being dipped into a cup of water. My dad basted them by dipping a branch of wood about as thick and long as an axe handle, with a big swab of cheesecloth tied at its end, into a clean metal paint can filled with olive oil, crushed rosemary and garlic, and big chunks of lemons. He then mopped the lambs, slowly, gently, and thoroughly, back and forth with soft careful strokes like you might paint your brand-new sailboat. Then the marinade, too, dripped down onto the coals, hissing and atomizing, its scent lifting up into the air. So all day long, as we did our chores, the smell of gamey lamb, apple-wood smoke, and rosemary garlic marinade commingled and became etched into our brains. I have clung to it for thirty years, that smell. I have a chronic summertime yearning to build large fires outdoors and slowly roast whole animals. I could sit fireside and baste until sundown. Hiss. Hiss. Hiss.

The rest of the meal was simple but prepared in such quantities that the kitchen felt hectic and brimming and urgent. There were giant bowls of lima bean and mushroom salad with red onion and oregano and full sheet pans of shortcake. Melissa, with a pair of office scissors, snipped cases of red and black globe grapes into perfect portioned clusters while my mom mimosaed eggs—forcing hard-cooked whites and then hard-cooked yolks through a fine sieve—over pyramids of cold steamed asparagus vinaigrette. Melissa and my mom worked quickly, efficiently, and cleanly—mother and daughter together in the kitchen, both in bib aprons each with a dish towel neatly folded and tucked into her apron string, "doing the bones" of our lamb roast.

Todd gave the lambs a quarter turn every half hour. Simon parked the cars. Jeffrey politely kissed the older guests, who arrived more than punctually, on both cheeks. And I plunged in and out of the stream to retrieve beer and wine and soda.

Then they started pouring in, all these long-haired, bell-bottomed artist friends of my dad's and former ballet dancer friends of my mother's, with long necks and eternally erect posture, and our friends, too—the Drevers and Mellmans and Bentleys and Shanks—the whole pack of us dogs, muddy, grass-stained, and soaking wet in the first fifteen minutes. I hardly recognized the washed and neatly groomed Maresca brothers with their father, Mr. Maresca, out of their butcher coats.

Slowly the meadow filled with people and fireflies and laughter— just as my father had imagined—and the lambs on their spits were hoisted off the pit onto the shoulders of men, like in a funeral procession, and set down on the makeshift plywood-on-sawhorse tables to be carved. Then the sun started to set and we lit the paper bag luminaria, which burned soft glowing amber, punctuating the meadow and the night, and the lamb was crisp-skinned and sticky from slow roasting, and the root beer was frigid and it caught, like an emotion, in the back of my throat.

2

I HAD NO CLUE THAT MY PARENTS WERE UNHAPPY WITH EACH OTHER until I was sweeping up cornichons and hard salami and radishes off the kitchen floor. It was a Sunday, and my dad had been outside building a stone wall all morning, which was a decades-long kind of joke because of the nature of the burnt-out old mill, which we called "the ruins" for good reason. He had come in for lunch.

My mother had been cooking that morning, standing at the six-burner in her apron with her wooden spoon in hand, as usual, something elaborate and involved with her many ingredients laid out at her reach on the butcher block kitchen table. My dad came in from out-side, powdery with lime and concrete and sand, washed his hands in the deep stainless sink, and then opened the refrigerator. He eked out some space among the diced onions and paprika and wine and cubed beef my mother had arranged on the table, and set up his Kronen-bourg beer and his salami and a hunk of Jarlsberg. He pulled out of the fridge some radishes and butter and some cornichons and Dijon mustard and set these things out, with a Sunday's unique sense of pleasure, in front of his wooden chair. Impossibly, he managed to arrange the fat Sunday *New York Times* right there next to him on this small, already laden table. Triumphantly, he spread out his elbows and sat down. They did not seem to speak to each other.

I had been sitting on the little padded bench in the kitchen writing in my treasured red leather diary that locked with a real key and canoodling with Ralph. He was a large tomcat, indifferent to us unless we had food, and we replaced him whenever it became necessary, after death by car wheel or dog chase, with exactly the same cat, and named him the same. For the nearly dozen years that I lived with my family, we had one cat named Ralph. I hoped inordinately each day that the cat would forgo mousing out in the dark nights and instead find my room and my bed and sleep with me. And when he did and he fell asleep dead in the center of my slim single bed, leaving no room for me, I curled up and contorted my own body to sleep around him even if it meant I was hanging on to the outside edge of the mattress and one whisper of the covers. My mother could never understand this. She kicked the cat away from her ankles and said, "Ah la la la la la la. The problem with kittens is they become cats!"

I heard the thick Sunday newspaper hit the kitchen floor with a thud. And then my mother, who had yanked it out from under my dad's elbow while he munched the radishes and had dropped it on the floor at his feet, actually smiled when he swept his arm across the entire table and sent every item on it clattering and shattering onto the terra-cotta tile floor. I had no idea what was happening between them. My mother, still smiling, then clasped her hands together in front of her like a schoolmarm waiting for the spitballer to hand over his straw and paper wads, her head tilted disapprovingly down and to the side forming an extra wrinkle under her chin. Turning to me, as if we were old, old friends grooved in a routine of sarcastic observation, she said, "Oh lovely."

Looking directly at my father, but addressing herself to me she said, "Gabri, could you please pick up your father's wonderful display." And my dad pushed back his chair and walked out.

Until this moment, more or less, I sat in her lap after dinner every single night. For a period I was too young for after-dinner chores—clearing, washing, drying—and possibly too favored, and so I eagerly crawled up and took my place in her lap, barefoot and drowsy. I leaned back into her soft body and listened to the gurgling as she chewed and swallowed. I breathed in her exhale: wine, vinaigrette, tangerines, cigarette smoke. While all of the others were excused from the table, I got to sit, alone with my mother and father as they finished. I watched her oily lips, her crooked teeth, and felt the treble of her voice down my spine while she had adult conversation and gently rested her chin on the top of my head. She cracked walnuts from the Perigord and picked out the meats, extinguished her occasional cigarette in the empty broken husks, shifted my weight in her lap; she squeezed the tangerine peel into the candle flame and we watched the oils ignite in yellow and blue sparks. I sat in that woman's aproned lap every single night of my young life, so close to the sounds and smells of her that I still know her body as if it were my own.

I went everywhere she went. In the car, in the woods, in the market, in the kitchen. She took me to the farm to get our milk. As only a Frenchwoman can—in heels, a silk scarf, and a cashmere skirt—she'd pull up the long driveway of the dairy farm in her chocolate brown antique Mercedes-Benz, and without a single awkward gesture, get down and fill four rinsed-out gallon plastic jugs with raw milk from a stainless steel tank while forty woolly Holsteins chewed and pissed in the over-humid next room. We left our money in the honor system coffee can. And I sat in the back of that old car, while she struggled with the mechanics of a shifter on the steering column but no clutch on the floor, and inhaled as deeply as I could the stink of the farm and the cow shit that lingered on our skin.

I still very much like that smell of manure. I like it in my food and my wine and even in certain body odor. That milk was so thick and shitty that the cream separated and rose to the top and we siphoned off three inches from every gallon of milk we brought home. My mom used a turkey baster to extract the cream, and she kept it separate in a jar in the fridge. This entire errand she could run, effortlessly, in suede heels.

The Stecks were among many French friends my mother had cultivated in our area, and lived a few rural towns away, north of us following the Delaware. Theirs was a deep woods overrun with chanterelles, and we couldn't ever eat in one sitting all that we had collected. Jean, so recalcitrantly French that he wore a beret, espadrilles, and a blue canvas jacket, sturdily greeted us in his driveway, on damp opportune mornings. His wife, Hilda, with the watery, sagging blue eyes of a basset hound, emerged from the house, a little wobbly. They were old enough to be my mother's parents. In aggrieved tones, they spoke to each other in French about entirely pleasant subjects, but Hilda's jowls jiggled with every "*oui, oui, oui,*" that she offered—in that way that the French have of speaking on inhaling rather than on the exhale, "whey, whey whey"—in apparent commiseration with everything Jean or my mother uttered. And Jean made deep, disapproving faces with the exaggeratedly downturned corners of his sharp mouth. My own mother huffed out phrases I'd been hearing my whole life, "*C'est pas vrai!*" And "*Mais, non?!*" and "Oh la la la la la la," sounding quite miffed and then, abruptly, we cheerfully kissed everybody on both cheeks, and parted ways, calling out, "*À bientôt!*"

"Okay, Prune, let's get going!" she prodded, using her pet name for me, and I followed her into the damp woods where we picked all morning.

My mother could loosely fill a paper grocery bag—could that be fifteen pounds?—ferreting out the true chanterelles from the poisonous orange look-alikes, and I was taught how to differentiate them by the time I hit first grade. The smell of the moist, loamy dirt and pine needles clinging to their stems and gills permeated the car as I held the paper sack on my lap the whole car ride home.

In the spring, in the surrounding woods, we walked, and she pointed out to me the Johnny-jump-ups and jack-in-the-pulpits also just coming up at that time of year, and with paring knives we cut the fiddlehead ferns still tightly coiled like snail shells and took them home for a quick blanche and then sauté. Dandelion grew everywhere in our back meadow once summer came on fully, and occasionally she'd pick it and make salad, using lots of fat and eggs and bacon to temper the bitterness.

She taught me to eat common clover—the purple and white blossoms that grew in the grass in the meadow, which you could chew on and suck the sweetness from while searching for a four-leafer. From her I learned how to pull the pistils out of the honeysuckle flowers and eat the one small bead of pure clear sugar water. While many mothers were ever alert and poised to keep their kids from shoving sticks and rocks and bugs in their mouths, ours, on the contrary, locked us outside every day even in the rain and demonstrated to us how to eat slugs and grass. We'd tromp around in the mud and taunt the geese in the meadow who'd lower their necks and come at us hissing mad, try to spear fish in the stream, and pick the big black berries off the mulberry bushes near our mailbox while inside our mother would whistle along with the classical music station, stir pots of fragrant stews, and repose in her chair, howling out loud, a *New Yorker* open on her lap and a particular cartoon cutting her in half.

One summer my mother took just me out of all the kids, just me, to Greece, and it was with her on that trip that I accidentally got drunk for the first time, even though we'd had watered wine at the dinner table plenty of times.

"We'll split a big bottle," I remember her saying, referring to those mega beers they serve in Europe that you rarely saw in America. We were inside the kitchen of a tiny taverna on the island of Ios, she in Jackie-O sunglasses and a bright patterned headscarf, looking in the pans on the top of the stove while the cook held the lids. I was flat-chested in my T-shirt, in boys' shoes, such a tomboy that I was always given the key to the men's room when I asked at gas stations or restaurants to use the bathroom, and not quite nine years old.

I pointed to the pastitsio, as I did at every meal that I didn't order the moussaka, as it was so greasy and delicious and the closest thing to Hamburger Helper I'd ever get to see. We sat at a little wooden table outside under a tree. She poured the tall beer into our two short glasses and when we finished our lunch and got up to head back to our whitewashed rented rooms, we discovered I was bombed.

I weaved while she stayed the course back to our cool, spare rooms where we napped through the hottest part of the afternoon;

outside, a small war of blue sky and wild oregano and buzzing bees and someone's lone donkey up the hillside, shrieking out his bray in that train-tracks-on-steel-rails way, was waged. Voula, our smiling thick-middled proprietess, sun-dried her own grapes and figs on straw matting right on the roof above while her husband, Iannis, cleaned his fishing nets in the shade. Even through my disoriented beer high and in spite of my age, I could see in them that unspeaking way that married people who live directly from the ancient land, with only olive trees and fish from the sea and tomato vines, have of moving around each other and their life's chores, of pausing briefly in the afternoon and squinting out at the same horizon where the sea meets the sky and becomes indivisible, like themselves.

HERE IN OUR KITCHEN, with the mustard streaked across the floor and the cabinets and my dad's uneaten lunch and my mother's half-prepared dinner scattered about the floor, I watched while my mother smiled unemotionally, surveying the debris of their own life's chores, her eyes resting for a moment on the few dusty cement footprints left by my father's boots and I thought, *What a fucking bitch.*

I scrambled off that bench and was down on all fours as fast as the cat. There was adrenaline pumping through my own heart, but for some reason I was smiling, too, and had to hold back giggling, I was so startled and so awed and exhilarated. I had never felt such profanity come into my thoughts with such effortlessness. I had never been this alert or this awake in reality. The cutting board that Todd had made in ninth-grade shop class that looked like a racquetball paddle made of solid maple, the bread knife, the bread, the hunks of dry cured salami, the Jarlsberg cheese, the radishes, his beer bottle, butter, hard-boiled eggs, and cornichons were suddenly scattered across the kitchen, and I was on all fours gathering it all up.

Still, I had no idea their divorce was coming. None. "Family Meeting," my mom called out, and late in the afternoon, with dusty yellow sun slanting in, we assembled in the long narrow dining room, all of us at the dark wooden table that had so many leaves it could be extended to seat twenty-four. Simon and I were lying down on the oriental rug, Ralph between us, vying for his attention by pattering our fingers on the carpet and making little *psst*-ing noises. The cat ignored us both and I turned my attention to the very large bushel of apples my mother kept in the coolest part of the room. My mother shopped in bulk, like a restaurateur. With five kids in the house she never had a small decorative still-life type of fruit bowl on the dining room table with just two pears, a melon, and an apple. She bought whole legs of lamb, four gallons of milk at a time, whole wheels of cheese.

I was gazing at that full bushel of apples when she made her stunning, preposterous announcement, which I have possibly never recovered from. "Jim, it's over, *and the kids and I* have decided you should go."

3

IT PROBABLY TOOK OVER A YEAR, OR ALMOST TWO, TO DISMANTLE THE family. But I was eleven turning twelve, and I felt as if I fell asleep by the lamb pit one night and woke up the next morning to an empty house, a bare cupboard, the leftover debris of a wild and brilliant party, and only half an inch of Herbal Essence left in the bottle on the ledge in the shower. At that age, washing my hair and how I was going to wash my hair with no parents and no shampoo felt utterly important to me. I walked around the empty ruins of the mill that was our home, looking in all the cabinets and drawers and closets to see what there was left that I still recognized, and claimed for myself anything I fancied, not unlike a looter the day after a blackout.

I don't know how they technically worked it out, my parents— what the actual physical arrangements were that they had made for us when they decided to split up—but I think it's probable that my dad was supposed to be in charge of us that next summer the year following their finalized divorce. And it's possible that he wasn't entirely up to the job. Because that first summer after their divorce, my seventeen-year-old brother Simon and I were left alone—and this I remember acutely—for weeks. This may have been an oversight, like leaving your cup of coffee on the roof of the car while you dig out your keys and then drive off. Or wishful thinking on my parents' part that their two youngest children were old enough to fend for themselves. Either way, Simon and I were on our own. And we were better off, we seemed to agree without discussing it, each to fend for himself.

If this happened now, a government agency would have been called. But not in 1979 in our small benign town, where we were a big, well-known family. The older kids were accounted for, in a relatively natural way—Jeffrey, at eighteen, had taken that anthropological impulse of his and hitchhiked to Africa. By the time my parents were splitting he was already deep in the Ituri forest in Zaire, a wannabe Colin Turnbull, in a loincloth, hunter-gathering with a tribe of pygmies. Todd, with his collection of electric and acoustic guitars, was already popular on the Skidmore campus, even as a sophomore, in his band Tempo Tantrum. Melissa was finishing her first year at Sarah Lawrence and spent that summer in New York City in love with her first real boyfriend, a smoker, a literary snob, and, I always thought, a little bit mean.

Our mother had moved to a profoundly remote and rural part of northern Vermont. Something about that setting she—at that time a rage-prone, menopausal, highly distressed woman with the ink barely dry on her divorce papers and two sullen teenagers in tow—found soothing. But it was one that held no appeal for me and Simon, whom she had pulled out of school and taken with her. And after a long winter school year in Vermont, which we joined a couple of months after it had already started, we returned, decisively and definitively, to our dad and the remnants of the house we grew up in for our first summer after their divorce.

My father, for his part, had bought the Barry Gibb and Barbra Streisand *Guilty* album and played "What Kind of Fool" over and over and over, like a much younger man, or even a heartbroken boy, might have done.

It was kind of tremendous timing to hit adolescence just as the family was disintegrating. It's not too bad to live out your Pippi Long-stocking fantasy right when you most seek independence from your parents and are practicing it so ardently. There was no curfew and no dress code. My distracted, self-absorbed dad was probably trying to figure it all out himself—how to be forty-five and single after all those years of being married to a woman I believe he loved emphatically and who brought such concrete order to his otherwise watercolor life. He worked forever hours, then fell asleep in his bed with the light on and the crossword puzzle half-finished, and his felt-tipped pens left large black ink spots where they bled into the sheets.

But that summer happened to coincide with one of my dad's worst financial periods ever. Some had been bad, but this would not be bone-issimo. Nor bone-ified. This would be the summer of bone-less living. Gasoline was being rationed and you could fill up your car only on odd or even days, according to the date on your inspection sticker. My father was being so aggressively pursued by banks and creditors that our home phone—the bone phone—began to ring punctually every morning starting at seven-thirty. My dad went to New York and hid there for the bulk of summer, launching a show for which he'd designed the sets. That show just made it through previews and all of eight performances before they were taking down the marquee letters "Got Tu Go Disco!" and nobody got paid what they were owed. I answered the phone every morning and gave truthfully vague answers concerning my dad's whereabouts, not to derail the creditors, but because I actually didn't know where he was or when he would be able to be reached.

There followed one of the many, many fall semesters when we each arrived on our various campuses only to be barred from registration and directed to the bursar's office, where the administrator shook her head "no" unsympathetically and seemed to enjoy, on some level, that cocktail of panic and humiliation and despair blooming in us. Private schools for all five children, both in high school and college, in spite of the artist's paycheck?

Overreaching? Not in our vernacular. *De-Bone-aire.* My father has said a hundred times, and I have paid attention, that it's stupid to let money be the reason you don't do something.

By the time my parents might have realized—a glance in the rearview mirror—that they'd abandoned us, we were not to be recovered. That summer was the definitive end of some things and the rather hastened beginning of many others. While Pippi charmingly moved her horse onto the porch and wore mismatched striped socks when she found herself alone, I smoked cigarette butts salvaged from public ashtrays and sidewalks and retrieved from the asphalt from passing drivers who flicked them out the car window. I wore Candie's spiked heels that I shoplifted and a watermelon-red tube top. I did my first line of coke, and then my second and third, and made lots of "friends" in town who, like me, had no curfew and nobody watching, but who, unlike me, were twenty and not thirteen. I hastily grazed through the menu of adult behavior and tried on whatever seemed attractive, for whatever inchoate reasons, as they occurred to me. It was a spectacularly scattershot and eclectic approach, as I found myself still going to Little League practice in the afternoons while reading D. H. Lawrence's *Women in Love* at night, because it had a photograph of naked people in bed on the back jacket.

But quickly I realized that I would need money. I had entered a few of my neighbors' houses by crawling in windows when I knew they wouldn't be home or sometimes even just walking in the unlocked front door and for reasons unknown to even myself, made off with some of the strangest things, like wine that I didn't even yet care for, and adult's clothing that didn't fit me. I had managed to lift a few silver objects—ashtrays, a birth cup, candlesticks—and had pawned them in town, but even so, I understood I needed a job. So with the hardly faint traces of all the parties we'd thrown still swirling around in my blood—the laughter of drunk adults still echoing in my ears and the lingering powerful aroma of roasted lamb smoke still clinging, practically, to my skin—I walked the mile or so along the train tracks into town to find work.

What can a thirteen-year-old do in a heavily touristed town of a hundred bad restaurants? Cut bread. Haul bus tubs. Take out the garbage. Wash dishes.

I did all of those things for a few weeks at The Canal House. I applied there because, I realized thirty years later on a walk through town with my own young children, it was the first restaurant you came to when you got into town along the route I walked. It was picturesque, perfectly located, a tourist trap with unintentional food, a piano player on the weekends, and outdoor seating romantically arranged right along the canal where the tourists could throw bread from their dinner baskets to the ducks below, and with geraniums growing in planter boxes hanging from the railing canal-side. With portions designed to signal value, the waitresses asked, when clearing your plates, "Did ya get enough to eat?!" It was a very, very busy restaurant.

Johnny Francis, the owner, knew my father, but I didn't know this. He was probably only forty years old or so when I walked in and asked for a job on a hot summer weekday. I thought I was talking to an old man, his years of restaurant life hung on him so. I was extra polite as I had been raised to be. Johnny wore glasses that got darker in sunlight. He sat down in the now-empty canal-side dining area and looked me over while puffing on long white cigarettes.

"This'll be a summer job? Part time? What position are you applying for?" he asked, rather gruffly, I felt.

I totally panicked; I didn't even know the names of the jobs in a restaurant. I'd never heard of busser, salad girl, runner. We ate in restaurants when I was a kid, but not like families do today; to dine was an exception and a special treat. We had to sit in our chairs the whole meal, say please and thank you at every exchange with the server, and eat everything on our plates with a fork and knife. We ate at the Lambertville House, the Colligan's Stockton Inn, and rarely, Conti's Cross Keys Inn in Doylestown, where they made Caesar salad tableside, with both egg and anchovy. As a reward for our good behavior, we were allowed a Shirley Temple, just one, and at Colligan's we were allowed to throw pennies in the wishing well outside and, until we got too big, to sit on the owner's especially giant St. Bernard dog named Brandy. At the Lambertville House, we were allowed to be excused from the table to go visit Fritz the bartender in the back of the restaurant and eat pretzel mix.

I said to Johnny with a straight face, "I'm sixteen, and I was thinking of being a waitress."

I had just started "borrowing" cars from the repair and body shop up the road, which would be left in the lot with the keys in the ignition or under the floor mat in those days, waiting to be serviced. I would go up at night, now that I had no curfew and no chaperone, and first just sit in the cars. And then turn the engine on. And then finally, I crept the cars out of the parking lot and onto the road. I went everywhere that it used to take me hours to get to on my bicycle or on foot, and places I'd been to with my mother, keenly alert the entire time to the route and to being sure I could find my way back, which I'd never before had to actually attend to. For a few days there was a pale blue Volkswagen bug that I so thrilled to drive—it fit me so well—that I felt heartache when it was finally serviced and no longer in the parking lot. I returned it, my body wrecked from the exquisite exhilaration of having bathed in such unknown freedom and the nearly narcotic, depleting relief of not getting caught, having burned out the clutch and run out the gas. With the headlights off, I coasted the car right back into its spot at the gas station, put the key back under the floor mat, and walked home alone down the dark back road. Somehow, because I could do this, because I possessed some of the talents of an average sixteen year old, it felt effortless to claim it to Johnny Francis.

In that thirteen-year-old way of understanding the world, I didn't realize somehow that New Hope was a small town, and that if it was small enough for everybody to know almost everybody and that my dad was kind of a big fish in a small pond, then the very thing I was hoping for, that my last name would help me, could also work in the reverse. That Johnny Francis could easily pick up the phone or run into my dad at Smutzie's lunch counter and say: "Gabrielle came looking for a job a few weeks ago, claiming to be sixteen."

Luckily, he didn't. He sat with me and just talked for a while. "You're Jimmy's youngest?" he asked.

"Yes, that's right," I answered, a little spooked that he would know that.

"I knew your great-aunt Helen Louise." He smiled warmly. She had been kind of legendary in town, my father's aunt. She drove a black antique Thunderbird, wore coral-frosted lipstick, played Burt Bacharach on the piano—rather well—and kept a vintage bric-a-brac shop in town that was considered quite stylish and elegant. We reminisced about her, and it was as subtle as the way his lenses lightened in the cool shade of that terrace that his face and demeanor softened during the talk. Then we went out onto the sidewalk in front of his restaurant, in the blazing sun, and surveyed the scene. He asked me, from behind his now-black lenses, what I saw.

It was probably not later than eleven a.m. on a weekday. I didn't know what to say. What was I supposed to notice? The tchotchke store across the street was just opening up: The Ember Glo', filled with glass menagerie and incense and the kind of trinkets that end up at yard sales across the country. A few tourists straggled along the cobblestones, window-shopping.

"Look at those people," Johnny said. "Where are their shopping bags?" He dragged on his cigarette easily, blew out with a little fatigue, irritation, world-weariness. "It's a tight season."

But by the end of our conversation, he let me come and try to be a busser on a Saturday lunch. I didn't know to wear an ironed shirt. I didn't know how to properly pour ice water. I didn't know the right way to clear a plate. He had me off the picturesque, canal-side serving floor and back in the kitchen within an hour, and as soon as I saw the three-bin stainless steel pot sink, exactly like ours, I felt instantly at home and fell into peeling potatoes and scraping plates for the dishwasher like it was my own skin. And that, just like that, is how a whole life can start.

It almost didn't happen because, at that age, I didn't understand that a schedule was a rule not a suggestion and so I didn't show up one day, when we, the green-capped Mets, had a game against the yellow-hat Astros. Only three teams in the league had a girl player, and the Astros' girl was a pitcher. I was our third baseman. It was not the first year that they let girls play Little League, but it was only the second, and I was acutely aware of the skepticism and also the shame for some of the parents when I tagged out a runner at third and drilled the ball to first for a double play. Joanie Carrozza, the black-eyed, thick pony-tailed Astros' pitcher, easily struck out boys twice her size and of course plainly heard the taunts aimed at the batter who walked, fuming, to the bench. *You got struck out by a giiiirrrrll?* It was not possible for me to be absent from this game. Nor could I reveal to my employer, who was supposed to be taking me for a sixteen year old, why I couldn't work the shift. Of course there was no job waiting for me at The Canal House when I went, audaciously, to pick up my pay.

But I got another job, this time as a dishwasher at the Picnic Basket, and listed The Canal House, on my application, as Previous Experience. When I saw two women making out in the kitchen—a chef and a line cook deeply tongue kissing up against the walk-in freezer door—my heart raced so fast and I felt such a prickling of adolescent embarrassment that in the middle of the shift I quickly changed out the garbage in my station, hauled the half-full bag out to the Dumpster behind the restaurant, and sprinted home along the train tracks. Afraid to be caught, I ditched my apron in the woods.

On so many occasions, vestiges of my real chronological age and all its attendant ignorance and confusion tapped a disruptive finger against the smoke rings I was convincingly blowing on the exhale of a Marlboro and must have startled so many people who took me at my word even though they surely perceived, on some level, the cleavage between the girl and her doctored-up story. Simon had found meal-time surrogate family life in the homes of some of his friends whose mothers were the more-the-merrier types who good-naturedly added another plate to the table and fed their broods Pop-Tarts and frozen French bread pizzas. There must have been some adults who might have liked to have put a strong warm hand on the back of my neck, to walk me gently off the field for a quiet talk, and then to walk me back into the game, with better focused purpose and direction. But I was meeting only the kind who were enthralled and titillated by me in a red tube top, who were lavishly entertained by the way I said "cunt," "fuck," "dick," "ass," "bitch," and "shit" in a single conversation, and who gave me just the enormity of attention I was so seeking. "She's eleven going on twenty-two," my dad used to say, proudly, to a stranger when introducing me.

During this summer I learned how to cook. I spent most of my time in our home in the kitchen, opening old jars of stuff my mother had left behind in the pantry. It was the only room in the large house that most resembled what it had looked like when my mother and family all lived in it together. How complicated it must be to separate out a vivid and fruitful marriage of twenty-five years. Half of the furniture, the photographs, the sheets, and the books had made their way to Vermont, and nothing had taken their places. When you split up, and you are struggling with the very meaning of everything said and promised in love itself, who is able to divvy up the contents of the pantry?

Our mother had her own double-tiered, potbellied couscoussier, and she made tagines with preserved lemons and cardamom pods, pigeon pies with sultanas and pine nuts, painstakingly brushing each fragile layer of phyllo dough with melted butter using a special brush made of white duck feathers, which would neither leave loose bristles in the dough nor perforate it. She knew to serve mint tea and sliced oranges with onions and olives, if she was making a bisteeya, and never put a meal together in a careless, eclectic, or incoherent way. The meal was always organized correctly, traditionally, which I now appreciate, but as a kid, pigeon was not a treat, even if it was served with the traditional condiments.

On certain nights, she gave us baths and then hair washes and then dessert, sort of. Side by side, however many could fit, we knelt at the edge of the tub after we had bathed, leaning over a drainful of suds, just as we had waited in that same huddle every Christmas morning at the top of the stairs before being allowed down to see the tree and attack the pile. Huddled there, we pressed washcloths to our clenched eyes until brown curlicues and stars formed from pressing too hard while she hosed water over our heads and shampooed us. When we were clean and dry, we stood in the kitchen while she stood before the pantry, its shelves laden with red boxes of raisins and cashews; crinkly yellow bags of sweet baker's chocolate; metal tins of flour; sugar; green, yellow, and orange candied fruits; glass jars of oatmeal; dark bottles of olives, vinegars, and syrups; salt; strange cans of fish, beans, and crackers; tubs of peanut and almond butters. The boxes leaned against the stacked cans, and the stacked cans towered over the jars that sometimes lay on their sides.

One at a time, she blindfolded us with a dish towel, spun us around a few revolutions, and then set us in front of the shelves. With blind outstretched hands, each of us in turn surveyed the shelves and from behind came the shouts, "Cold! Cold! Lukewarm! Okay, Warmer! Warm! Hot! Hot! You're burning!" of the siblings, trying to guide each other to something good.

Whatever we blindly landed on, that was our dessert. It was a game of roulette. You could have a can of cling peaches or escargots, equally. If you picked the wrong package—Trenton Oyster Crackers—tough shit. The older kids were better at this than me, obviously, rehearsing the layout of the pantry shelves ahead of time, peeking out from under the blindfold.

Our sweets were mostly of the "natural" kind: a piece of fruit, yogurt mixed with jam, sliced bread with butter and granulated sugar, the occasional little square of good chocolate. And our school lunches were just plain embarrassing: leftover ratatouille, a wedge of Morbier cheese, a bruised pear. We were given one piece of Saran Wrap for the week, to be reused and brought home each day, washed and left to dry in the dish rack over the back of an upturned ladle or wooden spoon, ready to wrap our lunch in the next day. My mother turned soured milk into buttermilk with the help of a tablespoon of cider vinegar, and then it went in the blender with strawberries for our breakfast. Stale heels of bread became bread crumbs, made by grating on the toothy holes of a box grater and then kept in the freezer. Mold was cut away until the creamy tender edible part of whatever thing was revealed.

Now without her, but left with the strange contents of her pantry, which my father had not cleaned out—the way a griever won't empty the clothes closet of the deceased spouse? Or the way of a man who has not had to do any cleaning his whole married life?—I relied on what I had seen her do and improvised from there. I ate tinned white asparagus with capers and some of their juice and olive oil and parsley from the garden. I ate canned sardines and chewed through the spines and the silvery unpleasant skin until I finally realized how to skin and fillet them gently with a paring knife, placing the meaty bodies on horribly stale Triscuit crackers with sliced shallots and mayonnaise. I washed lettuce from the garden in warm water so my hands wouldn't get cold and watched it wilt but ate it anyway. I added Dijon mustard to milk and tried to make a pan sauce which curdled but I still ate it, poured over rubbery cold-and-raw-in-the-center chicken breasts which I had placed, still completely frozen, into the pan, reasoning that this would all just take a little longer to cook. When we ran out of Dijon mustard and olive oil, I used tomato paste in my salad dressing, and raspberry jam, and once even some chicken broth.

As my mother had shown me, I picked the Japanese beetles off the bean plants in the garden and dropped them into a mason jar of gasoline and harvested the lettuce from outside of the core so that it would regrow and continue to yield. I climbed into raspberry bushes and picked the fruit, getting stained, stung, and ripped apart in the doing. Our abandoned garden produced all summer, in spite of my inexperience, and I ate whatever it offered. I learned to cook a lot of different vegetables the way my schoolmates learned to put together a PB and J.

I finally got another job, where I managed to make my home for a few years working summers and after school and during holidays, at a restaurant on the main drag called, ironically, Mother's. There I grew into a teenager and a beginning cook and even worked as a waitress and bartender for a stint when I dropped out of college. I started by helping in the retail bakery, cutting and rewrapping the two full cases of cakes for which the restaurant was rightfully well-known. They made everything from scratch in the bakery upstairs and produced gorgeous tall cakes that drew in thousands of customers who planned their meal around saving room for one of the twenty buttercream castles on display in the gleaming refrigerated case near where you waited for the maitre d' to take you to your table. But I soon wanted to be back in the noisy, hissing kitchen, behind the two swinging doors with round ship windows—enter left, exit right—and so I washed dishes. Then I helped with salads on extremely busy or understaffed days, and I eventually even made it on to the hot line by the time I was fifteen. Mother's had a popular dish called a seafood chimichanga, which was a big pile of sauteed seafood—scallops, shrimp, and salmon, all mixed in with minced jalapenos, and then draped with a couple of slices of Monterey Jack cheese melted under the broiler. Instead of wrapping the seafood up in a tight package of flour tortilla and then deep frying it like a fast-food chimichanga, at Mother's the cheesy filling was tipped right from the pan hot from the salamander into an edible bowl made of a deep fried flour tortilla that looked like a giant bloom or clam shell. The sauté guy then garnished the gluey seafood with an orange half-moon and a sprig of curly parsley and sent it out the swinging doors.

I made stacks and stacks of those chimichanga bowls by dropping the flour tortilla into the deep fryer, where it would float and sizzle on the surface for a moment like a lily pad on a pond. Then, with a deep ten-ounce ladle, I pushed down in the center, and the tortilla came up around the bowl like the long dress and underskirts of a Victorian woman who had fallen, fully clothed, into a lake, her skirts billowing up around her heavy sinking body. We served, I am sure, two hundred chimichangas a day on weekends in this quaint town with its endless antique and art shows and mule barge rides along the canal, and I garnished every single one of them with its orange wedge and curly parsley sprig.

On the walk home from town, after the mats were hosed down, and the stainless steel scoured with soapy green pads, then toweled off as Chef Joe and Chef Tom supervised, I held in my hand my paycheck from Mother's—$74.11 after its inscrutable and unwelcome FICA and FED WT—and had precocious thoughts about who was in charge of me now, if I was earning my own money and everybody else was hiding in New York City or the hills of Vermont. No future graduate-level feminism seminar would ever come within a mile of the force of that first paycheck. The conviction was instant and forever: If I pay my own way, I go my own way.

4

I N June 1982, I graduated from alternative high school, barefoot and in an ankle-length white gauze dress that I'd shoplifted
from a store in town. Even though the school was only two miles
from our house, I was enrolled as a boarder because there would be
consistent adult supervision, regular meals, and "structure." I'd sort of
skipped some of ninth grade and some of twelfth grade at that school
where, at the time, you could substitute sports credits for science credits and theater credits for history credits, and where my English credits were strong enough to stand in for all the others. "Life experience"
and "individual character" were also taken into consideration, and
after my interview with the heads of the school, I was allowed to
graduate at sixteen. I moved to New York City the day after the ceremony with $235 in graduation checks that friends of my parents had
sent me. Both of my parents came to the ceremony and struggled
with the awkwardness of having to pretend to be perfectly comfortable seeing each other, while I flitted away as often as possible to have
ultra-jaded, ultra-sarcastic huddles with my teenage friends until the
whole thing was over, and everybody left campus and I went and
packed up my dorm room. It took four roundtrips on the Hunterdon

Bus Line, its underbelly stuffed each time with my bags and the odd wicker hamper full of miscellany, while I rode inside with a desk lamp on my lap. I also had a huge jar of change that I kept in the apartment I moved into in Hell's Kitchen with my older sister, Melissa, who was away for the summer, and I lived off that change for the first three months. The apartment had a cockroach infestation of such magnificent proportions that I have never ever encountered the like since. They even scattered, by the dozen, from the bed when you pulled back the covers.

The little grimy apartment was on Twenty-ninth Street and Tenth Avenue directly across from the Morgan General Mail Facility, where all of the city's correspondence passed, and one block south of an entrance to the Lincoln Tunnel, with its constant reciprocation of traffic—commercial and domestic—between New Jersey and New York.

Some of the astonishingly underdressed hookers who worked the tunnel would hang out on my stoop, in good weather, and have egg-on-a-roll sandwiches from the Terminal Food Shop Deli downstairs. I did not know about egg-on-a-roll sandwiches. They didn't exist where I grew up. For ninety cents you got a griddled buttered roll, split in half, into which the deli man set a fried egg, a slice of cheddar cheese, and a couple of strips of bacon. With a sweet and light deli coffee in a blue cup designed with the Acropolis on it, and that sandwich, I started each day of my first summer in New York City.

"Iassou, Dimitri," I said each morning to the owner, proud of my ability to pronounce his name correctly and to speak a few words in Greek. Everyone called him Jimmy, which is how he introduced himself, but I'd been to Greece and wanted to show him how clever I was. Whether he was charmed or annoyed, I could never tell because he had that utterly Greek way of being friendly to everyone.

"Iassou, Gabriellaki." He smiled every morning and sometimes *tsk*ed and raised his very bushy black eyebrows as a way of refusing my ninety cents, which I had nervously counted out from the dwindling jar upstairs. It must not have taken him very long to notice that I never once pulled out a crisp five-dollar bill to pay for my breakfast, but always arrived, instead, with a stack of dimes.

Delis were still run by Greeks then, not Koreans, and they were not the twenty-four-hour salad bar affairs they are today. You could get a can of ground Café Bustelo, cat food, toilet paper, cigarettes, and a turkey sandwich but that was it. There was no Annie's sesame-ginger salad dressing and precut packages of watermelon on ice. No fake crab leg sushi rolls. No vegan cookies or wasabi peas. The corner deli was a carefully edited experience in those days. Egg on a roll and coffee were the measure of a good deli, and a good deli man.

I took my foil-wrapped sandwich and the *Times* and sat with the ladies on my stoop, counting the Ninas in the Hirschfeld while feigning total nonchalance regarding the elaborate production going on around me involving Charisse, and the laying out of a single baby wipe on the step before placing her totally naked ass on it.

My jar of change was running low. I bought rotten and bruised fruit from the little stand on the corner of Eighth Avenue and Twenty-ninth Street, which was kept in a separate bin and sold for only nineteen cents a pound. The fruit was easily salvaged with a paring knife—with a quick bit of work, you could remove the offending, unsellable bit of brown—which the few West Indian women and I who bought this waste often exclaimed about, with great pride.

"Look at these plums! These are perfectly good plums!" we shrilled, willfully ignoring the large brown bruises at the tops.

I stole fistfuls of ketchup packets from all the McDonald's on Eighth Avenue and I'd make pasta "sauce" with it. The *Village Voice* advertised bars that held happy hours with free hot hors d'oeuvres. After walking around all day from job interview to job interview, saving myself the subway fare by walking, I would make my way to them for dinner, from five to seven p.m. With my purchase of two beers for five dollars, I would eat my two little plastic plates of complimentary—and to my frame of mind, utterly delicious—buffalo wings, which had just become "the new thing" in culinary New York City, and then walk as many blocks home as I was far from it.

I lived on canned sardines cheaply bought at the grocery store for thirty-five cents each.

I had strategically sworn off the habit of shoplifting, because I had this naive idea that in New York City, I would be sent immediately to women's prison if I got caught. I'd heard stories, exaggerated and magnified just as you'd imagine, back in Lambertville, that quite convinced me to not shoplift.

I pounded the pavement, instead, looking for a job. Because I didn't know my way around New York and because I didn't know what I was doing, I pounded it a little harder than was necessary. I ushered two nights of a performance way downtown for twenty-five dollars and saw Kate Valk naked on stage. I stood on the corner of Thirty-third and Sixth and handed out fliers. I sold something brand-new called FrozFruit from a cart in Central Park during a No Nukes free concert. With my earnings I bought a dime bag at a bodega that had about three dusty candy bars in its case behind the bulletproof glass through which you passed your money and back through which they handed you the weed. The same friend of my sister's who had told me you could do this—buy pot at the store!—also introduced me to his "slug" dealer, a guy who sold little brown packets of fifty copper slugs that got you through the subway turnstile, at half the price of a real token.

On my way back home to Twenty-ninth Street from an interview at a Spanish restaurant on Fourteenth Street that I had read about in the *Voice* that morning, I casually wandered into a bar with a revolving door on Thirteenth Street. It's only now, in the retelling, that I realize I was lost, walking south and east, away from home rather than toward it.

The Lone Star Café had a giant iguana on the roof, looking down over Fifth Avenue. It was dark inside, with the glare of midday crushing in through the few windows the place had. There was a tall guy with a well-groomed glossy brown beard in denim and cowboy boots with a beer gut standing at the entrance talking to a young woman in a high ponytail, which swung around dramatically as she performed her portion of the conversation.

"I just have have have have to take it," she was saying, as I entered and stood slightly stunned at the door while my eyes adjusted. He looked pissed. Shifting his French-fry gut back and forth, arms crossed over his chest, he set his lips tight and said nothing.

"Okay, Donny, I'm sorry but . . ." she singsonged, untying her apron and kind of scooting away.

And there I was, in the right place at the right time, a warm body, sixteen years old about to lie to be twenty-one, and he hired me on the spot.

He looked at me standing there still disoriented both from the change of light and from quickly trying to understand what was happening before me. Was this a waitress quitting right this very minute?

He said, "What do you want?"

I said, "Hello, I am looking for some work as a waitress . . ." and he cut me off by barking, "What's wrong with your eyes? Why are they so red?"

This was decidedly not Johnny Francis letting me—kindly and gently—lie my innocent thirteen-year-old lies. This was no pleasant sunny interview by the canal with ducks. But I mustered myself and said, "There's nothing wrong with my eyes. What? Do you think I'm stoned or something?"

And he actually smiled, and his face turned into a good-looking warm face, and he was pleased with my comeback, and he gave me the job of waitress, the job I'd tried to bluff my way into three years before unsuccessfully.

Suddenly, I was in a navy blue Lone Star Café T-shirt with white lettering, a short denim skirt, and cowboy boots.

My first few weeks had been entirely wholesome and uneventful, working the practically dead lunch shift, with this beautiful, friendly, seasoned waitress named Lori who taught me how to use a credit card machine, how to write an order on a dupe pad, how to check out my paperwork at the end of my shift, and how to tip Billy, the daytime bartender, the required 15 percent of my daily tips. Hardly anyone ate lunch at the Lone Star Café—it was a nightclub after all—but there were a few businesses around and not many other options, so we served chili and chili burgers and beer, slowly and easily, all afternoon to the few who did join us. When I tipped out Billy my 15 percent, it was not more than ten bucks. I left it at the service end of the bar, calling, "This is for your help, Billy. Thank you," as Lori had taught me. Not even a year had passed from the time I was still in high school plays, and so I said my line to Billy the same stiff way I said my lines, in tenth grade, in *Hedda Gabler.* And Billy waved from the middle of the bar where he was talking with an early happy-hour customer, "Thanks, hon!"

In the fall, I started my very first semester of college a few blocks away at NYU. I told Donny that I needed to switch to nights. And somehow he was persuaded. He handed me off to the night manager, Buddy.

It was incredibly loud, crowded, smoky, and great fun at the Lone Star. It was the original urban cowboy joint in New York at a time when urban cowboy was really hitting. Wall Street was off the hook, and young white traders from Goldman with not-thin stacks of hundred-dollar bills in their pockets would pile into the place while their black stretchies idled outside, waiting to take them to the Odeon later for steak frites and Cristal as a nightcap.

I clocked in for my first night shift just after Labor Day. There were six women over thirty in the locker room, spraying their hair, squirting Visine, and chatting easily, though I thought somewhat frantically, with each other. Not one of them said hello to me. Up on the floor, I worked my station as best as I was able, but with the aisles packed with guys screaming their conversations at each other and dancing and the live music and the tower of amps vibrating on either side of the stage, it was a whole new game compared to anything I'd played at lunch, where the loudest thing had been fifteen minutes of sound check. I made my way through the crowd by tapping people on the leg with my foot, while carrying a large and very full tray of longnecks over my head, high up in the air. Not unlike the way we had drilled at basketball practice—sweaty teenage girls with ponytails—just one spring ago.

The cocktail waitresses ran a cash-and-carry business. We bought the drinks from the bar ourselves, and then we sold them to the customer at the table and collected his money on the spot, making change if needed, from our own cash in our apron pockets. Sometimes the bartenders would be so busy that we just left our dupes there in a slot with everything we needed written down in funny code: arrows for "up" drinks and x's for drinks on the rocks, and when we came back in a few minutes our tray of drinks would be ready and our ticket rung up. In the mayhem of the place, I had sometimes received drinks I'd asked for but forgotten to write down and which the bartender had forgotten to ring up. When I found time later during my shift, I hailed the bartender, who oozed irritability, and squared up, as Lori at lunch had taught me.

I was the early girl out my first night. I don't remember the band, I don't remember how I made it out the revolving door, I just remember proudly handing Chris the bartender my tip-out—a whopping twenty-five bucks, unlike anything I'd done by day, and saying thanks.

He picked it up like it was covered in wet mucus and sneered at me, "What the fuck is this?"

I had never been spoken to like this.

"My tip-out."

"Twenty-five fucking bucks is your tip-out?" he spat, with a kind of sibilant "s" as he had a space between his two front teeth. His eyes were hard to see under the brim of his baseball cap, so to me he seemed like a dangerous raccoon.

I was electric with fear, with his unapologetic aggression. He seemed to have not one qualm about generating conflict with another human being.

"I made one hundred and forty bucks, that's my fifteen percent, what's wrong? What do you want?"

"I want you to learn how to work your fucking tables." He shouted and turned away and walked down the bar, his back lit by glowing liquor bottles like that black-pawed critter who has just ripped apart your garbage and now waddles off into the hedges, silhouetted by the little mushroom cap lights that line the driveway.

I turned seventeen during my waitress shift at the Lone Star Café, high on coke. And I made a big show of it. It made me feel something, something like bad and good, to run to the restroom in pairs, giggling with one of my new waitress friends, while patrons watched. I felt, somehow, as if I were sending a coded signal to potential admirers if I made an oh-so-casual point of wiping the little trickle of coke-laced snot from my upper lip and then licking my finger so as not to lose that last shot of tongue-numbing tingle.

We were partial to an after-hours club called the Zodiac, which I'm embarrassed to say that in spite of having been there dozens of times, I couldn't find today. Possibly it was in Soho, as I recall we always made a point to walk to Houston to get a cab home. I remember, with a kind of powdery nausea settling over me, coming out of it often and seeing droves of children coming *home* from school. Jake, the dealer, sat in a booth at the Zodiac and sold coke by the line. You slid into the banquette across from him, he cut out the line, you paid, snorted, and then vacated the seat after a soft and unpleasant hand-shake.

Duran Duran's "Hungry Like the Wolf" was a constant pick on the jukebox and the last time I walked out of that place, late summer 1983, it blared out the doors as I pushed them open and, wincing from the daylight, hailed a checkered cab, one of the last of a dwindling fleet. In that spacious backseat with so much room for your luggage and the round low stools for extra passengers, I lay down and thought, "Does anyone know where I am?" and rolled whichever way Tenth Avenue bumped me.

Obviously, I had learned how to *work my fucking tables.* Everybody was working their fucking tables, I soon learned. The girl at the door was selling tickets for the show while keeping half the "sales" for herself. The waitresses were *not* getting lost in the mayhem and accidentally not writing down drinks on their dupes and the bartenders were *not* supplying those unrecorded drinks unwittingly. They were in business together. I too, learned to sell them at the table, to keep the cash from the sale of a drink that didn't, on paper, exist, and to share that profit with the bartender, through tipping.

The tip-out at the end of a night when the waitress has pocketed seven hundred bucks is obviously a little more appealing than when the stupid sixteen-year-old lunch waitress hands over a "fucking" twenty. Chris and I had become, tentatively, friends. He slipped me an occasional shot of Cuervo for myself and only once spiked it with Tabasco.

There was a bartender upstairs, at the bar that serviced all the tables on the balcony with great views of the stage, who was rumored to have his own cash register, which he'd bring in zippered up in his duffel bag, set up under the counter behind the bar, and ring up drinks all night long that never made it into the company till. I never saw this, but the rumor was persistent and sworn to more emphatically the more I dismissed it as urban lore.

Even the coat-check girls were on the take. They invented a two-dollar fee for checking your coat and then were tipped as well for the pleasure. I was now cutting most of my classes at school but becoming friends with everybody at work. I, too, was frantically chatting away in the dressing room with Tooney and Duggan and Auntie Mary, the ninety-pound Englishwoman at least forty-five years old who kept right up with the coke and the job and the short denim skirts. Laura, an unexpectedly Upper East Side type of girl who kept her hair in a short pixie cut and wore penny loafers, had become an especially good friend. She always doubted her ability, after a certain point in the evening, to keep track of things, so she had the habit of bundling up her cash in hundred-dollar increments, rubber banding it, and putting it in the waistband of her stockings throughout the night so she wasn't walking around with half a grand in twenties bunched up in her denim apron pocket.

There was so much money being passed around at that place—legitimately and otherwise—that the owners had all of us bonded. We all went through a long, paperwork-filled process by which they insured themselves against theft.

Lloyd, the Jamaican night porter who drank warm milk with Guinness stout and a few drops of honey, had a whole substantial second income derived from doing our closing sidework, for which we tipped him lavishly. The sooner we got out of work, the sooner we could get to the bar at 1 Fifth, or the Zodiac, or a place on Tenth Avenue called Chelsea Commons, which would let us in after hours and lock the door with us happily inside because someone knew the bartender.

I never made it to the end of my first semester. I couldn't get to morning classes after what I'd done the night before. I dropped out. My dad, whose impeccably performed complaint to all of his friends at the time was that his kids only ever called when they needed money, was bone-ificently relieved to be sprung from the balance of the tuition he carried after my student loans and aid package covered what they could. I paid my mother's electric and phone bills that year, while she puzzled out how to be an independent, financially solvent divorced woman in blue jeans for the first time in her life. I gave her a wide berth. When Jeffrey had been questioned about the liberty he was taking by helping himself to a couple of eggs out of her fridge the morning after the long drive up to Vermont in his truck filled with her things retrieved from the split, furthermore making some derisive comment about our dad's inconsistent and inadequate support checks, I decided to just send the electric bill money and to avoid the fraught visits to her home. She mishandled a lot of things in those first years, but nothing more so than her evident inability to shield us from her significant fury at my father. I bought a stereo and got a Macy's credit card. I flew to Aspen and went skiing. I took home more than ninety thousand dollars that year and spent most of it on drugs.

At some point, urban cowboy started to slow down as a hot trend in the city's nightlife, but we didn't pay attention and we didn't scale back. Around this time a new girl started at the club, and I, for the first time in my life more senior than someone, ignored her in the dressing room. She carelessly left her book of dupes sitting in a drawer in the waiter station while she was having a pee break, and I stole them. Now I had a whole book of checks, marked in sequential order, which should have been returned to the office at the end of the night accounted for, wrapped up in her neatly organized paperwork. They had not been assigned to me, and I could do what I liked with them. It was the waitress's equivalent of having her own cash register. I used them judiciously over the next few months, getting my cash-and-carry drinks rung up on these checks that could never be traced to me. But things were slowing down so considerably that we began to scale way back and frequently, in fact more often than not, worked whole shifts on the up-and-up.

On a slow night, one month shy of a year to the week after I'd started, I arrived at work, almost late and out of breath. I had woken up late and hurting from a night of decidedly more sinister hue than average, most of it unrecoverable in my memory, and I was particularly disoriented from not being able to recall even one detail of how I had gotten home, and when it was time to leave my apartment, I was rushed and ill-prepared. I couldn't find a clean T-shirt or a clean apron. Melissa had left a brief note, in reference to the cockroach problem, "Remember Mr. Kornfeld when we were kids? A German *exterminator*! Get this: He drove a Volkswagen *bug*!!! No kidding. Ha. Ha. Ha." I grabbed an old dirty apron that still had bobby pins and matchbooks in the pockets and a couple of chili stains on it and ran out the door. I got changed in the locker room, put on my apron, and discovered in the pocket one of the old checks I had stolen from that new girl a few months before, who had not lasted even two weeks.

It faintly registered in my dull and harried mind to take care, but then the thought vanished, and I went up to my assigned station on the balcony. We were used to big acts, Jorma Kaukonen and Bob Dylan and Dr. John—I even worked an Osmonds gig once at which every customer was a Mormon female clutching a scrapbook and a ginger ale. But this was a quiet night, with an unknown onstage, and very few customers. Laura was working the downstairs station alone—they'd cut the second waitress. And I was the only girl assigned to the balcony. At seven o'clock I had only three tables nursing their drinks, and so I stood at the service end of the bar, chatting with the bartender.

"Things are strange," Tom, of the rumored cash-register-in-his-duffel-bag fame, said.

"Yeah," I agreed, assuming he was referring to how dead it was.

"Buddy's around," he said, with a barely discernible tone of warning.

"Okay," I said, letting him know that I understood that we would be playing by the rules tonight: No stealing. All drinks written down and rung up.

Buddy had been around a great deal lately. Something, clearly, was off in the numbers and the owners knew it, but they couldn't find it. Buddy is that guy in a restaurant or club, the general manager who walks around with a huge keychain and has no one to talk to his whole shift. He used to stand, silently letting his presence be seen and felt, watching the floor from the mixing booth, the curved staircase leading to the balcony, or by the pass-through at the kitchen where we picked up thousands of bowls of chili and spindled the paper dupes. He would look on, poker-faced under his cowboy hat, while we dodged in and out of Wall Street big spenders, and snuck each other shots of tequila, and giggled and sniffled like teenagers. He tried sometimes, awkwardly, to bridge the gap between his brusque authority and our compulsory approval, by telling a joke and laughing at it himself, or by strangely revealing something personal about himself and his wife, and it just felt miserable to have to stand there, politely paused in front of your superior, while he struggled with his aloneness.

Suddenly, he was walking directly toward me. I was carrying a tray with one hand, bearing only three drinks, but still involved in balancing the tray, and heading over to one of my tables to deliver them. Buddy reached into my apron pocket and pulled out my checks. While I stood there with the drinks, he scrutinized each one, and I could see his eyes scanning the serial numbers of each one on the upper right corner. Back and forth his eyes went, trying to understand their sequence. He and I understood at almost exactly the same moment that I had a check in my pocket totally out of sequence.

"What the fuck is this?" Buddy said, still looking at the checks, but starting to shake.

"Oh. My God," I said, putting down the tray of drinks on a nearby empty table. "I'm going, I'm going, I'm going," I said, backing away from Buddy, who was now looking almost purple in the face. I feared, truthfully, that he was going to beat me. I started running down the back stairwell, untying my apron, taking the steps two at a time. I ran to Laura on the ground floor, who was applying beige lip gloss from a long wand with a sponge tip, and grabbed her by the arms, hissing, "He got me! He got me! Fucking Buddy just busted me!" And without stopping to talk to anyone else, I pushed open the safety bar on the side doors that spit me out onto Thirteenth Street and ran a few steps down the sidewalk. I hid behind our Dumpster, shaking, until I saw Buddy open the door and look up and down the sidewalk and then go back inside. Laura came out five minutes later with my stuff from my locker, nervously smoking, but laughing wickedly.

"You are so busted," she squealed, her nose wrinkling up with glee.

"What the fuck's gonna happen?" I asked.

"I don't know but don't say anything about the rest of us," she warned, and flicked her butt to the curb before slipping back inside.

It was not even dark out. At seven-thirty or so on an August night, the city was alive and daylight lingered. I had thirty-seven dollars in my apron pocket. Tens of thousands of dollars in cash had passed through my fingers that year, and I ended up with thirty-seven wrinkled singles, shaking with the fear of having bluffed my way into a circumstance well out of my league, crouched behind a Dumpster on Thirteenth Street. I walked all the way home, north and west, wondering what was going to happen to me. What was left in the change jar?

The owners called in the morning. The bonding company called in the morning. And then Detective Sperro of the Sixth Precinct called to explain that he was the government official charging me with Grand Larceny and Possession of Stolen Property. He explained that the bonding company was the party pressing the charges, not the Lone Star Café itself. He advised me to retain a lawyer, and said, if I liked, he would send a squad car in half an hour to bring me in to his station on West Tenth Street. He read me my Miranda rights over the phone.

"Do you understand fully everything that I have just explained to you?" he asked.

"Yes," I said.

"Iassou, Gabriellaki," called Dimitri, as I entered the Terminal Food Shop Deli. He looked at me fully, with his eyes fixed on mine. "You are coming home too late, kooklamou," he said, like a concerned uncle. He had seen me many mornings, getting out of a cab, struggling to appear coherent, as he was opening the shop.

"I'm fine," I said. "Don't worry."

I sat on the front stoop with my egg-on-a-roll waiting for the cop car, not in a million years the way I imagined a felony arrest would be.

The next day, I called the only person I knew who had ever been able to help me out with money: my brother Todd. He had amassed a collection of guitars that filled a whole basement room in his Brooklyn Heights brownstone, but instead of becoming a professional musician, he had cut his hair very short, invested in a few work suits, and started a career on Wall Street, in Ginny Maes. A few too many bone-a-fied humiliations surrounding money experienced in his youth, perhaps, had driven the artistic impulse right into the basement, to be let out on weekends only. Hidden under his crisp white Brooks Brothers shirt, he wore a thin leather necklace with a sterling silver electric guitar dangling at the throat, and years later, when he was a very secure and well-compensated veteran of Goldman Sachs, he wore a silver bracelet and didn't worry that it was not hidden by his white cuff. Rather, that was his point.

"This is Todd," he said, picking up the line.

"Todd, hey—"

"Steve, two fifty! Two fifty!" he shouted to someone. "What's up?" he shouted to me, uncertain to whom he was talking.

We managed a clipped and perfunctory four-minute phone call, Wall Street traders shouting behind him in the background, and he shouting at them with me mid-sentence hanging in his ear, during which he put me on hold more than once. This was how all phone calls would be with him for the next dozen or so years that he spent on Wall Street, and they were, those phone calls, the very first step in an incremental distancing that would eventually lead to a complete and definitive loss. I knew it was too bothersome to call him during work. It was too alienating to try to talk, like siblings, with someone who is putting you on hold every twenty-five seconds, as his work demanded. The days of lucky rabbit fur leg massages were long behind us both. I learned to call infrequently and to talk fast when I did. But in those four minutes, while on hold, he had retained a lawyer to help me, for fifteen hundred dollars, and conferenced her in to the call.

"Jesus, Gabs. I had no idea this was going on," Todd said in closing.

"Right," I said. "I know. Sorry."

The lawyer and I then spent twenty minutes on the phone during which she asked me to describe the details of the scheme and how I had learned it, and then, in the final three minutes of our strategy conversation, she asked me my date of birth. When she put the math of the year together, she stumbled for a minute: "Are you telling me you're only seventeen years old and you've been serving alcohol at the Lone Star Café for the past year?"

As I explained that part of my story, I could nearly hear her smiling ear to ear through the wires.

It apparently took less than an hour of her time, billed against her retainer, to get the charges dropped, but when she called me a few days later to tell me the good news, she was not festive. She advised me, authoritatively, to get my life together.

"You need to enroll in school and get out of state," she counseled. "In lieu of juvenile prosecution they could consider you for a juvenile diversion program, with counseling for twelve months, and this will also show on your lasting record. But I can't guarantee it so you'd better do a lot of good stuff, Hon, and do it fast."

I never even met her. But this stranger, brought to me by my brother through that technological innovation the conference call, was that walk-off-the-mound coach I'd been in need of some years earlier. Her grip on my neck was not as soft and not as encouraging as I always imagined the concern and guidance of an authoritative adult would feel. She scared me. It was sobering to finally encounter someone who wasn't egging me on to greater extremes of outrageousness, for their own vicarious pleasure, and who didn't for one second take me for anything but the teenager I was. I knew that I did not want to go to that juvenile diversion program because I had an intuitive sense that it would turn me irrevocably into the kind of character that I was now only rehearsing to be.

"I'm going to bill Todd and you work it out with him, okay? And you need to follow up with me in fifteen days so I can report back to the assistant DA."

And within a few weeks, I was, indeed, enrolled in college. I arrived on the campus of Hampshire College in the middle of an apple orchard in Amherst, Massachusetts, via Peter Pan bus. I was like a deep-sea diver who does not take the appropriate time coming up from twenty thousand leagues. People all around me were discussing Third World feminism, doing shifts at the on-campus food co-op, building eco-yurts for academic credit, and playing Ultimate Frisbee in their bare feet in the rain. I was still in cowboy boots *working my fucking tables,* sort of.

Monday through Thursday I wandered around this rural campus, with no required classes and a highly politicized culture, and started to get steeped in the language of the place—*div's and mod's and integratives*—and I ate stir-fry and tempeh and tofu for the first time in my life, as it was what we ate in our cooperative housing units where we spun the dial on a shared "work wheel" to divvy up the household chores. I met no one who knew where to score an eight-ball of coke.

Immediately, I got a job in town at a short-order diner called Jake's, cooking eggs and hash browns on a griddle top ladled with liquid oleo on Friday and Saturday night shifts. When the bars closed at one a.m.—rather provincial, I thought, having just come from New York and its four a.m. closing time—hundreds of drunk and stoned students from the surrounding five colleges crammed in for big plates of greasy food and coffee, rowdy from the bands they had just been out to see, or morose and limp from the foreign films they had endured, but either way, closer to me in age than anyone I'd been near to in years. I couldn't take my eyes off them and feasted on their fully incubated youth.

On campus, Bob Dylan and Bob Marley wafted out of the dorm windows, but in the kitchen at Jake's we crushed it all night long to Guns N' Roses. On weekends I cooked side by side with Greg, a part-time, Republican, poli-sci student at UMass, and we cranked out a thousand griddle-topped omelettes and pancakes at a pace I had not encountered since my chimichanga experiences as a young teenager. In the middle of the rush, he once called me over to the pass to look out at a father and his young daughter having pancakes after a night they'd had at the roller rink. I was truly impressed by this out-of-the-blue tenderness, taken aback that Guns N' Roses Greg had such a soft interior that he could call me over to admire this father-daughter moment, and as I looked back at Greg, beaming, he tossed his spatula in the air and whooped, "I bet she's pretty tight!"

He was smart and dirty-minded and a perfect gateway friend for me between the larcenous crowd I had just been with and these obscure new classmates I was now soaking bean curd with.

I had not heard of the My Lai Massacre, the Sandinistas or the Contras, Pinochet or Allende, but in the exact same way that I had been able to put on the navy blue T-shirt and make friends in the dressing room with the waitresses at the Lone Star Café, and to recite my line to the bartender when leaving his tip, I quickly enough learned to say "regime of torture" and "system of apartheid" and "military-industrial complex" as the coke snot dried up and my hair grew longer and I tried to become a college freshman, all over again.

I was not good at self-initiated studying and worse still at navigating a place that had no required classes and nobody writing you a demerit for detention if you didn't show up and didn't do any of the work. The first time I cut a class and nobody noticed made me feel from then on that nothing mattered and nobody cared. It was the most ill-conceived—not to mention expensive—education model I ever could have imagined for myself, this one in which you spring loose totally aimless eighteen-year-olds on a campus designed much more like graduate school than undergrad, and then watch all but the most serious and exceptional of them flail and falter. But it seemed like a perfect match when I was scrambling for a solution to my Grand Larceny and Possession of Stolen Property problems. A good friend of mine had graduated from the place and was on some Committee of Campus something at the time that I was having my run-in with Detective Sperro. My friend got me the application and the over-the-phone interview, not to mention the over-the-phone acceptance, in a dizzying span of two weeks, during which time I never once mentioned to the school my impending felonies. We were the hottest spot on the planet to be for Halloween—Purple blotter! Windowpane!—according to *Forbes* magazine, or maybe it was *Esquire,* with Bennington coming in second—LSD dosed out from Visine bottles!—and we had, as well, an attrition rate as infamous. I was out in five semesters, ditched, with barely any of my basic requirements met. But I was brimming with all of the appropriate intellectual angst and political discontent that had at first been foreign to me when I arrived. Now I was a staunch Marxist feminist, a budding lesbian, a black nationalist sympathizer, and a literacy advocate. I was also, once again, a dropout.

5

A T FIRST, MELISSA LET ME HAVE A LITTLE OF THE WIDE–OPEN SPACE
of the dirt-cheap loft she'd moved to on Driggs Avenue in
Brooklyn, while I figured out what to do next. Together we smoked
Camel filterless cigarettes and let our all-black laundry pile up while I
wrote endlessly in my journals and she painted large canvasses of dried
flower pods, clearly influenced by the painter Terry Winters, whose
brushes she was cleaning for a living. The winter days were pitch-black
by four forty-five in the afternoon, and with my dropout's prerogative,
I did not ever wake before one, leaving what felt like half an hour in
which to rally one's wholesome life into shape. I could barely shower
and finish the crossword puzzle before the day was already over.

I did not seek out my old Lone Star Café friends, and my brother
Todd, in just that short time, had become truly wealthy, inaccessible
and hard to reach, but also unrecognizable, with the new relentless
and lacerating sarcasm of a young man come lately into a shitload of
power. Melissa, who had gracefully managed to barely grimace or
flinch while I was coking it up at our apartment on Twenty-ninth
Street now flexed her maternal muscle and suffocated me with instructions about the kitchen dish towels, the coffee pot, the correct

route to the subway, and the hours of the Metropolitan Public Pool. It was way too late in the game for me to be able to receive surrogate mothering with any gladness. Meanwhile, if there was any single inch of my own flesh or remote coil of my own brain that I have warm regard for at this time, I cannot recall it. We agree that I need to make some different arrangements—maybe a summer in the country—and when spring emerges some weeks later, I have left Brooklyn and moved back to my hometown.

By the time I am gathering a lame and terribly pecked chicken from the pen on my dad's property, readying it and myself for its slaughter, it's become clear that a full summer of country air has done nothing for my outlook. I've been out of school for almost a full year, aimlessly putting a paycheck together in a hodgepodge of strange ways—I cleaned the rooms of a charming and historic bed-and-breakfast, cooked hamburger patties and turkey club sandwiches at a local public golf course canteen, and picked up as many waitress shifts as I could get at my friendly old spawning ground, Mother's on Main Street. The earth and sun have somehow revolved around each other so many times that, again, it's already getting dark by five o'clock and I am not one gibbous moon closer to a life plan. I live in the cold basement apartment of my dad's house.

That fall, I was often outside in my canvas jacket sitting on the log pile at dusk smoking hand-rolled cigarettes, feeling shrouded in gloom. I watched the garden decay, and a frost settle, and thought about death and the inherent beauty of the cycle of life. How untragic it would be, I thought, if I just killed the mailman or maybe myself, and returned to the earth. I was reading Dostoyevsky—who arranges the timing of these things?—and identified too strongly with Raskolnikov's desire to have all feelings, all sensations, and to kill a human being. I had it confused at the time with some literary context but I think, in hindsight, I was just brittle with subcutaneous rage, and bone tired. I had been hustling for a long time. Eternal sleep had strong appeal. I've all but begged to kill this chicken.

There was no need for me to be killing chickens. This wasn't 1930 or anything. And we weren't out on the Nebraska plains. We were in what had been my grandparents' house, up on the hill overlooking Lambertville, on the Jersey side of the Delaware, where my dad had been living since he'd sold the ruins. The house looked over a cemetery and had a deep woods behind it. It's true that my dad didn't have TV—the "tivvies" as he calls them—a telephone or a microwave—but these were aesthetic choices. There were people on either side of us—normal New Jersey neighbors—who knew of things like ice-in-the-door-of-the-fridge, MTV, and instant ramen noodles. He kept chickens as part of his gestalt.

There was one chicken in the coop being badly henpecked. My dad said we should kill the chicken and spare it the slow torture by its pen mates. I said I'd *like* to kill it. I said I *wanted* to kill it. I said it was important to confront the death of the animal you had the privilege of eating. I said it was cowardly to buy cellophane-wrapped packages of boneless, skinless breasts at the grocery store—desensitized, sanitized, devoid of any semblance of its live form.

This was what two years at Hampshire College had done to me.

My father, wishing I would comb my hair more often and pass quickly through this particular phase, said, "You can kill the thing when I get home from work."

He claimed to have grown up with chickens and said he had killed many in his boyhood, so I let him coach me through it.

From a remote spot on the back kitchen steps, he told me how to decisively gather the chicken out of the pen. Adding my own bit, I spoke to it philosophically about the cycle of life. I held it firmly and calmly with what I hoped was a soothing authority. Then he told me to take it by the legs and hold it upside down. The chicken protested from deep inside its throat, close to the heart, a violent, vehement, full-bodied cluck. The crowing was almost an afterthought. To get it to stop, my dad told me to start swinging it in full arm circles. I windmilled that bird around and around the way I had spun lettuce as a kid in the front yard, sending droplets of water out onto the gravel and pachysandra from the old-fashioned wire basket spinner my mom used.

He said this would disorient the bird—make it so dizzy that it couldn't move—and that's when I should lay it down on the block and chop its head off, with one succinct whack. If you're as practiced as my father claims to have been, your ten-year-old brother windmills the birds while you are chopping off their heads, and no sooner have you tossed one chicken into the grass to run around headless, than your brother is handing you another dazed chicken to whack, and like a machine you just spin and whack, spin and whack, until you've got twenty birds ready for the icebox for the next five winter months of Sunday suppers.

In my own way, not like a machine at all, I laid it down on a tree stump and while it was listless and trying to recover, I clutched the hatchet and came down on its neck. This first blow made a vague dent, barely breaking the skin. I hurried to strike it again, but lost a few seconds in my grief and horror. The second blow hit the neck like a boat oar on a hay bale. The bird started to orient. I was still holding its feet with one hand and trying to cut its head off with the dull hatchet with my other when both the chicken and my father became quite lucid, and not a little agitated. The chicken began to thrash about as if chastising me for my false promises of a merciful death and a poignant logic to its demise at my hand. My dad yelled, "Kill it! Kill it! Aw, Gabs, kill the fucking thing!" from his bloodless perch up on the landing of the kitchen steps.

I kept coming down on the bird's throat—which was now broken but still issuing terrible clucks of revolt and protest—stroke after miserable stroke, until I finally got its head off. I was blubbering through clenched teeth. My dad was animated with disgust at his dropout daughter—so morose, so unfeminine, with the tips of her braids dyed aquamarine, and unable even to kill a chicken properly. As I released the bird, finally, and it ran around and around the yard, bloody and ragged but at least now silent, he shouted, "You weren't fair to the damned thing!" which I heard as, "What kind of person are you?"

For a solid minute, and for a significant distance, the headless chicken ran around in the yard before its nerves gave out, spent themselves, and it fell over motionless in some dead brown leaves. This sight is pretty arresting but I was familiar with it as I had been to the Kutztown County Fair many times as a child where Mennonites and other rural Pennsylvania agricultural folks convened to sell scrapple, souse, double-yolk eggs, and funnel cakes. Bearded, suspendered guys at the fair butcher live chickens and let them run around in the pen with their heads cut off before wrapping them in butcher paper for you to take home.

The other chickens in their pen, now silhouetted against the darkening sky, retreated inside to roost for the night. My dad closed the kitchen door and turned on the oven.

It's quite something to go bare-handed up through an animal's ass and dislodge its warm guts. Startling, the first time, how fragilely they are attached.

I have since put countless suckling pigs—pink, with blue, querying eyes—the same weight and size of a pet beagle—into slow ovens to roast overnight so that their skin crisps and their still-forming bones melt into the meat, making it succulent and sticky. I have butchered two-hundred-twenty-pound sides of beef down to their primal cuts, carved the tongues out of the heads of goats, fastened whole baby lambs with crooked sets of teeth onto green ash spits and set them by the foursome over hot coals, and boned out the loins and legs of whole rabbits that—even skinned—still look exactly like bunnies. But at the time of the chicken killing, I was still young and unaccustomed.

I retrieved the bird off the frozen ground and tied its feet and hung it from a low tree branch so it could bleed out. Then I went inside and boiled a blue enamel lobster pot full of water. Once the bird bled out, I submerged it in boiling water to loosen its feathers. Sitting out on the back steps in the yellow pool of light from the kitchen window, I plucked the feathers off the chicken, two and three at a time. When I finished, it was reduced in size in a way I hadn't anticipated. Its viscera came out with an easy tug; a small palmful of livery, bloody jewels that I tossed out into the dark yard.

There are two things you should never do with your father: learn how to drive and learn how to kill a chicken. I'm not sure you should sit across from each other and eat the roasted bird in resentful silence either, but we did that too, and the meat, as if scripted, was disagreeably tough.

Bones

6

I'D LIKE TO JUMP AHEAD. MELISSA AND I IN OUR SEPARATE HOMES, hers with her husband and two daughters in a white clapboard near our hometown in New Jersey, mine with my gorgeous androgynous girlfriend in an East Village one-bedroom tenement apartment. Melissa leaves me that phone message, "Bwahahhahahahaha!!!" about the bone density study. That era.

I've graduated from college on my third try.

Stopped stealing things.

Don't want to kill anybody or anything anymore.

I've been working in the most unsavory corner of the food industry, except for maybe poultry processing, which is to say, for the past ten years I've been a grunt putting together a living as a freelancer in New York City catering kitchens. For the last several of those grim catering years, I cooked every July and August at a children's summer camp in western Massachusetts.

If you didn't know it was there and you weren't hunting for it, you would easily miss the camp's gravel road, which twisted down from the highway, cut through the woods, and eventually opened up into meadow. At the bottom of this road was a hundred-year-old slate-shingled barn that had since been converted, gently, into the bunks and dining hall and theater space of the children's camp. Up at the top of the wide sloping meadow, butting up to the tree line, were a few A-frame houses for the administrative and senior counselor staff and a miniature, one-room faded-shingle Cape Codder cottage—for me, the camp cook—from which you could look out upon the entire campus below and Mt. Monadnock in the distance and the jet green forest for miles between.

While the cottage was only a single ten-foot-by-ten-foot room, it had paned windows on all four sides that made everything look watery and seemed to erase the boundary between outdoors and indoors. It had a tiny porch with a step down into the tall grass, which was just big enough for two people to sit smoking a cigarette without burning each other, but barely. In back, there was a fenced-in spot where I hung my towel to dry when I returned from the communal showers across the way, and in that miniature yard I always planted, for the summertime, outdoorsy hell of it, a few rows of cosmos. When the dew on the windows in the early mornings was so thick that it trickled like rain, I often felt as if I were sleeping outdoors, on one of the longest and best camping trips ever taken.

Every year, I arrived a few days before camp officially started, when the grass was still waist-high from the year's growth and the land was utterly still save for the wildlife. I spent those days down in the huge camp kitchen in what used to be the dairy barn, unpacking all the cooking pans and pots that we had so carefully washed and put away the year before at the end of August, and found all the cutlery and plates and cereal bowls and ran everything, anew, through the dishwasher. In silence, except for the kitchen radio, I swept out the chipmunk and field mouse droppings from the screened-in dry-goods room and made lists, and plugged in the kitchen phone, and scrubbed down all the counters until the place was ready to prepare food for, at first, the dozen or so counselors, and then right behind them, the one hundred campers of the first session.

With my teeth chattering uncontrollably from the deep chill of the early morning—it got cold in those hills in the summertime!—I tugged on my pants and heavy sweatshirt and readied myself to go down to the barn and finish preparing the kitchen. A most unnatural and frenetic rustling of the grasses just a few feet away beyond my tiny front porch sent a rocket of alarm up my spine. I froze, immediately and intuitively terrified.

One woman, utterly alone, in the middle of a woods, out of earshot.

I ducked down low—adrenaline coursing through my veins as I quickly calculated exactly how alone I was with no bodega, taxi cab, or pedestrian nearby—and silently but quickly stepped into my rubber boots. Fully dressed, I spider-walked to the backmost wall of the cottage and stood back up slowly so I could peer out the window without being seen by whoever was crawling through the tall grass. In those few seconds of involuntary adrenaline rush, I imagined, with total clarity, the derelict who had walked down from the highway, ventured along our gravel road, and was now creeping up to my cabin to torture me at knifepoint for the next four solitary days and nights. No doubt he was attracted by my car parked beside the cottage, a signal to him of potential prey, I imagined vividly how he walked past the uninhabited A-frames, ignoring them, and was now down on all fours, obscured by the tall grass, creeping up to my flimsy screen door.

I saw his stringy hair, his greasy sort of goatee, his dirty army surplus jacket, his jeans hanging off his thin frame, his partially unlaced sand-colored boots and his two socks, both white but one with green stripes and the other with orange.

And in an instant, there in front of my porch waddled a wild turkey as big as a Labrador. And behind it, one after another after another, came *sixteen* more.

I watched this procession in silent awe, my body deflating like an unplugged swimming pool mattress, and counted seventeen wild turkeys with prehistoric-looking heads, as they waddled their way through the tall grass covered in heavy dew and made their way down the long sloping meadow.

The work at camp was in an airy, wide-open kitchen with a view of camp life from every screened window: horses in a paddock;

"Birch" girls—the eight-year-olds—in flip-flops with their towels around their necks stomping down the hill to the pool; the "Willow" boys—twelve-year-olds—playing soccer just beyond the arts barn with about as much form and finesse as a kitten chasing a cotton toy at the end of a wire held by a slightly mean human. Wherever the ball went, they all went. The bunks were separated by age and gender and named after trees, from Birch to Spruce to Willow. It was such a welcome departure from the kitchens I had worked in all fall, all winter, all spring—all my life really—with its wide-planked wooden floors and wooden cabinets and the jubilant purply mural of happy children painted on the wall.

I felt like a severe arthritic—hunched and limping to Lourdes and miraculously standing upright, freed from joint pain—to be in a place where the pine-scented breeze swept through the afternoon prep shift, and the fireflies snuck in after dinner when the campers left the screen door open, and where early early in the mornings while I made coffee and turned on the ovens I would catch chipmunks, cheeks bulging, trying to make off with granola bars and loaves of sliced bread.

The catering kitchen where I had clocked most of my hours that season, where I had just been days before, was in a warehouse on the West Side Highway. I put together my paycheck among two or three of the highest-volume catering companies in the city, and they were all eerily the same. During the off-seasons, these operations kept a skeleton crew of a few cooks, dishers, and drivers to handle little dinner parties for publishing executives and Wall Streeters, but *in-season*—fall, holidays, spring, and that season unto its own: wedding—these kitchens teemed with freelance mercenary cooks who possessed few skills and fewer scruples, and I worked side by side with them for more than a decade. We moved around from kitchen to kitchen, wherever the work was, got paid triple what restaurant work paid, and managed our flexible schedules by simply not booking in for any days we needed off.

In composite, as an entire organism, we had the skills to pull off what was required—there would be someone on the crew who could produce by day's end an elaborate miraculous bûche du noël, studded with little perfect meringue mushrooms, and another who could brilliantly organize a plate-out for 350 that would saturate the banquet room in perfectly hot dinners on clean-rimmed plates in less than fourteen minutes start to finish, and perhaps another who really did have a feel for meat cooking and who might come in early and pre-season the birds or the loins even though no one asked her or paid her do so. But the bulk of what was served to party-going New Yorkers was ground out in a robot coupe—rosemary aioli, harissa hummus, white bean puree—by a revolving and ever-interchangeable warm body in a rented chef coat who knew not one thing about what a homemade mayonnaise might be. You would never be fired for throwing a cup of sour cream and a little walnut oil into your breaking aioli because you didn't know a thing, just like a hundred catering hackers before and a hundred after you, about the relationship of raw garlic to egg yolk and blended oil, but even if you were, there was always another right behind you to take your place.

These windowless kitchens, all of them, were lit with harsh fluorescents, and when you entered at seven a.m. and didn't exit until two a.m. sometimes, having prepped all day and then gone out to chef the party at the museum or the gallery or the private home—I've done a shift that long easily a hundred times—you looked tubercular—by the time you clocked out.

The debris that accumulated in those kitchens—sneakers, hoodies, but also food left over from jobs—sat in the walk-in for weeks until an energetic and anal-retentive cook with a little hustle and who happened to still give a shit, tossed it. She spent a quick hour, her jacket on over her chef's whites, inside the huge refrigerated walk-in tossing clear plastic quart and pint containers labeled with masking tape and black Sharpie into the garbage. The containers had names of places, not names of foods—the places where they had been on that day's dizzying roster of multiple events leaving the warehouse kitchen in six different vans at about the same time. BOTANICAL. MONH. LIBRARY.

She could not guess what was moldering away inside each pint container, but she knew, when tossing the shit out, that the event had been at the botanical gardens, the American Museum of Natural History, or the New York Public Library.

The food we produced in these kitchens was often bad but not as bad as what had to be done to it to get it from the warehouse kitchen on the West Side Highway to the botanical gardens, the museum, or finally into the mouths of the wedding guests in Amagansett. Catering, in that era, was not cooking. It was factory work in a refrigerated truck or cargo van or even the four-car garage of an oceanfront property in the Hamptons, if that's where the event was and if that was the only viable place to set up our makeshift kitchen with Sterno ovens and propane burners and coolers filled with evaporating dry ice to keep the molded ice-cream flowers frozen.

The smoked salmon and cream cheese pinwheel—that steadfast staple of all catering kitchens throughout all of time—had been touched by four or five people by the time the guest ate it: the guy who opened the salmon and laid it out on sheets of plastic wrap, the guy who spread whipped cream cheese on it and rolled it up, the guy who later unwrapped and sliced it, the guy who garnished it with chopped chives and arranged it in careful circles on a sixteen-inch round silver or fourteen-inch square black-lacquered tray, and probably even the waiter on his way out to the cocktail reception bearing that tray and in his other hand a small stack of artfully fanned out cocktail napkins.

The bruschetta under the three different toppings—tomato-basil concassé, Tuscan white bean, and Sicilian tuna salata—which was to sit at the Italian station, was nothing more than sliced baguette that had been laid out on sheet pans and blitzed in the double-decker convection oven, then sprayed with cheap blended olive oil, using the kind of spray bottle commonly used for Windex and houseplants. I had seen those toast rounds sit out on a rolling rack in the warehouse kitchen all week.

At some point in the catering world of the late '80s and early '90s, someone thought of putting food into a shot glass, and thus the hors d'oeuvre shooter was born. And so, all season long, I portioned mucusy preshucked tub oysters with lemongrass mignonette, or minted pea soup, or vodka-spiked gazpacho into two-ounce shot glasses. We set the filled shooters back into their slotted dish racks—one per person of each menu item multiplied times three hundred guests is nine hundred shot glasses—and stacked the interlocking dish racks in a neat, sturdy tower in the walk-in refrigerator, where they sat for hours and hours. At the load-out, someone wrapped the whole tower in commercial plastic wrap, shimmied it onto a hand truck, and wheeled it to the refrigerated truck to make the journey to the Hamptons. This can look just like a dockworker with a pallet at a warehouse and nothing like a white-jacketed chef artfully coaxing the best flavor from your food. Apollo, meanwhile, whose smile was sunshine itself in an otherwise weatherless world, diced and smashed limes with sugar in coffee cups, filled them with ice and cachaça and introduced us, decades before it was wildfire, to the caipirinha, the national drink of his home country, Brazil. We arrived at our parties a little lit.

Once at the party, the cook working the cold appetizers station—an eight-foot rectangular table with a cloth thrown over it—simply pulled out a rack at a time from the back of the truck and set the glasses by the dozen on a silver round tray, and they were whisked away by the waiter, a tuxedoed guy wearing shockingly blue contact lenses, who then had to stand in front of the wedding guest explaining its contents.

"Chilled pea soup! Yes! You drink it! Just like a shooter!"

After the shot glass came the Chinese soup dumpling spoon.

The edible sugarcane skewer.

The espresso cup.

We used all of these gimmicks for portioning the hors d'oeuvres and serving them to the guests on a garnished silver tray.

Self-contained items that required no skewer, toast round, or shot glass—like pigs-in-blankets, curried beef mini-empanadas, and sushi, which we always contracted out to a commercial producer in Queens—the one that supplies grocery stores and delis with those little to-go boxes of "assorted sushi"—sailed out of the back of the truck, got reheated in the garage if necessary, and were sent out on a heavily garnished bamboo-weave tray right into the bride and groom's tummies.

When the intended couple had agreed on this menu, back in January, after a private tasting in the little nicely dressed and furnished showroom of the catering company, it had been prepared for them by the chef of the company, in just enough quantity for the tasting—not more than four portions of each thing—and each ingredient had been hand-selected by the chef and prepared the same day as it was eaten. In fact, it went from stove to table during the tasting and it, indeed, looked and tasted very good. I had been assigned to execute dozens of those tastings over the years and felt genuine pride in what we produced.

But by the time the bride and groom, now betrothed, and their three hundred guests were enjoying this same meal on a beautiful June evening, we were now on a very different scale of production. A whole crew of mixed talent and fluctuating demeanor—catering cooks—had been booked in for the week to produce it. To be sure, this couple was not the only one to have decided on June fifteenth as their ideal wedding date, and not the only one to have been nudged by the party planner toward the "grilled salmon filet on a bed of leek compote with preserved lemon relish" as their entree. We were producing six to ten jobs at the same time, every day, at the peak of the season. Food for thousands of wedding guests and college graduates and US Open attendees—all the accounts the full-time party planners up in the front offices had spent all year cultivating—was being cranked out of those warehouse kitchens on the West Side all at once, by slightly crazy people. The party planners, to a one, had mono *and* shingles by the end of every June.

On the kitchen crew there was always a Patty—the chemically cheerful girl who could work a twenty-two-day stretch of doubles without blinking. She would chirp, "Sure," with her eyes unnaturally wide open when asked, on day thirteen of her doubling marathon, if she could run the hors d'oeuvres for one thousand at the Brooklyn Botanical Gardens, then get up the following morning and set up the brunch in Banquet Room C at the midtown Marriott, where the International Planned Parenthood Chapter Heads would be having back-to-back conferences. She would agree to come in at five a.m. and bake off all the mini-muffins, mini-scones, and mini-quiches and to roll up the mini-black-bean roll-ups without even checking her book or calling her boyfriend. She would go out and drink White Russians all night but still work every hour she committed to. Her paychecks were knockout.

There was also always a steady lethargic prep cook like Nancy, and usually several of her friends and cousins, who sat around an island of stainless steel prep tables all day, like factory workers, assembling goat cheese in phyllo dough purses by the thousand. She refused to work parties, and so had arranged her schedule to end at five o'clock every day. Humming a little calypso tune as she smiled and waved kisses good night to us all at the end of her shift, she would walk out with gallons of bleach and dish soap that she'd stolen from the unlocked cage downstairs near the changing room, and sell it on Eastern Parkway to her West Indian neighbors.

There was also always a Rich, the guy who used to walk quickly and purposefully from one room to another, giving us all the impression that he was banging out a job, a prep list, a pack sheet, a van load-out, or an equipment pull. When in fact that was just his strategy for earning his $17.50 an hour to prep while accomplishing little. He was always the one dicking with the boom box in the kitchen, incessantly popping in CDs he was so psyched to "turn us on to," as if he were our unsolicited mentor. Rich had that characteristic compulsion I frequently encountered in catering cooks, that incessant and pressing need to declare his credentials as a real cook.

"Yeah, man, I'm just doing this shit for a short stretch, until I find the right place to jump back into restaurants. It's gotta be the *right* place with *my* kind of quality." He'd blow that same hot air for years, while taking a cigarette break on the back loading dock. "I mean, look, I tried to show 'em aioli, but I just gave up, man. . . ." It was not only impossible for him to accept his complicity in the crap we were producing, but he was also driven to inflate his own credentials to such dimensions that it made us all squirm, stomp out our cigarettes, and rush, for relief, back to our cutting boards inside.

"I *invented* aioli, man. . . ."

The wedding meal itself, a sit-down dinner for three hundred that followed the butlered hors d'oeuvres hour, had sat in the warehouse kitchen refrigerator, some components of it for days, and then in the back of the cargo van in bumper-to-bumper traffic on the LIE. On the long ride out to Amagansett, three cater waiters assigned to ride with us, so they can help us unload cases of Sterno and staff cola and seltzer at the destination, sat on their garment bags containing their waiter tuxedos and sang show tunes. In the way, way back of the cargo van—perched on a five-gallon bucket of leek compote amid stacks and stacks of disposable aluminum hotel pans packed with salmon filets portioned at four ounces and already partially blasted in the convection ovens back at the warehouse—sat Andrea, the freelance chef assigned to run the party.

He, dear bride and groom, was the bitter and viciously funny guy chain-smoking Marlboros, about to oversee your very expensive love meal. For the eighty-three-mile ride from our loading dock to your spread on Mill Pond Road, he bitched all the way about how shitty this company is and wondered aloud the whole way to the Hamptons why he should give a shit if "they" don't give a shit, all the while doing a caustic and exquisite interpretive dance on those five-gallon buckets. And the rented hackers? The freelance kitchen assistants assigned to assist him, to shove shot glasses onto trays and to reheat salmon in five side-by-side Sterno-fueled proofing cabinets that we've dubbed "the wall of fire"? They think he's fucking hysterical. Me, too. He's *very* funny. The death of your party but what a van ride!

That swarm of truly mediocre cooks, after constant repeated handling of this bride's food in preparation for her Hamptons wedding, clock out at the warehouse thirteen hours later, leaving their old dirty shoes and Saran Wrap belts all over the locker room floors, and the next day they head uptown two blocks to the next company and their next four days of booked work. Or in my case, to the Berkshires to cook for little kids at two months of sleepaway camp.

And I had just seen seventeen wild turkeys!

Not that hiring for camp was a piece of cake. We advertised both locally—in the *Berkshire Gazette* and the *Northampton Star*—but also in New York City in the back of the *Village Voice*. I spent a few nervous days culling out the few unsavories who had applied for the job, wondering if I was going to have a crew at all. You have to ask yourself what's wrong with the local townie guy who submits his application for a summer cook position at a remote children's camp, thirty miles from any nearby town—especially when he turns out to be thirty-five years old and arrives on a girl's 3-speed bicycle for the interview. I was disinclined to hire some guy with a driver's license revoked for DUI, needless to say, on a campus with a hundred plump nubile boys and girls sleeping soundly in their unlocked smelly-sock bunks. I also nixed the applications of grown-up former campers who had always thought it "looked fun" to work in the kitchen, and although they'd had zero experience working in any kitchen, anywhere, really wanted to "check it out." Everyone thinks cooking is "fun." Everyone who doesn't do it professionally thinks it's fun. And it is fun, but not for the same reasons they think it will be. They think it's the same as trying out a new recipe for brownies like you do at home, with the radio on.

In the end I was able to cobble together a pretty wholesome crew. Finishing up for the day, I put salt in all the salt shakers with grains of rice to absorb the humidity, filled all the soap dispensers, and fried myself three eggs for dinner, which I ate on the back stoop of the barn, looking out over the empty horse paddock and the surrounding fields. Ending my long last day of preparing the kitchen, I turned out the lights and went back up to my cottage and got ready to greet all the counselors and the kitchen crew as they made their way to camp the following day.

At midday, bleary-eyed and not a little spooked by the enormous and powerful force of nature itself engulfing him, Shaun arrived by bus from New York City.

"I need to get back to the Bronx," he joked when I came out from the barn to greet him where he was standing in the fresh air and sunshine with his neat duffel held close to his body. Shaun was a Jamaican guy with the most delicious jerk marinade I've ever encountered, which I still use frequently in the summer. It has about twenty-five ingredients in it, including stout, honey, and scotch bonnet peppers.

Shaun spent the long hours after the kitchen was clean and shut down each night—while I was making lists and ordering and sipping bourbon and cokes in my cottage—making fruit carvings. He was afraid to return to his room where there might be bugs. I think he slept with the sheet pulled taut over his head, like a body in a morgue, the entire summer. In the morning I would come down and find elaborate apple swans and watermelon dragons in the walk-in.

And from just a few miles down the road came Debbie, a local mom. She enrolled her girls for free at the camp while she worked in the kitchen each day. It was always a happy and strong hug between us when we reunited each summer. She was that classic rural woman who, with her husband, does every job she knows to meet their bills and keep their three daughters in clean clothes and neatly combed pigtails. Between them they plowed roads, drove the school bus, baked specialty cakes in the shape of a baseball diamond with a Red Sox logo, had a public notary license, and worked in the school cafeteria during the year. I loved her.

She knew just the nearby farm to go to when we had a shortage of milk and needed dozens of gallons immediately. Much of the stress of the job with children was in figuring out the pars—how much of each item, like milk for example, would a campful of kids go through each day, each week. A lot, it turns out. And so I bought it by the five-gallon plastic sack, ten sacks at a time, once I understood how they'd suck it down.

Running out of milk in the middle of the dark woods with no town nearby and a hundred kids far away from home—some of them for the first time—rattled me but left Debbie calm and even-keeled.

"But what the fuck am I going to give them to fucking drink?" I asked, discovering that the milk "cow" in the dining room, that refrigerated stainless box with the two heavy levers that spout milk when you lift them and stanch its flow when you lower them—had run dry. Two swear words in one sentence had become as effortless a part of me as my own saliva.

"Kool-Aid!" Debbie replied cheerfully. She was used to opening big number-ten cans of corn and beans and mashed potatoes that they served at school lunch, and I didn't know anything about this, and I knew even less about kids. I naively didn't understand that they would *prefer* Kool-Aid to milk. Debbie grew her own tomatoes and zucchini in her garden at home but was no foe of processed foods. I loved that she gave her kids homegrown vegetables and big glasses of sugary processed Kool-Aid right alongside. That is my favorite kind of integrated person. Some of each thing and not too much of any one.

These two rocks, Shaun and Debbie, I could totally rely on. The other four helpers were the only former campers, now turning eighteen and nineteen years old, who had not written "fun" on the application. And here they all were.

By four o'clock in the afternoon, all the counselors had arrived, having filtered in slowly throughout the day, some on the morning bus, and the rest in their parents' hand-me-down Camrys and Saabs. They passed through the kitchen area of the barn on their way to and from setting up their bunks, carrying sleeping bags and Hackey Sacks and hiking boots, and all stopped to say hello. The girls kept their hair long and loose, all the way down their backs, and they wore pajama-bottom pants all the day long, not just for sleeping. Most of them had been campers themselves and so knew each other since childhood. I'd heard of this kind of enduring bond but had nothing to relate it to in my own experience. I was firmly in the out-of-sight-out-of-mind camp, and had cogent, unflinchingly honest declarations I frequently made about losing a shared context, and sentimentalism, and the general faintheartedness of most people—but I knew there were people in the world who remained friends, for life, with bunk mates from sleepaway camp, and this was that group of people.

Among them, there was so much deep hugging and excited shrieking to be seeing each other again, I often stopped in the middle of my food prep to marvel at the show.

I made a nice big meal with lentils and lamb leg and fennel salad and roasted cherry tomatoes with bread crumbs. I'd been told ahead of time that almost all the counselors were vegetarian. The girls, at least. The guys seemed happy to see the meat. And dinner with all twelve or fifteen of them gathered around three picnic tables pulled together to make one lasted a couple of hours. A long dinner then turned into an even longer evening of fireside guitar and deep serious conversations that were constantly punctuated by more deep hugging between them all. I had not seen such a thing since I myself was nineteen and working two simultaneous hits of Ecstasy.

Shaun and I cleaned up the kitchen and made our plans for the next week, while the guitar player strummed away in the next room. Until now, it had just been me and the turkeys and the camp director, who spent the last of her free days painting abstract paintings in her A-frame before the onslaught of campers and their parents arrived.

This was the last meal I could prepare that still had adult appeal to it, because the next morning, the four-foot-tall "nothing green, nothing spicy, nothing healthy, nothing dark, nothing but nuggets" crumb snatchers arrived and for the rest of the summer we cooked little more than plain spaghetti and plain chicken.

It's hard to cook for kids, and when something doesn't appeal to them, instead of saying a polite *no thank you,* they instead break into a giant yuk face and shriek "eewww" right in front of you, as if you had no feelings at all. There were moments that summer when I felt more distressed by a nine-year-old's disgust with a fleck of basil in his tomato sauce than I had in the entire previous decade when ostensibly more serious failures had occurred. Somehow, a crack in my fully cultivated antipathy toward children and their insipid tenderness had formed, and without even the slightest understanding of why or how, I felt worse at the thought that I might be undernourishing the kids than I did when, for example, all the quenelled saffron-pistachio ice cream melted onto the gold-rimmed plates when the king of Thailand spontaneously rose from his seat at the luncheon honoring his presence and gave an unscheduled and wordy toast. Worse watching a homesick Birch boy walk away disappointed from the empty milk cow than watching that line of tuxedoed waiters standing there with plates in their hands, ice cream pooling, strictly forbidden to move.

We cooked from scratch, and even though it was only baked chicken and buttered noodles and spaghetti and meatballs we made it all ourselves. I worried that I wouldn't have enough peanut butter or breakfast cereal and that I was thirty miles from the nearest town with only a once-a-week appearance of that giant eighteen-wheeler that Sysco would send up from Boston on Wednesdays. Bearing everything I needed for the kitchen, except vegetables, that gleaming monster of a truck would slowly make its way down the winding and meandering gravel road, the driver in a blue uniform with a name patch sewed on his breast pocket and a blue Sysco trucker's hat, taking his time. This would not be a good place for an eighteen-wheeler to get stuck in a ditch. The counselor girls in their pajama bottoms and the counselor guys in their Greenpeace T-shirts paused their hackey-sack games and made a human chain from the back of the truck to the kitchen where they good-naturedly hauled in the huge weekly order and stacked it.

The produce came from a local organic operation out of Amherst. Their truck was a battered mustard yellow panel truck with a big butternut squash logo on the sides, and the drivers were all good-looking and polite and incredibly friendly guys in dungarees who had quite possibly just graduated, not in traditional cap and gown but in Birkenstocks with a bell-ringing ritual, from my alma mater, Hampshire College.

Kids don't eat vegetables but I bought them the best anyway. I had accepted the logistical fate of ordering meat and dairy and dry goods from Sysco when I understood that being on a hundred wooded acres out in the pine forests of western Massachusetts took me off the delivery routes of better purveyors. But I couldn't bring myself to buy vegetables from them, too.

Many of these kids had suspicious food allergies that I had to carefully work around. At the beginning of every session, I passed around a survey to all the bunks—Birch through Willow, boys and girls—and asked each child to alert us to any special dietary needs, any allergies or diabetes or issues around food. Every year for the four years that I was the chef at this camp, there would be one boy with a very serious peanut allergy, who really would swell up and die if I carelessly used the same spoon at the make-your-own-sundae bar for jimmies as I had used for peanuts, while every session I had no fewer than sixteen girls with "allergies" to dairy and wheat—cheese and bread basically—but also to garlic, eggplant, corn, and nuts. They had cleverly developed "allergies," I believe, to the foods they had seen their own mothers fearing and loathing as diet fads passed through their homes. I could've strangled their mothers for saddling these girls with the idea that food is an enemy—some of them only eight years old and already weird about wanting a piece of bread—and I would've liked to bludgeon them, too, for forcing me to participate in their young daughters' fucked-up relationship with food. I was obliged to attend to the allergies. For the first time in probably the entire decade that had passed since I had seen or spoken to my own mother, I thought warm and grateful thoughts about her. She instilled in us nothing but a total and unconditional pleasure in food and eating.

There were a couple of girls at this camp, however, who were quite different. And many nights during dinner these sisters would come up to the huge open kitchen window—the pass-through—where we the kitchen crew served out platter after unbreakable melamine platter of pale, bland, innocuous, and inoffensive foods to the kids assigned as that night's table waiters and then stood there waiting to refill their family-style platters with "seconds." These girls would come up to the window and ask, politely, for "the balsamic vinegar, please." Oh, little Emma! With her chubby cheeks and some braided thing around her wrist that she had made that afternoon in the crafts barn—I could've kissed her every evening for appreciating the food and even daring me to make it a little more "adult" at every meal. Those kinds of kids can be obnoxious, too, I admit, with their oversophisticated tastes, turning up their noses at good old fried chicken, claiming to prefer "a paillard, quickly sautéed," and insisting on extra virgin olive oil. That kind of cultivated taste could be sort of unbearable in an eight year old, but not this girl. She was pleased to please me, almost aware of how charming she was, in her little way, asking for Parmesan cheese, or fresh black pepper. But most of the one hundred or so kids ate like pigs—and just as fast and just as loud, and made big gruesome messes of their meals by pouring milk into their food and stirring it around giggling uncontrollably while their counselor pretended to keep some order at the table.

Three weeks into it, just when I thought I would die from tater tots and baked chicken, we had session change, and all the parents came up to camp for Parents' Visiting Day. At last, I could really roll out a spread—a spicy, slimy, wiggly, bitter, green, and bony spread. I couldn't spend any real money—it wasn't in the budget—but I could cook anything I wanted. We were giddy, Shaun and I, to have our hands in stinky Vietnamese fish sauce for the vegetarian spring rolls, which we packed with cilantro and jicama and carrots and cucumbers. The four kitchen helpers were maybe not so enthused to be pulling the beards out of and scrubbing twenty pounds of mussels for the chilled mussels on the half shell with vinaigrette, but if working in a kitchen was something they all had wanted to "check out," this was a perfect introduction. As best as we could, using the butter-yellow melamine plates, we artfully arranged soppressata, Alfonso olives, hard cheeses, and bread that had crust and body—that could actually hurt the roof of your mouth if you were unaccustomed. We fried fatty, bony duck wings and coated them in toasted sesame seeds. We untangled mounds of curly bitter endive and tamed it with pear and walnuts and vinegar with bacon fat.

It was a perfect New England summer day, hot and breezy and a saturated blue sky made more beautiful by puffy white clouds. Parents in clogs and Tevas, having almost all arrived from Brooklyn in Volvo station wagons, were swarming the campus, moving from bunk to arts barn to theater to see all of the clever and crafty things their kids had been doing for the past three weeks. I was transferring a whole side of cold poached sea bass from a sheet pan onto a serving platter—the fish a little longer than our largest platter, unfortunately—and getting ready to dress it with some parsley oil, when I noticed one of these parents standing at the pass-through, watching me with amused curiosity.

"Hello there," I said.

"Are you responsible for all this?" he asked, pointing back to the buffet.

"Um, I guess so. Yes."

"I'm Emma's dad. She's been telling me about you all summer."

"Emma's dad!" I cried, lighting up. "I love Emma!"

I put down my spoon and went to the pass to shake hands.

"I'm Gabrielle."

He said so many kind things about the food, and I felt so rewarded, but I noticed that he spoke about the food the way that only someone who works with food could. There is a way, a distinct way, that people who work in the industry speak to each other about food and you can tell, within minutes, that they are part of your extended clan. It's not like an obnoxious foodie talks about food, ostentatiously throwing around kitchen terms and names of ingredients they have researched at length. It's not like an appreciative eater talks about food—awed and enamored and perfectly happy to speak of his enjoyment without having any idea of what he's just eaten or how it was achieved. It's the way only someone who works in the industry talks about food, by almost not talking about it, but just throwing out a few code words and signals—like a gang member flashing you his sign. Every single time that I sit at a restaurant's bar, order the txacoli or grüner veltliner rather than the sauvignon blanc, ask for the razor clams and not the calamari, I am sniffed out immediately by the server as an industry peer. Having said nothing.

"Who are you?" I finally asked, having picked up every single one of his gang signs.

"I'm Mark. Mark Bittman."

The father of Emma turned out to be Mark Bittman, the cookbook writer and New York Times columnist. Of course she loved balsamic vinegar and Parmesan cheese and fresh ground black pepper.

At the end of every summer, I was asked to prepare a lavish and special dinner for the staff. The tradition was to have lobster, that creature that most signals luxury and splurge. After the last weeping deeply tanned kid had pulled out of camp, with his Popsicle-stick cabin and tie-dyed T-shirts in the trunk of his parents' car, waving out the dusty back window to all of his beloved counselors the entire length of the gravel road until he was out of sight, we were all left alone on the beautiful campus. We had to clean up and close down. Between this very minute and sundown the next night, the canoes needed to be hung in the shed and all the life vests washed and sun dried and then wrapped in heavy black garbage bags. The glue and glitter and pipe cleaners in the art barn had to be neatly arranged in their tight-lidded two-pound coffee cans. The mattresses and springed cots needed to be stacked in the barn attic. And when that was done, everyone could come down to the fire pit for an outdoor feast in appreciation of their hard work dispensed all summer long.

Each year, I butterflied and grilled whole Maine lobsters over real wood charcoals and basted them with smoked paprika butter. I grilled leeks and red onion, and corn on the cob in the husk after soaking it in one of the horse's water tubs filled from the garden hose. We had sliced tomatoes and cherries and watermelon. And in this instance, with the kids gone, we drank a lot of cold beer.

In Northampton, a twenty-five-minute drive south on a quiet set of roads, there was a good seafood guy. I got my lobsters from him every year. It was a fun excursion and a total change of pace and scenery to head into town with its foreign film houses and organic coffee roasters and summer session Smith College girls riding their bicycles around. I resurrected a routine I had established when I was in college nearby and working at Jake's, of stopping at Steve's ice cream for a scoop of malted date and a scoop of sweet cream ice cream—two flavors like your birthday and Christmas morning rolled together—and then proceeding on to the seafood wholesaler to pick up my thirty clawed beasts, neatly packed and sound asleep in chilled Styrofoam "coffins," as they're called. I'd return to camp in the late afternoon, put the Styrofoam boxes of live two-pound lobsters right into the walk-in, then grill them the following evening down at the fire pit.

My last year as camp cook, I decided to skip my normal routine and instead of going into town myself, I passed the errand off to the whole gang of counselors who were taking the van into town to bum around and do laundry and drink beer. I was really looking forward to a quiet vacated campus. The impending return to my cramped New York City apartment and that grisly catering workload was weighing on me differently than years past and I wanted to stay on campus as many of these last hours as I could. I asked Laurel, one of the long-haired, pajama-pants hippy girls who was assigned to drive the van, if she could go to the wholesaler and pick up my lobsters, which I'd already ordered.

"Sure, man," she said, ignoring my gender. "But, like, we're probably gonna get back kinda late, y'know?" She giggled.

I understood this to mean that they were going to hit a bar for a while before returning to camp.

"No problem," I said. "Just throw the boxes into the walk-in when you get back if I'm not still up. That's all you have to do."

"Okay. Cool," she agreed. And soon, the campus was nearly empty. Even Shaun, a teetotaler, had joined the group just to get away from the insect-ridden wilderness that he'd been enduring for six weeks.

I spent the whole day in silence cleaning and wrapping up the kitchen. Debbie and the kitchen crew had done a major job in washing all of the plates and cups and cutlery and putting it all away in the attic. And they'd taken a vanload of surplus dry goods over to the school, where it would be put to good use in the coming weeks. I was left to clean the stoves and scour the walk-in and unplug the phone and de-lime the dishwasher. Tasks I love, as they keep your hands occupied and your mind free to wander.

I watched the horse ladies back up their trailer to the paddock and load the horses into it and then drive away, slowly making their way up the long drive. Suzette, the maintenance gal who walked around all summer with her toolbelt on, nailed closed the barn shutters and padlocked every outbuilding on camp, finally hanging all the keys in their labeled spots in the office, and went home. I left myself a couple of cutting boards and the few things I would need to produce the meal the following afternoon, but since I would be grilling almost all of the food down at the fire pit, I had the rest of the kitchen pretty nicely put down. I emptied all the salt shakers and the soap dispensers and scrubbed out the milk cow with bleach. At dusk, a bluer and earlier setting dusk, I noticed, this late in August than it had been in June when we arrived, I made a small meal out of a few leftovers in the fridge and headed for the screen door to sit on the back stoop. Something made me stop short, and hang in mid-stride. At first I smelled an incredibly pungent kind of ammonia as I froze my hand on the door just about to push it open. I could hear someone breathing, heavily and irregularly. I stood dead still. And then a full-grown black bear ambled by, not ten feet away, with nothing but screen door between him and me and my bowl of dinner. He continued on his way down past the barn and across the field and disappeared into the woods, just as it was getting too dark to easily make out his shape in the distance. I opened the door, sat down on the stoop and ate my dinner.

The kids were not back from town, so I turned out the light and went up to my cottage, loudly clapping my hands the whole way in the dark to scare off any other thing that might appear. At around midnight I heard the van creeping down the long road to camp, its headlights and taillights the only illuminated things in an otherwise pitch-black night. Silence everywhere except for their drunken laughter and the car radio blowing out the windows. I heard them park and kill the ignition. And then I heard the slam of the screen door to the kitchen, as it echoed up the hill to my cottage. Feeling secure that they had just deposited the lobsters in the walk-in, I turned out my light and went to sleep.

I was always the first one up at camp. I had to get to the kitchen by six to make sure waffles were made and coffee brewed and the canoe trips packed out with their crates of food. The director rang the camp bell at seven-thirty, and each morning there was a camp-wide assembly outside the dining hall, before they would all pile in for breakfast. I did this every morning. First one in, to be quite ready.

So even on the last day, with the kids gone, and nothing but our end-of-year counselor appreciation dinner to pull off, by habit I still was up and heading down through the wet grass in my tall rubber boots at around six the following morning. I pulled open the screen door, ducked under the pass-through to enter the kitchen, and nearly crushed a lobster lying right there at my feet. I couldn't comprehend what I was seeing. What was a dead lobster doing on the floor at the entrance to the kitchen? Had it fallen, unnoticed, out of one of the coffins when the kids were putting them away last night? How drunk could they have been not to notice?

I followed my eyes across the kitchen floor and I'm not sure if I moaned out loud or physically gasped out loud. In the middle of the kitchen floor I saw another lobster. Dead. And just next to it, another. And then, a couple of feet behind him, two more. I was losing my breath. I looked up and there, clinging onto the edge of the three-bin pot sink, but having expired mid-journey, another lobster. With a clenching knot in my stomach and welling up with tears, I cautiously made my way to the sink, and there found the rest of the thirty lobsters, drowned in cool tap water. The ones on the floor had crawled up on the backs of the others, scrambling for freedom, for oxygen, and had clawed their way out of the sink and onto the floor, before dying midway across the wooden planks.

I was sick. And I could barely breathe. And even when I pushed myself outside into the fresh air and the rising sunshine and the wet dew, I couldn't feel cleansed or well or recovered from the stupid death I had just picked my way through. I felt as if I had been poisoned. They were just lobsters but it takes a lobster more than fifteen years to grow to three pounds. Grown men die harvesting them. The boat moves along as the lobstermen stand in back hauling up the pots and dumping the lobsters on deck. You can get your leg caught in a line and go overboard. It happens. And forty-five pounds of massacre of anything is hard to stomach, giant stupid seabugs even. Lobsters live in deep cold ocean water. Ocean water, as most of us know, is salty, and not the stuff that runs out of the tap of a camp kitchen sink.

But how could this have happened? Shaun would have surely known exactly what to do with the lobsters. I had given Hippy Chick clear instructions. I went back into the kitchen and started to collect them all and place them back into the Styrofoam containers they had arrived in, which were sitting open on the counter. I scanned my memory for the events of the night before. Hadn't I heard the screen door slam? Didn't that mean they had entered the kitchen? But I had clicked off my light and gone to sleep before I heard the screen door slam again, signaling that they had left the kitchen. I drained the water from the sink and put the rest of the lobsters into the coffins, the irony of the word we use to describe these rectangular containers for keeping fish fresh not lost on me. And Shaun appeared but I couldn't even talk. He was also stunned.

"Gab," he said quietly. "We put them in the walk-in and I went to bed. I don't know what happened here."

But by now, of course, I did. I could imagine the whole thing. A vanful of blotto, stoned kids returned to camp and stayed up all night drinking and smoking and hugging long meaningful hugs with their camp soulmates whom they might not be seeing again for a whole year.

In between bong hits, one of them, maybe the guy with the hackey sack says, "Dude, like, how cool are these crazy lobsters?"

Somebody coughs and exhales smoke at the same time.

"But aren't they like, gonna die, without any water?" wonders aloud the guy in the Greenpeace T-shirt.

"Hmm. Oh man, dude, you're totally right."

But Laurel, shaking her waist-long curly hair, says, "Gabrielle said just to, like, put them in the walk-in."

"Hmm."

Choke. Cough. Exhale.

"This is some harsh bud, dude."

"We should put them in some water, I think."

"Definitely."

"Yeah."

"Def."

So instead of leaving the perfectly packed, sleeping, vital lobsters in the walk-in as I'd asked them, they started to worry. And worry, wrapped up in the gauze of a marijuana high, turned into crystal clear paranoia about animal cruelty. And just behind that paranoia came soft, waxy thoughts about animal rescue that drove them to fill the kitchen sinks with cold water, pull the Styrofoam boxes out of the walk-in, drop each sleeping lobster into the makeshift tank, and inadvertently suffocate all of them to death.

Proud and relieved, they snapped off the kitchen lights and went and passed out in their stinking bunks, while the lobsters, panicking, now thrashed and clawed up and over each other to get out of their death pool.

After burying the thirty dead lobsters in a little grave I dug between the arts barn and the soccer field, I shut down the kitchen for the season and let the screen door slam behind me. I drove north to Pittsfield and I bought ten boxes of Kentucky Fried Chicken, left it at the fire pit, and then I drove off campus for good. Heading down 91, making my way back to the city, to the West Side warehouse kitchens, to what I was starting to think would be another twenty years of everyday life, I hoped the bear would find the KFC and the counselors and eat them both.

7

I HAD, WITHOUT EVER DECIDING OR DESIRING TO, RACKED UP NEARLY twenty years of kitchen work—if we start with my dishwashing stint at the Canal House that adolescent summer. And now I was good at it. In college, I had met the Southern writer Jo Carson and she said, "Be careful what you get good at doin' 'cause you'll be doin' it for the rest of your life." And that had forever stuck with me. I thought it would be useful, as my thirtieth birthday neared, to discover if I had any talent other than churning out the twenty-hour shifts without complaint, smoking filterless cigarettes, and out-cussing my male colleagues. I had always imagined I would end up as a writer, but I'd never made the time for it or discovered a way—sapped and depleted after those long shifts—to dedicate myself to it. All I had were boxes and boxes of notebooks accumulated over the years—grown-up versions of that silly, cherished red leather lock-and-key diary I'd kept as a kid—the pages filled with, well, nothing remotely disciplined. For the genuine effort of real writing I was never able to find the time. Yet I was the girl who put on her coat over her chef's whites and spent an extra hour cleaning out the cruddy walk-in refrigerator. Aside from an iron-clad work ethic born of an early understanding of self-reliance, I was wondering if I had anything else to offer. I was wondering if there was still time for a life of my own choosing.

What had started as a quick and urgent necessity—that nearly empty shampoo bottle and even emptier house driving me into town to look for a job—had become a lifetime, a life style, and a life lived gazing over at the greener pasture. I had wanted to do so much more, somehow, than spend my days with my hands thrust into a bowl of micro-greens lightly dressed with aged balsamic and garnished with toasted pumpkin seeds and roasted apricots. I had always wanted to contribute in some way. Leave a little more than I took.

The ironic and disaffected stance toward life had not yet closed its full suffocating grip on the throat of the world, and at the time I remember, it did not feel embarrassing or over earnest to say that you hoped to make a difference. It did not feel hopeless—or even futile— to declare your deep and total admiration for the million-man marchers with their sons and fathers walking together or the radical ACT UP kids who were lying their own fragile bodies down on the freezing pavement of Times Square at rush hour, stopping traffic with their die-ins, or the brilliant visionaries who were unfurling that ever-expanding quilted acre of bottomless sorrow and getting arrested for trespassing on Bush's White House lawn in the doing. My heart caved in a little further every month when the popular food magazines hit the stands and in them were articles entitled "What to Wear to Your Favorite Expensive Restaurant," or "Chef's Favorite Kitchen Tools," or this urgent topic, "French Chef Doesn't Use Butter at Home."

This may sound like badly written parody, but I am quoting actual food magazines. It's hard to work in an industry where these are the headlines. Or at least I was finding it kind of demoralizing to feel like my most significant contribution to the world each day was that I made enough baby artichoke ragout for that night's wedding rehearsal dinner. People who were thinking of ways to guide me when I would describe to them my jam—*I'm not interested in my industry but I'm locked into my industry*—*I don't know how to do anything else*—tried to talk me out of my pessimistic and cynical place by pointing out how important food is in our lives, how important it is to sit around the dinner table with friends and family. I argued back that people who sat around dinner tables these days were discussing nothing more than the food that was placed in front of them and marveling at its spiral of pin dots of pistachio oil administered with a squeeze bottle around the rim of a fourteen-inch plate. When I described what I felt was so achingly missing from my line of work, namely Meaning and Purpose, they would encourage me to go cook in a soup kitchen or a hospice, or to get a job cooking for an agency that delivered meals to the homebound elderly. But there was not one molecule in my body that was engineered to ladle out low-sodium, low-fat, compartmentalized meals designed and overseen by a nutritionist and an officer from the Department of Health and Human Services. I felt less than useful doing it but, nonetheless, I loved the baby artichokes and the vivid green pistachio oil I was handling. Large-scale high-end cooking—with all of its imperfections and corner-cutting—at least put me in contact with ceviche and Israeli couscous and mushroom duxelle and robbiola cheese and was still preferable to just plain institutional cooking—in a hairnet and latex gloves—no matter how empty of meaning and purpose.

But what began as a nagging discontent in that green forest of western Massachusetts had become a dark preoccupation back in New York City and finally turned into a full-blown crisis as I was wheeling a proofing cabinet of two hundred boxed lunches—goat cheese and arugula pesto roll-ups—up the service entrance ramp to the building where, if I recall correctly, the National Book Foundation's fall conference was taking place. Trying to quietly roll this metal cabinet filled to the top with the neatly packaged sandwiches and cookies, I squeaked down the hallway just outside the auditorium toward the lobby, where I was instructed to set out the self-serve lunches and then depart. The auditorium doors kept opening and closing as attendees came and went, and every time they opened, the voices of the panelists and their gorgeous words—Grace Paley? Galway Kinnell? Jamaica Kincaid? I thought I recognized so many of them but couldn't be certain—floated out into the hallway. It felt almost cruel, to be schlepping this metal box on wheels down the corridor in my chef whites and black clogs, while inside that auditorium was a roomful of people I wanted to be. A roomful of people who did just the kind of work I wished I could do. For the first time in my twenty years in a kitchen I felt a real sting to be feeding, and not mingling with, the roomful of people.

Dave, the driver, was waiting in the idling van with the radio fixed to Hot 97 and blasting so loud that the windows vibrated. I banged on the side of the van, and he popped out and helped me load the empty proofing cabinet into the back. Shaggy blasted out of the cargo van's speakers, "I'm Mr. Boombastic, say me fantastic. . . ." Over which Dave yelled, "Back to the shop?"

"I'm done, Dave. This lunch gig was my only booking for the day. Can you clock me out when you go back? I'm done."

I had no ties to anyone or anything—"outta sight outta mind"—so I was not conflicted, in elapsed time sequence, to clock out on my last freelancer shift at one of those warehouse kitchens, sublet the East Village tenement one-bedroom, kiss the girlfriend good-bye, pack the matte black Volvo, and head out to grad school. I had applied for a spot at Iowa—which everyone I asked advised me was the best and most famous writer's program in the country—but instead had gotten a spot at the University of Michigan in the master's program for fiction writing. That September, I rolled into Ann Arbor to start a whole new clean and kitchen-free life.

The very first thing I did when I got there was land a kitchen job. Because I can't sleep at night—let alone aspire to write National Book Award–worthy prose—if I don't have a job. Misty, when I met her, was grilling boneless chicken breasts for U of M tailgate parties wearing a stained, faded V-neck T-shirt and a dirty apron. I didn't see anything in her but the tired, slightly beaten chef of a perfectly decent catering company in downtown Ann Arbor. While I had a ten-pound knife kit brimming with tweezers and Q-tips, fish spatulas and needle-nose pliers, she was assembling rigid, odorless cheese platters for university functions. I had cooked for the king of Thailand. She was, I thought, simply the source of my future paychecks and nothing more.

The next day I went to register for school, and when I walked on Michigan's campus for the first time, strolling the Diag with its pristine landscaping and swiping my student ID at the library, which looked like one of those buildings in Thomas Jefferson's America, I was ebullient. I had not visited any campus during the application process. I had just cast my net and hauled in the best offer and then followed it to Michigan, for whatever awaited me. When I saw the one-hundred-year-old columns of Angell Hall, I skipped up all twenty-five of its granite stairs. I sat in every single leather chair on all four floors of the Rackham Graduate School. I stared at all the oil portraits. If I entered a room with a Persian carpet, I took off my shoes and socks and walked barefoot on it. If there were cheese cubes in the writer's room, I ate them with delight. Alternative high school and alternative college, housed in old barns or in prefab modular units of click-together plywood, were a necessary and important part of my development, but had trashed my own sense of validity. But this—this highly polished marble floor, this leather chair, these brass banisters, these chandeliers—this was Total Legitimacy. Everybody I met referred to the school as *the Harvard of the Midwest* and it took me only two-and-a-half minutes to follow suit. Check me out! A dishwasher matriculated at the Harvard of the Midwest! Entered through the front door by invitation!

And I picked up my first fellowship check—one thousand dollars!—and walked around like someone whose lottery ticket is called on the evening news. I could not get over my luck. *They were paying me to read and write.* I got a thousand dollars a month just to sit around the grad writing room eating cheese and discussing metaphor, to gaze out from a big leather chair *thinking,* to read as many books as they assigned, and to teach freshmen how to write a tight five-paragraph college essay. An academic workday was only six hours long. As if that weren't lavish enough, for a certain stretch of my commute to and from school each day, the speed limit on the Michigan highway, unlike anywhere else in the United States that I had lived, was seventy-five miles an hour!

There were a few signs of weirdness but I shrugged them off. My fellow program mates seemed unaccountably anguished when I met them at our first orientation. Also, this was my first time in a university football town. I thought it was bizarre that grown men wore Maize and Blue parkas, hats, and golf socks, often all at once. I had never seen this before and it spooked me, the way that seeing too many civilian children in scout uniforms also made me nervous. Misty sent me out to chef a few parties in my first weeks there, and when the guests asked me where I was from or how I had come to Michigan or when I had gotten my tongue pierced, they smiled emptily and said, "Oh, that's nice," without meaning it, and the conversations stopped before they even started. But there's weirdness in New York, too, so I shook it off.

My route to rehabilitation—starting anew, not as a dishwasher but as a writer—seemed to be a straight shot.

Except that I had never heard of the *second person static point of view.* And had completely forgotten the meaning of *indirect interior discourse.* My sullen new friends had read so many books that I hadn't and had already, by twenty-three years old, become fluent with so many terms, ideas, and words that I had never heard of. And they could put sentences together in class using so many of them that I was sure if I tried to contribute to the discussion, it would be instantly discovered that I had been accepted by accident, that someone had messed up and put my application in the wrong pile. In the world I had occupied before coming to this campus, *I* was the one with the words. In those kitchens filled with transient part-timers, it was an obvious testament to my potential for high intelligence that I completed the crossword puzzle each day of the week, including Sunday, *in pen.* That I could remember and recite a few stanzas of Chaucer. In this new world, where twenty-three-year-olds discussed *Barthesian tropes* and *post-Hegelian moments* with the same ease with which I boiled water for pasta, I smarted with the realization of my own amateurism. While I had taken the part-time catering job with Misty just to pay my rent, I noticed as the semester progressed that I started to depend on it as a buffer from the sting I often felt on campus during class discussions of *narrative strategy* and *diction*. These people were not fucking around.

It was like a salve to have a few hours each day where I understood the terms, like *sauté* and *roast* and *sweat to translucent*. And to hang out with thirty-five-year-old cooks who hustled past with sheet pans hot out of the oven yelling, "Hot Behind," as we all sniggered cheerfully at the sexual connotation. There was no sexual connotation among academics and when I, out of habit, tried to throw some around, it just fell on the marble floor untouched.

I was having a hard time embracing my new tribe on campus. They kindly pretended to admire my experiences with hot ovens and lobsters and they over-generously allowed me to get around whatever intellectual blocks I faced—I will never confidently understand a post-Hegelian moment—by allowing me to dismiss it as elitist and esoteric. They even paused to agree with me, and then went right back to their work. But there remained, and I was somehow committed to, a cleavage between "me" and "them." I was friendly with a fiction writer named Elwood, who had hunted, fished, bartended, and played U of M football—not as a walk-on but as a recruit—and I think once had stapled dollar bills to his own bare chest at a frat party. And I was getting to know Geoff, a poet who played in a band and drank all the amber liquors without getting sloppy when most of the guys in the program called it quits after two beers. He also, to my eternal gratitude, unequivocally confirmed what I had always intuited about sex scenes in novels written by older men.

"Yeah, that stuff is creepy," Geoff said. "It's just plain wrong."

Whenever our director, a famous-ish and prolific writer, would publish a new book—like, every three months it seemed—Geoff would roll his eyes and smile during wine and cheese hour, and point to the page where, in all twenty-three novels, our blue-blazered director would write a sex scene and describe the woman's nipple.

I was also relieved to meet Kate, who had as much frustration with grading the freshman papers as I did. The freshmen were poorer writers than I remember being when I was a freshman and yet expected much higher grades than they had earned—but maybe all people feel like the generations after them are depraved. Kate, who was also teaching Intro to Comp sections, held office hours across from me in the afternoons. We kept our doors open when waiting for students and chatted in between appointments.

But these new acquaintances were a year ahead of me or busy otherwise, and I didn't see them as much as I needed to.

Meanwhile, Misty and I were working away together under the fluorescent lights, with cold smoked chicken in apricot glaze and sirloin tips in molasses black pepper sauce. The Midwestern requirement of well-done meat and well-done fish was certainly not the lowest place in catering I'd been. I'd already known the lowest and the dullest: oyster knives jammed through the webbing of your hand between thumb and forefinger, steam burns, twenty-three-and-a-half-hour days with just a thirty-minute nap on the office floor with my head on a pile of folded aprons, pack a day cigarettes, ring molds, braziers, propane torches, roulades in Saran Wrap, and shelled lobster claws dramatically crowning the seven hundred fifty martini glasses of ceviche. Misty's catering was organized and calm, and the food was, under the circumstances, totally respectable; she smartly navigated the terrain while hewing to the decidedly unadventurous popular taste.

I wouldn't go so far as to say I *missed,* but I did feel lucky to have already known some of the killer highs of catering as well as the catering brilliance that had come up in my past twenty years, because even the most extravagant events that we now catered, at the art museum or the dean's house, were dull and unambitious. There was tremendous wealth in Ann Arbor but the charity balls and even the private wine dinners we were doing resembled tailgates, in a way, with miniature ham-on-cheddar-biscuits hors d'oeuvres and a driveway parked bumper to bumper with the most giant cars that have ever been made on earth—SUVs manufactured by the Ford Motor Company. I had been exposed to some of the most amazing things that catering presidential inaugurations, the weddings of the daughters of the uberwealthy, and the ultra-rare concert of Barbra Streisand at Carnegie

Hall can yield: edible gold leaf floating in the champagne flutes, pale green sugar glass blown into the shape of apples under a heat lamp and later filled with apple mousse, and Russian Imperial Service, in which the entire dining room is surrounded suddenly by two hundred fifty waiters—exactly one waiter per guest, each bearing one silver-domed plate—and at the signal of the captain, all two hundred fifty waiters step forward, in stunning synchronicity lift the domes high into the air to release the steam trapped by the cloche, and place the hot magret entrée perfectly in front of the guest.

That kind of magnificence—that expertness of choreography and timing—would have been dismissed as *fancy*. There was no customer base in Ann Arbor for handblown sugar glass. The company's service captain was so disabled by palsy that to watch him ferry a sloshing and rattling silver tray of crystal champagne flutes around to the guests at certain black-tie events was excruciating enough and as much of a challenge as he could take on, even if some event organizer *had* called, improbably, inquiring about the possibility of Russian Imperial Service. I dressed for work every day in clean check pants and my own clean chef jackets, as I had my whole life, and with some regularity I sharpened my knives and even those minuscule expressions of professionalism, of respect for the trade, made my new co-workers bristle with what they perceived as excessive self-regard. They wore T-shirts and blue jeans and dirty aprons. It's possible that I now found myself in an unspoken, undeclared polite mutual disapproval with both of my new tribes, Town *and* Gown, but I will never know for sure because no one would ever say something as straightforward as "I don't like you."

I missed my expressive, volatile New York tribe—not because I like conflict and aggression, but because it is abundantly clear where you stand with the guy who leaps onto the hood of your car and calls you a stupid bitch.

When the initial exuberance of landing in Michigan began to wear off, I thought I started to hear all kinds of disapproving tones and implications of distaste in that constant pallid refrain, "Oh, that's nice," that everyone recited through empty smiles. It was meant to soothe, to go along to get along, to mask the heavy odor of one's true opinions, but it had the opposite effect on me. I stayed awake at night, paranoid, and wondered how I was going to be sure anyone was telling the truth. One night, I slept in my car in my own driveway. Paralyzed by something I'll never be able to name. I just pulled into the drive, killed the ignition, reached for the door latch, and suddenly couldn't go through with it. I slumped back in my seat until I woke up the next morning, very early, and finally allowed myself to move onto the porch, get out the key, and go into my little empty apartment.

I went crazy for an opinion. I was starved for opinionated opinion. That I had so many, and offered them in such abundant mouthfuls, made me feel eleven feet tall and garish.

Misty found no end of hilarity in this when I reported it to her the following day.

"You nut!" She laughed. "You slept in your car? Oh dear." Misty had a taciturnity of impressive measure. I've never met a person who could not talk the way Misty could not talk. My extroverted East Coast demeanor was met for the first six months in that catering kitchen from across the prep island with her shy and vaguely grunted, "un-hunh" and her six-word halting sentences. But there was something, something I had not at first picked up on in Misty and I was not deterred. She did not spook me.

She set up her board each day at one corner of the large prep island, and I looked forward to finding a place across from her, and eventually we started to exchange a few words over the easy pace of the prep day. The conversations, while punctuated by pauses in the walk-in or loading into the van—were evolving from grunts to full sentences, and what she knew about food and cooking was immense. If I mentioned something uncommon I'd cooked or eaten in Turkey, where I'd lived and worked for a period in my early twenties, she knew of it and didn't even hesitate. "Oh, Manti? I've read about that." When I admitted that I loved the pine-sap taste of the retsina I'd had in Greece during that same period, she chuckled, and revealing that she knew exactly how it is always served, added, "in those cute copper cups?" Through conversations about food, it was possible to gain glimpses of her.

Because Misty didn't talk or emote or express anything such as gladness to see me or passionate interest in our conversations or satisfaction with my work even though we had actually been working together for some eight months, I had to rely on other signals that we were maybe becoming friends or at least that she was glad to have a set of capable hands with her in the kitchen. *Misty kind of laughed at something I said! Misty let me make the menu and do all the prep for the edible flower dinner at the Arboretum! Misty offered to give me a tour of downtown Detroit!*

She did in fact offer to give me a tour of downtown Detroit, and one weekend night in the dead of winter, with her wildly talkative husband in tow, we crossed 8 Mile and drove into the city. I was not quite comprehending what we were driving through and could not stop staring at the ruin—mile after mile of burnt-out homes, boarded-up storefronts, all the husks of an abandoned city—inexplicably desolate on a Saturday night. Nestled in every so often, we saw a well-maintained home, the glowing lights of inhabitants, little patches of life eked out of what, especially in the dark, looked like nothing. Even when we got to the hub, it was deserted. All these gorgeous buildings and no one on the street. I was used to Greenwich Village on a weekend night where you have to fight the throngs to even get down the sidewalk. Bill narrated the entire experience from the front seat in a kind of free associative poetry-slam manner, rolling his own cigarettes from pouch tobacco, and bringing everything he had to the mic—which included his own upbringing in Dearborn, his formidable knowledge of Allah and the Muslim world, a long thesis on automobile versus train travel in *Amerikkka*—and Misty deftly downshifted when we hit ice patches and occasionally tapped her husband on the knee and said, "Easy, William."

We ate a forgettable dinner in Greektown, had a great drink at The Rhino Club, and enjoyed each other. I think. In my paranoid condition, it seemed more than possible that she was just being hospitable to the unraveling out of towner who had just slept in her car in her own driveway as she might be to, equally, some neighbor's homesick Swedish au pair.

But I still wasn't sure, even by the following spring, and when she invited me to her home for a meal, I took it as a declaration and was thrilled.

Her collected pack of six stray dogs all came racing out and barked their heads off when I pulled up the driveway and stood, pretending not to be afraid, behind my car door. She came out and calmed them all, getting down herself on all fours and kissing and hugging some of them more intimately than I have ever seen her interact with a human person, including her husband, either then or in the fourteen years since that I have continued to know her. I hardly recognized her.

Their home was a hundred-year-old brick house with rough-hewn beams exposed in the basement, surrounded by farmland and part of a land conservancy started by Bill and some friends and neighbors. There was a hand-me-down working John Deere tractor in the driveway and the spring night air smelled of tilled earth. There were budding fruit trees scattered around the fields, flower beds surrounding the house, and there, sprawling out behind the shed, was an organic garden just two mules shy of a farm. She had her own duck prosciutto hanging between the racks in her refrigerator. Shell beans from the year before had dried in their pods in bushels in the garage.

At this first dinner, she had brined a capon, and then roasted it on a tightly sealed grill by indirect smoky heat. It was possibly the most delicious thing I had eaten all year. We sat on the sun porch, surrounded by all the dogs and cats and houseplants that she devoted herself to, and she poured us some rosé wine, an excellent Bandol. Another glimpse of herself.

"Misty, nobody drinks rosé but my mom! Americans think it's déclassé."

"Un-hunh," she nodded. "We had this one in France. We liked it."

I walked around her warm, beautiful house, snooping everywhere with the same disoriented fascination as meeting someone's identical twin for the first time. Her pantry shelves had dried anchovies, salt-packed capers, homemade vinegar, and homemade brandied Michigan cherries. Her kitchen cabinets were filled with heavy Le Creuset pots and clay earthenware from Mexico. There was a whole room packed to the rafters with cookbooks. Bill recited half-remembered poetry and filled in the half he couldn't recall with whatever he could make rhyme. Misty drank the wine and spoke in full paragraphs and laughed full-throated laughter and I could not believe this whole other person before me. I began to feel the stirrings of a remote past, a someone I had been a thousand lifetimes and fluorescent-lit kitchens ago, and suddenly I found myself digging deep, way deeper than the PVC ring molds and the Silpat mats and the propane brûlée torches of my entire adult life, to find the language to keep up with her. I had to remember the exhale of Bandol rosé while my mother talked to my father after dinner, not the edible gold leaf in champagne flutes. When Misty put clafoutis on the table for dessert, I had to remember that I knew the taste of the almost muddy, sweet, ripe black fruit of that mulberry bush by the mailbox of my childhood home.

Meanwhile, I was starting to have misgivings about going to the writer's workshop. It wasn't that it was too hard for me; once I got a grasp of the words everyone was using, I, too, could make my halting way through Derrida and Lacan; I, too, could understand *language as a subjective construction*. It had been like a year of Friday crossword puzzles, cautiously undertaken in pencil, but I was getting it. My misgivings were about something else; something less defensive than protecting myself against my own inadequacy. At our final meeting of the semester I arrived late, having come from work, reeking of roasted bones, onions, molasses. As a group, we had decided to meet for the last time at someone's house instead of the grad lounge and to make a party of it, and I was not very much in the mood.

It was a textbook student pad—scented votives, framed posters, a futon folded up into a couch—and everyone was sitting in a deep hush when I arrived. There were folks on the floor, three on the futon in stockinged feet—everybody had removed their shoes so as not to damage the Salvation Army throw rug. I quietly push open the door, let myself in, silently wave and signal my apologies—one of the students is reading her work, and continues while I settle in. After a year of Monday nights with these guys I still barely know them.

The reader reads aloud, with a sing-song up . . . then down . . . then down again cadence. My mood shifts from merely reluctant to derisive. It's a tired reading style. I'm sick of it. It attaches more importance to the words than the words themselves—as they've been arranged—could possibly sustain, and it gives poets and poetry a bad name. Which is not what I came to graduate school for; I want to forever admire poets. I arrived believing there was meaning and purpose in this work, that this work gives more than it takes, that it helps out. But the longer she goes on in that self-important sing-song way from the candlelit corner where she is perched on a purple and gold pillow, her black eyeliner thick and greasy, stopping on occasion to explain a few of her references—for those among us who may not know the term "chiaroscuro" or who are not familiar with the "tropes" she is exploring in her prose, the more I fear it's no more a contribution than arranging salmon roulade in a ring mold with tiny dots of pistachio oil garnishing the plate. I feel wholly condescended to when she is explaining her work, but backpedal slightly on my position as soon as I realize that, in truth, a year ago I did not know the word *trope*. Before I packed up the Volvo and arrived on that Michigan campus I would not have been able to use it in a crossword puzzle.

Unbelievably, she's reading from pages of pale green rice paper—they remind me of hundred-dollar bills—on which she has written by hand. We have computers, of course, in 1997. Her poem is not good but good-looking and well-dressed. She's missed the point. She should be in bookbinder school. Blindfolded and spun around by her obsession with the handwritten word, the feel of paper, and the smell of ink, in this round of the game she's pinned the tail far away from the donkey, right into the mantel. She still thinks that writing is about self-expression; I can just picture her, with a favorite calligraphy pen, sitting at her desk in front of the window where a spider plant hangs, a large tablet of expensive hand-wrought paper before her and a big bowl of milky sweet tea. And there in the weakening sunlight, she maps out a description of an old man's hands—her own grandfather's perhaps—*with knuckles like like like . . . and ah, the metaphor comes, like pecans. Knuckles wrinkled and brown like toasted pecans.*

She finishes reading and looks up at the room, smug and afraid simultaneously. We remain silent, some people's eyes are closed, though a couple of people sigh crisply, audibly, as if to say *you have pierced my soul.*

I wish we could just read the words out loud and let the stories speak for themselves, but somehow, in just a year, we all know to singsong, and to load the thing up with tropes, to spend whole paragraphs describing an old man's hand, and to bow our heads and close our eyes when *listening.*

Awww fuuuuuuck, I think to myself, trapped in this girl's living room, in this middle state, in the middle of my crossing, now totally convinced that the route I have chosen is wrong. I will have to survive one more year of this if I want to walk away with the master's degree from the Harvard of the Midwest. To my left, just out of reach, I notice the crudités—raw broccoli florets and those baby carrots washed in formaldehyde, and some bread and cheese. I'm starving. Our leader, who's sitting in the apartment's one comfortable chair, raises his head, and announces, "Perfect. Simply perfect." The poet glows brighter than the ginger-cranberry candle she is sitting next to. Someone from the futon chimes in: "Truly. That moment with his hand on the back of the kitchen chair—I mean you really captured that moment perfectly." I go for the cheese cubes and hope for a more generous mood. Elwood hauls his huge football player body up off the floor, where he's been gamely sitting, and comes over to the cheese platter. Conspiratorially, he says, "I gotta go. I've got dandruff." And my mood instantly lifts to discover someone else here who's struggling with this shit.

In the fall, I went to another—much larger—dinner at Misty's house, and I met lots of her friends. She had me cut down the last of the rhubarb from the garden and grill the sardines outside by the light of car headlights, while Bill smoked pot and filled the birdfeeders, and I was proud and honored to be put to use. I would've walked into the cold stream barefoot if she'd asked me. I had sharp transportive flashes to every party my parents had ever thrown. Misty was inside, not quite ten years my senior but just old enough to not be exactly my peer, with a kitchen towel draped over her shoulder and in a bib apron, drinking a mojito with mint from her garden, as she arranged cauliflower and zucchini and onions into earthenware baking dishes. All of their friends—philosophy of religion professors, hairdressers, Ford engineers—surrounded her to watch and chat or wandered in the garden or stood by the charcoal fire where I was grilling and their voices and laughter drifted out over the Michigan landscape.

At work we were cooking the required filet mignon with horse-radish cream and super fudge chunk brownies but at her home, where I had become like one of her stray dogs picked up on a back road, she cooked all the dark and oily fishes like bluefish and mackerel and sardines. She served pork shoulder, pork shank, lamb tongue, lamb legs, and lamb sausages. She made true duck confit.

When she emptied the garden and started the enormous labor of pickling, canning, and smoking enough to fill a room in the cellar with hundreds of Ball jars, dated in her handwriting with Sharpie marker, I sometimes helped. I was in the thesis stretch of my degree, so I had fewer classes and more time. We made cordials, cornichons with the tiny yellow blossoms sometimes still attached, and concord grape juice, except for the year that Michigan concord grapes were wiped out from Pontiac to Petoskey. We grilled thickly sliced bread and ate it right there in the moment—warm and charred—nothing like that air-blasted baguette that sat out on rolling racks under the fluorescent lighting at work—and we made, by hand and not in a robot coupe, toppings from olives or swiss chard or beans. We shucked many varieties—yellow steubens and tongues of fire and flageolets—of fresh shell beans from her huge garden. In the winter, we hauled what she hadn't had time to shuck out of the shed, these last beans still in their pods, though drier, and merely cooked them longer. She combined meat and fish in the same dish. She deep-fried as regularly and with as little hesitation as you or I might brew coffee. The cheeses she ate at home sat out unwrapped on the counter and stank and oozed, and al-ways, always, she offered a well-made, well-researched cocktail.

I had met a girl at work, a big butch Michigander who had never once lived out of state, and I was loving her so much that it made the weirdness of Michigan and the uncertainty of my whole enterprise there suddenly bearable and even sometimes a total blast. I also had made the crucial successful move to make some friends outside of the English department, and there were people in the school of environmental sciences and statistics, like my friend David for example, who were not anguished at all, whatsoever, and who played excellent pool, drank bourbon, and built large fires outside as a pastime. With him, I had more fun with language than I was ever going to have in that building with the oil portraits.

"You're such a tree hugger!" I taunted, when he went on and on about the ozone layer and renewable resources.

"Only the cute ones!" He grinned.

In the university program where I was supposed to be emancipating myself from the kitchen, preparing myself to go back to New York having at least answered the question of my own potential, the novelty and thrill had thoroughly worn off. I could not find the fun or the urgency in the eventless and physically idle academic life. It was so lethargic and impractical and luxurious. I adored reading and writing and having my brain crushed; but those soft ghostly people lounging around the lounge in agony over their "texts," endlessly theorizing over experiences they would never have, made me ache to get out of the leather chairs, to put my shoes and socks back on, and get back into the kitchen, which I increasingly found practical and satisfying. The work may not have held much meaning and purpose, but I was gunning the motor of my car to get off campus and get to it each day.

To tackle a prep list at eight a.m. and have it knocked out by four p.m., black Sharpie line crossing out each item on the To-Do list:

~~6 quarts aioli~~
~~brown brisket~~
~~butcher salmon~~
~~toast walnuts~~

felt so manageable and tactile and useful. I could wake up and tackle that in a way that I would never be able to wake up and take a crack at certain literary pursuits, like, for example, illuminating the fog surrounding the human condition. This is not to suggest that I accepted this understanding about myself gladly, with just a sneering dismissal of the pursuit in the first place. *Human condition.* It's a blow to have to admit to yourself that you are not quite cut out for something that matters so much to you. More than a blow—it's a knockout. I had to lie down on the floor of my apartment for a very long time letting that one sink in. *Did I have something more to offer, any other talent than a strong work ethic? Did I have something in me other than dishwasher?*

As it turns out, I did not.

To stand at the prep table with other cooks who were just doing mundane things like fixing the car over the weekend, cleaning the house, and shuttling their kids to doctor's appointments felt newly satisfying and meaningful enough. I liked these people and their lives. But more to the point, I came to understand that I liked People and Life. After sitting around for too long in those leather chairs, I welcomed the intense pressure of getting a dinner for two hundred plated quickly, and came to see that there was a rush and a method in that that I hadn't quite known to what extent I liked and needed in my life. And I will admit, spending that chilly hour cleaning out a cluttered walk-in and putting impeccable order to it is still, thirty years later, my favorite part of kitchen life. I bring my mother's compulsion for concrete order with me wherever I go.

My resolve to start a new kitchen-free life was further weakening in the direct warmth of Misty's home style of cooking, her bumpy, misshapen tomatoes ripening on the back steps, her cabbages shredded and broken down with salt and vinegar, her hunks of pork swimming in smoky, deep, earthy juices. Unwittingly, she was untethering me from my ten-pound knife kit, propane torches, and ring molds and showing me that what I had been doing these past twenty years— and what I had come to think of as cooking—was just the impressive fourteen-ring string of a twelve-year-old exhaling her first lungfuls of a Marlboro. Nothing more than the tricks of the trade. She was waking me, in her nearly monosyllabic way, out of a dark and decades-long amnesia.

But then, without telling me and worse, without taking me, Misty worked her last day at the catering company and went across town to pursue an opportunity to open a restaurant. Misty, without letting on in the slightest, was in the early stages of opening a restaurant across town, with her brother as co-chef, and because she would never behave in such poor form as to poach cooks from the catering company, she did not offer jobs to anyone there. She just left. Her spot across from me at the prep island remained empty as we continued to cook the old familiar menus on autopilot. We watched as the owner apprehensively auditioned new chefs. One chef came, and then another, and one more still, and I stuck it out at the catering company for a few more months. The last chef I worked for introduced his signature dish in the first week or two—a pounded veal breast with a blueberry-Frangelico sauce topped with prosciutto, Parmesan, and pine nuts—and I clocked out on that dish and ran to Misty. I begged her for a job. Decent, timid catering food was one thing, but blueberry-Frangelico sauce . . .

They were planning a pan-tropical place, which allowed her to cook dishes from countries around the Equator. I could feel and see her excitement and fresh energy not only to be in a new place, after eight years in the old one, with permission from the owners to really open up, but also to get her hands on new ingredients, and to read incessantly about unfamiliar dishes and cultures. The giant pile of books on her desk was heavily marked with yellow sticky memo tabs. The whole experience gave her demeanor a brightness that made the stained V-neck T-shirts that she still wore seem almost clean. Within weeks, she was happily exhausted rather than hopelessly worn down; she was almost *talkative*. For the first time I had picadillo, the slightly sweet ground meat hash popular in Spanish and Latin countries; and chimichurri, the green Argentinean sauce with chopped herbs; and asafoetida, the pungent, sulfuric Indian flavoring. Reluctantly, I tried Malibu coconut rum in cocktails, and they worked. She made pho, lemongrass ice cream, macadamia nut tartlets with lime curds, coconut creams, and passion fruit syrups. It was legitimate and well-prepared and delicious. We tested dishes over and over until we got them right, and they seemed, in spite of their Vietnamese origins, not out of place there on State Street across from the university. She found a local tortilla maker in Detroit, and she persuaded the famous Michigan store Zingerman's to make chipotle challah for her rock shrimp club sandwich. She found fresh kefir lime leaves. She went through cases of nuoc mam. And enough galangal to fill a boat at the Bangkok floating market.

I saw fresh turmeric for the first time in her new kitchen and so learned—a bit late in my cooking life, I thought, for someone who thought for sure she knew everything—the difference between a root and a rhizome. Misty was able to distinguish between an Indonesian, a Chinese, a Vietnamese, and a Thai ground shrimp paste. It was the first time I heard a chef say, "I don't know, let me look it up." It was the first time I saw a chef solicit the opinion or experience of her staff. She was willing—always—to learn from any source. If the dishwasher's mother had made posole for twenty years at every family reunion, Misty would ask him about it. If not to learn something that she didn't already know, at least to benchmark her own experience against it.

It was a good kitchen. She ran it well.

It was the first time I saw a chef ask relevant questions of job seekers at their interviews. *How long is your commute? Your fiance lives in Chicago? This is your third DUI? Between jail and TGI Friday's you worked salads at Bombay Bicycle Lounge for how long?* She knew well that the cooking end of things would be apparent in these applicants as soon as they entered the kitchen, and that it was a waste of interview time to ask them about their kitchen skills, which everybody lies about anyway. She was keen to discover if the rest of the package existed— the part where you need your crew to be somewhat sane, logical, and reliable. I learned from Misty that when a cook tells you that his girlfriend is moving to L.A. to break into movies, you had better start preparing for the departure of the boyfriend, as well.

When I had my final reading for my thesis, she knew well, and I knew that she knew, that my own move back to New York was not far behind. "And the lovebird? Is she going, too?" she asked, referring to my Michigan girlfriend.

"So it appears," I said. "She's packing her boxes. But I'm going to have to teach her how to drive faster and to give people the finger or she'll be eaten alive."

Misty chuckled.

"Well, I guess I'm going to have to come visit."

Once during that miserable school year with our mother in Vermont, my seventh grade class took a school trip to New York City and visited the famous sculptor Claes Oldenburg's studio in Soho. When we entered, there was a large white horizontal plank in the center of the room. And he had put a peephole in the center—exactly like the fish-eye peephole in every New York City apartment door. When you bent over and peered through it, you saw the back of your own head where you would have expected to have seen your own feet. It was so disorienting that it actually took several moments for you to understand what you were seeing. Some people took a long time figuring out what they were looking at. It's not as assured and graceful as you might think to recognize the back of your own head when you see it. Especially when it is not where you expect to find it.

I had been staring right at Misty across that prep table and didn't even recognize her for what she would come to be. It took me a long time to figure out what this woman in a dirty T-shirt grilling chicken breasts was teaching me. Or to even admit that I had learned something from her. One does not fend entirely for herself starting at puberty, and then gladly and easily turn around and credit just anyone who happens to come along later in life with having helped out. These kinds of admissions are careful. Gradual. Delayed. To call Misty my mentor isn't accurate. I suspect it makes us both kind of uncomfortable—the implied intimacy of it for her and the fealty of it for me—and yet, if you squint with one eye, and look through that peephole, that is what she, for a certain important period, became.

8

I WAS NOT LOOKING TO OPEN A RESTAURANT. THAT WAS NEVER ON MY mind.

I was just dashing out to park the car one spring morning, when I ran into my neighbor Eric, a guy I knew only peripherally from years of living on the same block. I didn't even know his last name, but we often saw each other during that hectic morning ritual of alternate side parking that New Yorkers, or at least East Villagers, seem to barely accomplish in time to beat the meter maid. It's a twice a week early morning ritual, Mondays and Thursdays or Tuesdays and Fridays, depending on which side of the street you're on, in which everyone on the block with a car comes rushing out of their building to move their machines, still wearing their pajamas and with pillow creases still marking their faces. Eric was sitting on the stoop in front of a long-shuttered restaurant space mid-block, and as I zoomed by in my sweatpants and hastily slipped-on clogs, we waved. He said, "You still cooking?"

I was, technically. I had taken an interim chef job at one of those huge West Side Highway catering companies where I had formerly been a freelancer while they performed a thorough talent search to find their real next chef. I was just a three-month placeholder, during the dead season, which is why I felt fine taking the job. I reasoned that it was a moderate way for me to make some money while I continued to write and to resolve my last lingering uncertainties about my place in a kitchen.

"I am, sort of," I said.

"Wanna take a look at this space?"

I was off that day, with big plans to sit on my couch procrastinating the writing of my novel-in-progress.

"Sure. I'll take a look. Why not."

There was a faded yellow typewritten letter in the window from the former tenant—a French guy who had run a bistro that thrived for a brief but bright couple of years—advising customers that the restaurant would just be closing for a two-week vacation and renovation. They looked forward to seeing you soon! *Bonnes Vacances!* Two weeks had turned into two years, and I could see, from the second we stepped inside, that there had been no vacation planned at all.

"Bankruptcy," Eric said.

It looked like the restaurant had desperately done business right up until 12:01 a.m., when the city marshal came and padlocked the place, leaving the coolers full of lamb shanks, dairy, and crème brûlées. There were racks of dirty dishes sitting outside the machine, which sat ajar, as if the dishwasher had just run downstairs for a few more clean towels and a gallon of pink liquid before running his next load. The pot sink was packed with dirty sauté pans. The pastry station had black shriveled pastry in the coolers, and the espresso machine had hard, spent pucks of powder fossilized into the ports. Next to the machine sat a stainless steel pitcher with long spoons in it, as if a café machiatto was in the works just as the city's assessor walked in the door with his huge ring of keys. There were cigarette butts in the ashtray, as if the early waiter had already sat down and begun his paperwork and tip sorting at the end of his shift.

Eric, who owned a couple of units upstairs in the co-op and who was now putting some effort into sorting out the mess of the abandoned storefront, showed me around the restaurant as I held my

T-shirt pressed over my nose and mouth. The place was putrid. The floors grabbed the soles of my shoes with every step. So much rat shit had melted in the summer heat and commingled with the rat urine over the two years that the space had sat there idle that it was like walking on old glue traps. I had to run outside for gulps of fresh air after several minutes in the restaurant.

The electricity, oddly, had not been cut off but the light bulbs had died, and most egregiously, the freon had run out in coolers that still had running fans. When I opened a door on the sauté station reach-in refrigerator, I was hit by a blast of fetid warm air coming from de-composed lamb shanks and chicken carcasses. There were legions of living cockroaches. The basement was very dark. Only one tube of a fluorescent flickered overhead. It was impossible not to jump out of your skin with the creeps with every brush of your own hair on your own neck. In the walk-in, by the dim light of a weak flashlight, I stupidly opened a full case of apples only to have a gray, sooty cloud of spores—like a swarm of gnats—fly up into my nostrils and eyelashes. Twenty-five pounds of apples had rotted away to black dust.

And yet, even with the cockroaches crawling over bread baskets and sticky bottles of Pernod, I could see that the place had immense charm. There was an antique zinc bar with just four seats that had been salvaged from a bistro in France and shipped over. There were gorgeous antique mirrors everywhere, making the tiny space seem bigger than it was, and an old wooden banquette, and wrought-iron table bases. The floor, under all that sticky rat excreta, was laid with the exact same tiny hexagonal tiles that had been on the floor of a crêperie in Brittany where I had worked for a brief period in my early twenties. Even when gulping the comparatively fresh New York City air once back on the sidewalk, thinking I might have been poisoned in some way, I knew the space was exactly "me." There were ten sturdy burners. Just two ovens. And fewer than thirty seats. I could cook by hand, from stove to table, never let a propane brûlée torch near a piece of food, and if it came down to it, I could just reach over the pass and deliver the food myself. I knew exactly what and how to cook in that kind of space, I knew exactly what kind of fork we should have, I knew right away how the menu should read and how it would look handwritten, and I knew immediately, even, what to call it.

"Any interest?" Eric asked.

A thin blue line of electricity was running through my body.

"Maybe," I bluffed.

I had no idea how to open a restaurant. I had that work ethic and that nearly strange mania for cleaning and organizing kitchens to forever re-create my own mother's. And I had just spent a few good long years understanding my relationship to kitchen work itself and could, with a certain calmness, claim to have put the question to bed; the greener pastures I had been straining my neck to gaze at all those years were not, predictably, as sweet and filled with clover as I had always imagined. But in all the most pertinent ways, I had nothing. For starters, I had never been the chef of a restaurant. I had never even been the sous chef of a restaurant. I had never cut a check for more than a thousand dollars or balanced a checkbook that ever had more in it than a thousand and fifteen. All I knew about a walk-in refrigerator was how to tidy it up and the most I knew about an oven was how to turn it on and roast a brined turkey in it. The only lawyer I'd ever retained was the one who'd bailed me out of my grand larceny charges as a seventeen-year-old. To imagine that a newly jogged memory about the few dishes and food experiences I had managed to collect at my mother's apron strings would be enough to sustain a restaurant would be naive. And to open a restaurant with nothing more than an idea for a menu, a clean kitchen, and an apt name would have been certain failure.

As we parted on the sidewalk, I said to Eric with a distinct doubtfulness, "I'll think about it. Let's talk again later." But once back in my apartment, I felt very nearly combustible with something I could not tamp down with any blanket of reason or logic I threw in front of it. I doodled menus. Pulled some plates down from my own stack and set a mock table. I opened the windows to the new spring weather and cranked the stereo with songs I fantasized would bust out of the speakers at my new restaurant. To try and disrupt this electric hum of "rightness" that had taken hold in my gut and was now spreading through my being, I recited, at length, my lack of restaurant experience. I punctuated every thought with that famous statistic that 80 percent of new businesses go under in the first year. I pointed out to myself that I had never fired anyone. And noted that I certainly had never been involved in the even more complex parts of boss-hood that crop up in between the beginning and the end of an employee's tenure, like issuing a W-2, understanding FICA taxes, and articulating a sexual harassment policy.

In spite of my efforts to be rational, the birds and the sunshine were in concert outside, as if egging me on, and while I told myself over and over that I couldn't possibly open a restaurant in New York City, the most critical and sophisticated place on earth where I would be eaten alive by some restaurant reviewer within the first fifteen minutes of unlocking the doors, I nonetheless merrily pulled out all of my wooden salad bowls and wooden cutting boards and wondered if it would be a health code violation to use them in my restaurant instead of the heavy white plastic ones. As I reminded myself of my total lack of credentials, not to mention my total lack of one thin dime, let alone the fifty large I would need to put toward such a venture to play "serious," I simultaneously fantasized ripping out the fluorescents and replacing them with incandescents. While anyone who actually knew what they were doing would have come right home and crunched some numbers involving square footage, check average, and an ROI for her backers, I sprawled on the couch in my bare feet, staring into the middle distance, and wondered how I might serve walnuts from the Perigord and a small perfect tangerine so that the restaurant patrons could also sit at their table after the meal and squeeze the citrus peel into the candle flame to make fragrant blue and yellow sparks as I had done on my mother's lap as a child. By dusk that same evening, I called Eric and said, "I'd like to take another, closer look."

EVEN THOUGH I HAD NOTHING, in the traditional sense, to qualify me as a chef or a business owner, I had something convincing and compelling from my early twenties. From that era with the chicken, and my dad shouting at me from the back steps, and me wanting to sleep the long permanent sleep. I had something from that time.

From all that sitting on the woodpile that aimless fall, imagining the death of everything from garden tomatoes to small animals to the mailman, that time when I loathed and despaired of the self I had become, whatever self that was, so hastily cobbled together in an emergency, I had something persuasive.

Those gloomy thoughts at dusk with the cigarettes turned from thoughts of my own death, which I, an otherwise healthy and robust and well-mannered nineteen-year-old, couldn't in good conscience accomplish, to significantly politer thoughts of disappearing, which I could. And soon, out of pragmatic consideration for others and a deeply ingrained adherence to good manners, I had planned my own clever death without actual death. I would leave, disappear, send an occasional postcard and be done with the whole dilemma. Good-bye world! Good-bye New Jersey! Good-bye Family, God, and Country! Hello Eurail Pass.

My mother, still protractedly adjusting in Vermont, now dabbling in "women's groups" and long herbal-tea-soaked conversations of "spirituality," kindly sent a list of friends and family in France and their phone numbers, which I planned to tuck away and forget about. My father, now dating all sorts of ill-fitting but dazzling younger women, not only opened up his house for a farewell party to which I invited the whole crew from Mother's, but he also offered to take on my student loan payments for as long as I was gone. Todd offered a bon-voyage professional-model Nikon camera with a powerful lens that must cost a thousand dollars. And so equipped, I arrived at a youth hostel in Bruges from New Jersey on a one-way, $99 People Express ticket. It was January 1986. I had a heavy backpack, a heavy sleeping bag, empty notebooks, and $1,200 in American Express Travelers Cheques. When my idea was formed on the woodpile that fall— a slow and meandering two-year trip around the whole world where I might be swallowed and digested and composted by the earth itself, with the sum of my existence rolled up into a backpack—I failed to account for the weather. It was the coldest winter Europe had seen in fifty years. Each day in January in 1986 was, I recall, below zero. My feet were frozen. My hands were frozen. I just wanted to stay inside the youth hostel and write down my dark thoughts.

This youth hostel, the Bauhaus, was owned by two brothers who came in and out with cases of UHD milk and laundered fitted sheets, both of them tall, with strong features and unruly hair, and between them a cassette collection that included Pere Ubu, Brian Eno, Talking Heads, and Joy Division. The cozy little bar downstairs was pleasantly populated with a few travelers, mostly guys, mostly German and Australian. The girl behind the bar, Aimée, spoke a peculiar accented English that made it impossible to guess her origin, which I admired, and I immediately set about cultivating such an accent of my own. She was there each day and seemed helpful to the brothers in enforcing the rules that govern all accredited and certified youth hostels:

Hostelers out by 10 a.m. each day.
Hostelers may not reenter the hostel until after 4 p.m.
Hostelers must be 18 or older.

In the morning , there was an included breakfast of watery coffee, overly sweet cheese wrapped in tin foil packets, bread, and a few olives, over which you could not linger. Anxious about money, I ate the whole thing hungrily, unsure what else I would eat that day. Precisely at ten a.m., we were pushed out. I began to call it the "youth hostile." After a couple of brutally long and frigid days wandering around the deserted city, early and easily reaching my fill of the famous but only-decent French fries, I circled back in the afternoons, sheepishly noting that it was barely three minutes past four o'clock. In the almost empty youth hostel, for the rest of the evening I sat alone in the little bar downstairs at the reception area and wrote in my notebooks as a few fellow winter travelers trickled in and sat intensely discussing a certain guest house in Rangoon, while the exquisitely detached girl still behind the bar poured their drinks and braided colored thread into bracelets. Every evening, I ordered glasses of red wine from Aimée and sunk into the comfort of every cassette she played, from Suzanne Vega to U2, as if something familiar, something from your own life, even if it was just the soundtrack of it, could warm all of your frozen bones.

Amsterdam was what I had mapped out next that frigid winter, and I questioned whether it might be warmer or colder there, and if—taking into account the conversation the travelers around me were now having about bhang lassis in Trivandrum, and blotter acid in Goa on New Year's Eve—if I even cared. Within five evenings I had already filled one of my notebooks with questions of my purpose as well as my stamina.

Dead of winter is not the most wholesome time to backpack in Europe, and January in Amsterdam found me in a huge open dormitory room with only three other occupants, the other forty or so beds between theirs and mine empty. They'd been squirreled in there since October. The drugged-out girl and the two drugged-out boys—none of them native English speakers but all of them speaking to each other in English—were huddled together under one blanket on one bed at the alcove end of the room, near a trickle of brown water that was leaking from one of the two steam pipes that were intended to heat the room. The dormitory was as cold as outside but without the wind.

The threesome were slowly, very slowly, talking to each other. They were blotto. The girl, Israeli, was trying to get some drugs from the guy, Swiss, but it wasn't working out for her. She was too stoned to make a serious case, and he was too mean to not enjoy his small fleeting power—he had the dope; she wanted the dope. This wasn't the harshest he-has-the-drugs-she-wants-the-drugs scene I had ever witnessed, but neither was it the most benign, and it was the first in which I would have to spend the night trying to sleep in the same room with the transaction unfurling a few beds away. The third guy, possibly a local, wanted what there was of the Israeli girl and wasn't deterred, it seemed, by either her disinterest or the lack of privacy.

Even though this was the one single city in the world where the guesthouses, it seemed, allowed you to stay indoors the day long through if you wished, pouring it all out into your journal, I had to get out. That little gruesome threesome in the one cot with their blunted senses was enough to drive me to wander the empty city of Amsterdam, even in subzero temperatures. Like everybody, I was curious about the legal hash and the legal prostitution, of course, but back in New Jersey when I had been thinking of including Amsterdam in my route, I also had thought I might wander the canals and see houseboats and Anne Frank's house and tulip farms and spend a couple of days cycling around the city. I wanted to see if anybody wore the clogs, and if I could make it to the city of Gouda in a day trip to try the famous cheese where huge, round yellow wheels of the stuff are traded at the market like a commodity. I wanted to tip my head back and drop the new fatty herring down the hatch and drink beer from a tap. But it was just the wrong season for this kind of travel. In all my months of studying the atlas, and in my great victory in flying all the way to Europe for only $99, I totally had fucked up and arrived in the heart of the wrongest season. No bicycles, no clogs, and no herring.

After trudging around for hours, while the tall, good-looking, and sensually emancipated Dutch retreated inside their homes and kept warm, I wandered into a coffee shop—the Dutch kind with legal drugs for sale—anxiously calculating my money, already down to $1,000 from the $1,200 I'd started out with only a week before, and regretting the wastefulness of now having a few useless Belgian francs in my pouch, but determined to have a Dutch experience. I felt jittery from caffeine, from hardly letting myself descend into full unguarded sleep all of the nights before, and from a chill so permeating now made more deep by the dampness of canals and seawater. I stood for a long time staring up at the blackboard menu of drugs available and finally decided to try the spacecake, but the blond girl at the dealer's counter and the fact of her heavily applied silver eyeliner somehow suddenly made me feel unsafe. Someone at a little table had passed out from the force of whatever she'd sold him—he was slumped over and fully blacked out—and I found myself unable to go through with it. Of all the times I've needed to be fully in possession of my wits, here and now, totally alone in the world with my whole existence crammed into my pockets, was the most urgent of all. I backed out into the cold street, starting to really unravel and nearly defeated.

Several blocks later, I found a café—the European kind with coffee and snacks—and went in it to warm up and to sort out some of my anxieties. I ordered a sandwich and sat in the grip of my own fuckup—impossible to go back home, impossible to wander another frozen minute in another impenetrable city, impossible to last much longer on my dwindling traveler's checks and impossible to go straight to balmy, exotic and indecipherable Indonesia until I'd gotten some more experience as a lone female traveler in friendly western recognizable Europe—until the waitress put the plate in front of me. There was, as I'd ordered, a cold ham sandwich on good buttered grainy bread, but it came with a warm salted potato and a wedge of Gouda that had aged so much that it had gritty, very pleasant granules in it, which at first I thought were salt grains but then realized were crystallized calcium deposits from the milk of the cheese. I ate the little potato right away. Its pale yellow flesh was perfectly waxy, and its skin snapped when I bit into it. I don't know under what other conditions a simple, salted, warm boiled potato could ever taste as good as this tasted. Probably none.

Usually the food that meets your hunger sends you into a calmed and expansive state of deep satisfaction, but I instead sat in that café and became quite heavy and defeated. Yes, I had wanted to leave everything behind—I had grown to hate my country, my culture, my own first and last name—but the sharp and creamy cheese, the starchy, warm small potato, somehow made it starkly apparent how weary and lonely and physically uncomfortable one could become in exile. I had fantasized I would be gazing at the Van Goghs while my bicycle with the basket rested outside against a lamppost, unlocked. But instead I had just seen some guy in a coffeehouse fully blacked out at the table. I was about to return to three drugged-out and frightfully skinny roommates.

I needed a better plan. Slowly savoring the last bites of my ham sandwich on that corky pumpernickel bread, I pored over my travel notes and found the letter from my mom with the list of her relatives and friends in France. There was also a contact in Algeria—the family of one of the dishwashers from Mother's—but when I imagined trying to manage that phone call, shouting over the static from an international booth at the post office, our words overlapping in the delay, and trying to cheerfully introduce myself while asking if I could be their guest for, well, several weeks, I immediately opted for France. I would be welcome there.

Marie Nöelle had a crêperie, tabac, and bar des sports in the tiny town of Montauban-de-Bretagne. I was silently thrilled to get off the train and, not one other backpacker or drug addict in sight, be met by this luminously blue-eyed old friend of my mother's.

"Gabrielle!" she waved.

"Marino! Salut!" And we were off, my heavy pack in the back of the Volkswagen Rabbit and she, as if I were her peer, began to speak of everything—complex and troubling, simple and pleasing—that had arrived in her life these past many years since we had seen each other. We drove through small villages on our way from Rennes to Montauban, and pulled up finally to her little spot in the center of town. The bar was closed, on a Sunday evening, and so we went without interruption upstairs to her apartment and settled me into the attic room.

While I unpacked a little and arranged my things, Marie Nöelle put together a simple dinner of soup and cheese and brought it up to her room on the second floor, where she said she preferred to eat in the winter when it got dark so early and the nights were so very long. Her husband of a few years had just months before killed himself by mouthing a hunting gun and pulling the trigger—right in front of her.

I slept more that night than I had in thirty days combined, it seemed, relieved beyond description to not have to keep nocturnal watch over my traveler's checks and my passport and my expensive camera, which all of the winter drug addicts in every youth hostel I slept in would have razored out of the bottom of my sleeping bag while I slept had I not remained, even in sleep, alert. When I came down to the bar to find Marie Nöelle, the place was open and busy, and there was the smell of coffee being ground each time an au lait was ordered. The room was warm and simple, with a stand-up bar, a small area at the cash register for lottery tickets and cigarettes, and a separate area with a pool table and a table soccer game up a few steps in the back. The crêperie, with its heavy, black cast-iron griddles and just a few tables, was in another room open and adjacent to the bar.

She put me to work at the bar at first, pulling espresso and steaming milk. She introduced me to one of the stout and ruddy-complexioned farmers and as we shook hands, his rough and calloused clasping mine, I said, "Bonjour, Roger." And Roger bowed slightly and said, "Enchanté, Mademoiselle," revealing his brown teeth. Marie Nöelle taught me how to pour his little ballon of vin rouge ordinaire with a good splash of water in it, because at eight-thirty in the morning, he and all of the other blue-clad men with terrible teeth who now stood against the bar, with manure and red dirt stuck to their black rubber boots, were on their first of many to follow. Throughout the day they would stop back in for "un coup" while their tractors sat haphazardly parked on the side of the road just outside. Bottles of Pernod, Ricard, and my favorite, the bitter orange-flavored Suze, hung upside down from a clever rack, and I learned to push the glass up against the spring-fitted nozzle to drain out a perfect one-ounce pour.

The eggs sat out at room temperature in the kitchen and Michel, the crêperie cook who wore big thick-lensed glasses that made his eyes huge above his mustache, let the cigarette dangle from his lips as he cracked them into the crêpe batter, made of buckwheat flour each day. The salad dressing was made in the bottom of the bowl with garlic, mustard, vinegar, and oil and tossed in with the Bibb lettuce that we bought at the little open air market that set up every morning across the street.

I stood often with Marino at her post at the cash register and sold lottery tickets, Gitanes, Gauloise, and Rothman Rouge by the carton, and from the register I could look straight into the crêperie where Michel spooned out the batter onto the oversized black turntable griddle and then swirled his little dowel of a baton around like a dj scratching the beat. He was decisive and swift, and he cracked the egg right onto the galette and sprinkled the grated Gruyère and laid out a slice of that jambon with the white fat cap over and over again, working the two griddles effortlessly. To finish and plate each galette, he used his metal spatula to fold in the four sides, forming a square from a circle with the contents exposed still at the center, and deftly ran the spatula under the savory crêpe, delivering it to the plate. "Et voilà!" he said each time, and then turned to the next. That meal—with the salad right on top of the *complet,* and a bottle of the hard cider kept at truly cellar temperature in an actual cellar—was one I ate every day without ever getting bored with it. I had never before given a single thought to how different the lettuces and the cider and even the butter, bread, and eggs tasted when left at room temperature and never refrigerated, but now I was keenly aware of it.

For the duration of the winter I hibernated inside her warm little hub of life in that tiny village and earned a few francs by working every day in the bar or the crêperie or at the cash register selling cigarettes and lottery tickets. I fixated on the local shops—the boulangerie, poissonnerie, boucherie, fromagerie, and pâtisserie—and how they displayed their foods in that careful, precise, and focused way that never, in spite of all that precision and care, looked rigid or antiseptic or strained. Every piece of food in every store—no matter how artful, precise, and often jewel-like—begged to be touched, smelled, and heartily eaten. We bought bread at the bread store, meat at the meat store, dry goods at the dry goods store. There was a huge supermarket that had just been built at the edges of the town, but when we went there—to get something in bulk supply for the bar or crêperie—Marie Nöelle kind of smiled sheepishly and moved quickly across the parking lot to the car.

In town at the local boucherie, though, the rabbits and pheasants and geese were displayed in the cases with some remnant of their living life still with them. The geese were laid out with their long necks arranged in great question mark arcs around their totally plucked bodies as if they were not dead but simply deep in sleep, their black beaks and faces nestled in striking contrast to their bare creamy bodies. The rabbits looked like clipped show poodles, wearing fuzzy slippers, otherwise skinned, but their furry feet left intact while their little bloody faces revealed their tiny bloody teeth. Pheasants in full stunning plumage hung for a few days until their necks finally gave out, and you could see, physically, a kind of perfect ripeness to the meat when it became tender enough to pleasurably chew, as if the earliest stage of rot itself was a cooking technique. Boudin blanc and boudin noir overran the charcuterie and traiteur cases as Christmas and New Year and saint's days in the deep of winter demanded these traditional foods, made only at this time of year when animals are slaughtered not bred.

Young cooks who desired to be chefs went to auberges in the countryside of France and slept on cots and worked without pay for sixteen hours a day, six days a week. They did these apprenticeships called "stages," which I never heard of until well after I'd opened my own restaurant. Of course I had never worked anywhere in my life where young people apprenticed for free in hopes of learning something valuable; The Canal House and The Picnic Basket and Mother's were the kinds of restaurants where the only thing that mattered to anyone was their paycheck, their tips, and their free shift drink.

People who knew about stage-ing were French boys on the cusp of manhood who lived in France and spoke French, and when they were fourteen and clearly not cut out for the books at their lycèe, would wander down the road to their local two-star inn and tap on the screen door of the kitchen there.

They joined—at the bottom—the ranks of a brigade kitchen and did their little part learning how to be clean, fast, efficient, and perfectly repetitive. They plucked the feathers from partridges that arrived through the back doors of the kitchens, they quickly washed berries picked by local men and women from their own bushes, they scrubbed copper as punishments. I knew nothing of it. Not one detail. I didn't even know such an apprenticeship existed or that anyone would aspire to such a thing.

I was clearly in no two-star country auberges. The locals—Riton and Andrè and Yannick—all of them strangely cross-eyed, chain-smoking, semi-literate drunks—leaned too many days a week and too many hours a day against that bar where I was understanding for the first time the chasm between coffee ground to order per cupful and what I'd slurped every morning from Dimitri with my egg-on-a-roll, which came out of a stainless steel tank. The patrons and crew of our little sports bar cum crêperie on that gray corner in that drab small town resembled nothing of the fine dining clientele of a two-star Relais & Chateaux inn nor its brigade. Michel, always in street clothes with the same apron used for the whole work week unwashed, smoking while mixing crêpe batter, and Marie Nöelle, nervously sipping her tisanes to calm her ever since Yves had offed himself, and the barmaid Sylvie with her long black hair rarely washed and never pulled back, who seemed to know just the right time to pour a free round and who very warmly received the flirtations of the cross-eyed, toothless, shit-stinking admirers—resembled not one aspect of a toqued brigade meticulously fluting mushroom caps. Nonetheless, everyone had an opinion about the baguette at breakfast, and everyone knew how to prepare a simple roast chicken and a few potatoes cooked in the local heavily salted butter. Everyone casually tipped the last sip of the red wine from their glass into their dish of soup and mopped it all up with the crusty heel left in the bread basket. I was sucking something in. Something unmitigated.

This is the crêpe.

This is the cider.

This is how we live and eat.

This man with bits of straw stuck to his thick blue Breton sweater, leaning up against the bar for a ballon of vin rouge ordinaire with a splash of water in it at eight-thirty in the morning, is the farmer whose milk we have been drinking, whose leeks we have been braising. These are the knotty, wormy, quite small apples from which the cider is made. And here, as a treat to celebrate my last day before continuing on my journey, when we drove to the coast, past fields of shooting asparagus and trees about to burst forth, and we stopped finally at the water's edge, in St. Malo—here are the platters of shellfish pulled that very morning from the sea—langouste, langoustines, moules, crevettes, huîtres, bulots, bigorneaux, coques. These are the pearl-tipped hat pins stuck into a wine bottle cork for pulling out the meats of the sea snails. The tide ran out, and the fishing boats slumped in the mud attached to their slack anchors like leashed dogs sleeping in the yard. The particular smell of sea mud went up our nostrils as we slurped the brine from the shells in front of us, so expertly and neatly arranged on the tiers.

"Cin-cin!" Marino and I saluted each other, celebrating these past few months, and clinked together our glasses of Muscadet sur lie.

I AM AWARE, in hindsight, that no real chef or restaurateur, when signing the thirty-year lease on her first restaurant, thinks back suddenly to the miserable beginnings of her wintry backpacking trip and considers it as part of her business plan. I now fully understand that instead of conjuring peak food moments in my life and trying to analyze what had made them so important, as if that was some kind of legitimate preparation for tackling the famously difficult restaurant business, I really should have been crawling up into the pipe work, noticing the water damage in the basement, and asking hard questions of Eric about the infrastructure of the one-hundred-year-old tenement building. If I had even known what one was, I should have asked about the C of O. While I was dreaming of how I would someday get that Gouda and that warm salted potato into the mouths of future guests, I should have been researching the restaurant's Certificate of Occupancy, arguably the most basic important document your restaurant will ever need. I'd never heard of due diligence. But there I was, pacing around my apartment, puzzling out how I could harness a hundred pivotal experiences relating to food—including hunger and worry—and translate those experiences into actual plates of food and wondering if eight dollars was too much to charge for a wedge of aged Gouda cheese and a couple of warm, salted boiled potatoes.

Of course it wasn't a stage; it was not a real education in a real kitchen. It was just a few months of living at the source of something rather than reading about it in a food magazine or learning about it from a chef-instructor in a starched and monogrammed jacket at cooking school, in the lifeless context of stainless steel and insta-read thermometers. I didn't consider it, at the time, anything pertinent to my future. But I was emboldened to sign that lease, in part because I had learned about buckwheat galettes and white flour crêpes and room temperature lettuce and salted butter and cellared hard cider in a typical Breton crêperie.

And it didn't end, this inadvertent and unconventional stage, with our kisses on both cheeks on that train platform in Rennes as I said good-bye to Marino and headed on to Paris and then the rest of my life in petit exil as I had initially planned.

There was more than a full year ahead of me—three months in India, seven months in Turkey, one month in Thailand, six months in Greece—during which I came to understand the differences and eventually to even have preferences between the milk from a certain wallah in Delhi and one in Rajasthan, the cooking of eggplant in Turkey over the cooking of eggplant in Greece, the sugar derived from beets in Romania and from cane in Cuba—for example—that would become part of my education as a cook.

There were uncomfortable bus and train rides that lasted for several days and nights, which I relied upon repeatedly—that three-day ticket keeping me sheltered and moving, because it killed two birds with one stone: the cost of travel and the cost of shelter—and so I would find my seat and remain in it, not even peeing or smoking or stepping out onto the platform for a leg stretch for the entire journey from Paris to Athens, from Mahabalipurum to Varanasi, from Bangkok to Chiang Mai, from Istanbul to Ankara. And on those journeys, those crossings, I came to know extraordinary and particular hunger.

As my initial twelve hundred dollars in traveler's checks dwindled down uncomfortably, I stared out the window of that bus or train in three-day increments in a glassy, light-headed state wondering about those women in the fields in the bright headscarves, the acres and acres of lopsided sunflowers all draping over in the same direction as the sun shines, the small stone huts out in the fields, the gray-green dry trees with silvery leaves. Flattened out by the heavy fear of how I would make it with just a few hundred remaining dollars, I did what

I always do when I am afraid and went quite still, with a total slackening of will or need, and I thought all of my thoughts, sifted through all of my old nostalgias, while couples fell asleep on each other's shoulders, bus drivers honked friendly hellos at each other through those panoramic windshields of their buses, little brush fires burned at night on the sides of the road, and solitary figures rode bikes shakily on the shoulder of the highway.

I starved. And I starved so many times on this repeated three-day bus ride or train journey from somewhere to somewhere else that I came to know every contour of my hunger in precise detail. When I came to be actually holding the keys to my new restaurant, wondering what credentials I possibly possessed for owning and operating such a place, I counted knowing hunger and appetite as one of them. It became such a recurring experience during this period when I was twenty—to be starving and afraid of running out of money—as I wandered from Brussels to Burma and everywhere in between for months on end, that I later came to see it as a part of my training as a cook. I came to see hunger as being as important a part of a stage as knife skills. Because so much starving on that trip led to such an enormous amount of time fantasizing about food, each craving became fanatically particular. Hunger was not general, ever, for just something, anything, to eat. My hunger grew so specific I could name every corner and fold of it. Salty, warm, brothy, starchy, fatty, sweet, clean and crunchy, crisp and watery, and so on.

This kind of travel, so distinctly prior to ATMs, debit cards, cash advance credit cards, cell phones, Facebook, and international SIM cards is probably not even possible now. And it isn't right to romanticize it; you, with a feathery mind and a too light body, sitting on your heavy pack without a penny of local currency, down to your last two hundred sixty dollars in traveler's checks, with not one person on earth able to locate you on a map in any more than the most general terms, and the local American Express office closed until Tuesday because of some local holiday or labor strike.

To be picked up and fed, often by strangers, when you are in that state of fear and hunger, became the single most important and convincing food experience I came back to over and over, that sunny afternoon humming around my apartment, wondering how I might translate such an experience into the restaurant I was now sure I was about to open down the block. I so completely understood hospitality and care from a bedraggled recipient's point of view, that even before I came to understand how garbage removal is billed on square yardage of waste and that a commercial storefront should have a separate water meter from the building's, I knew I had to somehow get that kind of hospitality into this minor little thirty-seater in the as-yet-ungentrified and still heavily graffitied East Village.

MELISSA HAD GIVEN ME the address and phone number of a man in Athens before I'd left home with my backpack. And at one of those unromantic points, alone in a new country, wasted on the youth hostel experience, down to my last dollars, my expensive camera long since ripped off, I dug up Iannis's number. These calls were always hard for me. I had developed such an intense deal about self-reliance, I bristled against having to need or want anything or anyone. Ever. But here I was in Greece and I couldn't even read the alphabet on the signs in this new country. I'd eaten nothing but a raw red onion, a sack of salted pumpkin seeds, and a glass of warm dry vermouth in the previous five days, and so I gulped down all my embarassment about having to ask for help and called ahead to this stranger, Iannis.

He couldn't have made it easier for me. "Yes! Yes!" he shouted into the phone, speaking excellent Oxford English. "You are most welcome here! I will be at my offices in the afternoon. Can you make your way into Athens from Piraeus or shall I come and retrieve you?" he shouted.

"No! No!" I shouted back. "I can make my way. I will just make my way into the city and call you again, if that is okay with you."

"Yes!" he shouted back, his welcome palpable. "I will await your call! I will be waiting!"

Iannis, probably twenty years older than me, with a big mustache and laugh lines all around his green eyes, met me in Omonia Square, brought me to his apartment, and without even inquiring, set to work frying in olive oil two eggs with the darkest orange yolks I had ever seen, then sprinkled them with a coarse sea salt and cut a slice from a thick, crusty loaf of bread. In a blender he mixed apple, honey, and milk and set this incredible, refreshing meal in front of me, beaming his huge smile. I was craving salt and starch. Eggs and bread.

In the evening, we were joined by a friend of his, and we walked to a restaurant near to the Acropolis. They knew the waiter by name, and he didn't even bother keeping track of how many drinks we ordered, he just brought to our table the big bottle of ouzo, put a rubber band around the bottle to mark the level of the contents, and then let us self serve as we wished. However much we depleted from the rubber band mark by the end is what we paid for. Iannis, without wasting a moment on that awkward and tedious conversation that will unhappily precede so many hundreds and hundreds of future restaurant meals in all of our lives—whether to share or not to share and whether or not there are food phobias and dietary restrictions among us—simply ordered food for the table without even consulting a menu, and so set the standard for me for all time of excellent hospitality: Just take care of everything. Is it considered more hospitable to discover your guests' preferences, their likes and dislikes? Is it rude to deny your guests choice and control over their experience? I don't know, but I forever want to arrive somewhere hungry and thirsty and tired and be taken care of as Iannis took care of us. I want to be relieved of making possibly poor decisions, to be spared the embarrassing moment when I—the guest—am asked to state my preference for red or white wine, meat or fish, sparkling or still water, when I know that whatever I say will be a decision rendered for the whole table. Delicious food and drink arrived at our table, and it was immediately clear how Iannis hadn't needed a menu or a survey of our preferences to order because he simply presented a classic, traditional Greek meal. There was saganaki and taramasalata and skordalia to start, some grilled lamb and octopus to follow, a classic salad with feta cheese, and the best part, a couple of raw sardines on a stainless steel plate that we cooked ourselves in pure alcohol set alight, but not before Kostas, roaring with laughter, sent one of them back to be traded in for a female. I could not for my life at that time have discerned between a male and a female sardine, nor the gustatory difference, but I laughed too and felt one hundred months of worry and care lift from my head up up up into the orange-scented Greek night. Iannis said, "Tomorrow we will go to my house on the island. It is small but I hope you will like it." Kostas smiled his huge smile, the only blue-eyed blond Greek I'd ever met, and said, assuredly, "You will love it!"

Even if you hadn't been strung out in youth hostels for months, keeping constant paralyzing track of your dwindling dollars, repetitively checking the pouch around your neck that held your passport and your money with a kind of obsessive worry, you would drink up this warmth and this generosity like it was ice cold beer. Iannis was thrilled to show me his city, the food of his country, his house on the island, to give me a frothy glass of apple, milk, and honey to drink in the cool salvation of his terrace, where a small orange tree grew, giving off its perfume.

And Kostas was right. I did love the island. I loved it so much that I stayed for months, and found a job in a well-lit touristy restaurant in the center of the port that paid a thousand drachmas a day where I washed dishes and pots and cleaned all the calamari and made hundreds of koriatiki—the Greek salad with tomatoes and feta. The waiters wore black pants and white polo shirts and smoked a pack of cigarettes in a single shift. I made my home in a little hut I had built on the beach. I showered in the ocean, shat behind the rocks, slept under the stars, and spent those early days in Serifos wandering the mountainside. Chamomile, mint, capers, oregano, thyme, figs, lemons, oranges—these grew so rampantly that when you walked, the herbs crushed underfoot and released their scent into the air. I followed narrow goat paths, and the shiny, black licorice, jelly bean goat poops guided me to hidden fresh water and mountainside gardens tended by their owners who came and went on donkeys. At the top of the world, high up in the mountain away from everything, I would sometimes encounter an old man, a goat herder with his tinkling goats, coming down the mountain riding his donkey in a wooden saddle as his dog followed. "Xiarete!" I greeted him, and he said back "Iachera."

And every night when I finished work, I walked to the very end of the port, to the last light before the vast darkness beyond the mountain jutting up out of the sea. There was a restaurant there. A few tables scattered in the yard under the long-needled pine trees where the locals went. Tourists had been swarming the Greek islands for decades of course, and everyone knew of the wild nightlife in Santorini and the party yachts in Mykonos, but Serifos was a world away, a tiny island in the undiscovered Cyclades where only Greeks went, where the oven at the bakery in Livadi was still used communally and town women brought their casseroles to bake in the ashes after the day's bread had been baked, and Margarita's little place there at the end of the port will forever be my idea of a perfect restaurant. Her son went out in his boat and fished and whatever he netted and however much of it he caught is what was for dinner. If it ran out at eight p.m., it just ran out, and people ached to see some delicious thing on the next table that they couldn't also have because there just hadn't been enough. If you wanted the lamb, it came saucy and ungarnished—alone on a plate. If you also wanted broad beans or potatoes, you ordered them separately and she served them also on separate plates. Margarita, maybe only forty but looking sixty, with sun-hardened skin and thick working hands, rode her donkey, sidesaddle, up into the hillside and got everything she cooked from her garden. I walked there many times in the early mornings, and when you pushed open the little gate fashioned out of branches and bedsprings, there was a rough and casual Eden inside, with olive trees, grapes, fig trees, zucchini and eggplant and tomatoes, and the wild greens called horta that she boiled in salted water to tame drabness and then drowned—delicious death!—in her own olive oil. Her freshwater spring was covered by a heavy wooden lid, and in her shed she stored a few tools, some bags, and large vats of homemade, copper-colored wine. Margarita, like many on the island, made her own wine. There was no menu, no daily special, no appetizers, entrees, and no dessert, ever. You either went into the kitchen and lifted the lids to see what there was or let her come to your little table out in the dry grass and she told you the five or six things she had available.

She set out copper cups if you asked for retsina and little glass tumblers if you asked for her own wine, which she brought in a little metal pitcher. At the height of the season, when it got very busy for that push at nine o'clock, especially on Fridays when the ferry from Piraeus churned into port—spilling Albanian Gypsies with mattresses piled on top of their trucks and the weekly mail and trucks carrying fuel and dry goods and Athenian weekenders looking for a relaxing weekend on the silent, iron island, away from the traffic and pollution of the city, a five-hour ferry ride away—you could wait at your table ignored for an uncomfortably long time, as she hustled from the kitchen to the yard carrying plates to different tables, and the cicadas fell from the trees above onto your waiting plates and your hair.

And at the end of your meal, she would come to the table with a short pencil and start to tally your bill by scribbling directly on the paper tablecloth. She would ask you what you ate and drank, and she added up the numbers, accepted your cash, and after you left, she would clear the table and crumple up the cloth and stuff it in the garbage.

In my new kitchen I couldn't discern between a freon tube and a condensation line in a lowboy reach-in refrigerator to save my life, but I had crystal clear understanding about bringing the experience of Margarita—in translation—into it. So Eric began to put together an LLC and an operating agreement and a small group of investors to buy the lease out of bankruptcy court, and I signed all the papers the same way I took off on that one-way People Express flight—knowing absolutely nothing about what I was doing, but understanding that I had committed to it.

And in a very short time, I was power-washing walls in a floor-length rubber apron, rain boots, and ventilated goggles. I killed roaches, poisoned their nests, trapped rats, stuffed their little holes with steel wool and glass shards while my girlfriend, in her own way, walked through the place "purifying" it with a burning sage smudge stick and read me my Rob Brezsny horoscope in support. My best friends were stopping by after work, scraping the walls, scouring every surface, using skewers and razor blades to get into every crevice of every appliance. We papered up the windows and worked into the night at every opportunity. While I continued to chef for a paycheck at the catering kitchen, I kept two clipboards going side-by-side throughout the day, one for the catering crap and one for my exciting double life lived afterhours, and on that clipboard the lists went on for thirty pages and constantly renewed themselves even after I had crossed off the first thousand tasks in black Sharpie. Items I had never encountered in my professional life—

~~Determine 2nd Means of Egress~~
~~Establish Payroll Account~~
~~Attend LCB Public Hearing~~
~~Estimate Breakage~~
~~Recharge Ansul System~~

—I now tackled bravely.

In the evenings, people I didn't know at all passed by constantly, saw the cleanup, and popped their heads in to ask, excitedly, if the old beloved French bistro was finally coming back to life, and when I said "No, I'm sorry, this will be a new place," their faces sank in sadness and disappointment, and I struggled to feel confident. No fewer than a hundred passersby asked hopefully if this would be a vegetarian restaurant and pointed out that the East Village really needed some good vegetarian places. One guy suggested, earnestly, that we run the same menu as a busy and popular neighboring spot and hope for their overflow. Finally, I locked the door from the inside.

I didn't have an ounce of what typically matters, but I had all that. And I wanted to bring all of it, every last detail of it—the old goat herder smoking filterless cigarettes coming down the mountain, crushing oregano and wild mint underfoot; Iannis cooking me two fried eggs without even asking me if I cared for something to eat; that sweet, creamy milk that the milk wallah in Delhi frothed by pouring in a long sweeping arc between two pots held as far apart as the full span of his arms from his cart decorated with a thousand fresh marigolds—into this tiny thirty-seat restaurant. I wanted a place with a Velvet Underground CD that made you nod your head and feel warm with recognition. I wanted the lettuce and the eggs at room temperature. The waiter to bring you something to eat or drink that you didn't even ask for when you arrived cold and early and undone by your day in the city. I wanted the toasted manti from a Turkish wedding I'd been part of in Göreme-Nevşehir, the butter and sugar sandwiches we ate as kids after school for a snack, the tarnished silverware and chipped wedding china from a paladar in Havana, and the canned sardines I ate in that little apartment on Twenty-ninth Street. The veal marrow my mother made us eat as kids that I grew to crave as an adult. We would have brown butcher paper on the tables, not linen tablecloths, and when you finished your meal, the server would just pull the pen from behind her ear and scribble the bill directly on the paper like Margarita had done. We would use jelly jars for wine glasses. We would put a rubber band around the middle of the wine bottle like I had done with Kostas and Iannis in Athens, and if you wanted to drink only half, you could pay for just half. Like Margarita's place at that far dark end of the port in Serifos, when we ran out of lamb for the night, we would just run out.

There would be no foam and no "conceptual" or "intellectual" food; just the salty, sweet, starchy, brothy, crispy things that one craves when one is actually hungry. There would be nothing tall on the plate, the portions would be generous, there would be no emulsions, no crab cocktail served in a martini glass with its claw hanging over the rim. In ecstatic farewell to my years of corporate catering, we would never serve anything but a martini in a martini glass. Preferably gin.

I wanted all of that crammed into this filthy little gem that Eric was asking to show me as I whizzed by to park my car. The rest, I imagined I could figure out—the hot water booster and the right size grease trap and the payroll service and the proper way to process a credit card transaction. I had a master's degree, I had figured out more densely loaded text than a standard commercial lease. I called my sister to make my announcement. I'm opening a restaurant. She'd become the food editor at *Saveur* magazine whose offices were then downtown, near Tribeca, and she was commuting into the city from New Jersey. More than once a week, she crashed on our couch.

"Can you look at my opening menu and tell me what you think?"

"What are you going to call it?" she asked.

"Prune."

9

ONE DAY I UNLOCKED THE RESTAURANT IN THE MORNING, ROLLED up the heavy gate, got the ovens going, and then went downstairs to the basement prep area and turned on all the lights. I unlocked the office door and smelled it immediately and unquestionably: human shit. I looked around, checking and rechecking the soles of my shoes for dog crap. I saw nothing. I put on my whites, an apron, and changed into my clogs, and smelled it again—a big whiff of human feces. I checked the bottom of my clogs. Nothing. I unbolted the back door of the office, which leads to nowhere—a small passageway between buildings with an ultra-narrow and steep stairway up to street level. This is protected by a rickety chunk of chain-link fence so that random derelicts can't wander down off the street and jump up on the fire escape and rob the apartments above the restaurant.

As soon as I pushed open the rusty old back door of the office, I found what I was, reluctantly, looking for. Someone with very loose bowels had managed to crawl over the chain-link fence and squat in my office doorway, unloading his guts onto the stoop and the door itself. It was half a mountain of soft, crusted-over, dark brown crap on the outside, where it had been left to dry, and soft, mustardy brown inside, the way guacamole gets when exposed to air.

I'm not, unfortunately, the kind of person who would ever ask someone else to do something that I myself am not willing to do. So rather than save the delight for the Mexican porter who would arrive in a few minutes, I went and got the gloves and the dustpan and the pine-scented industrial cleaner and began. Some of the shit had settled into a pool in the gravel and debris outside my door. This I could more readily scoop up with the dustpan and knock out into the waiting garbage bag. But the rest of it had to be dealt with in hand-to-hand combat. With a kitchen side towel wrapped around my nose and mouth like an old-time bandit, I scraped and scrubbed and shoveled and doused the whole contaminated area until the whole world, it seemed, smelled so much like pine cleaner that it was equally unbearable. For days, like some kind of olfactory chiaroscuro, we breathed pine cleaner, but then, there, at the very bottom of the inhale, there would be a subtle note of human shit.

As I was finishing and surveying my morning's work, I looked up the narrow staircase to street level and lurched a couple of steps backward. On the second step from the top was a rat, a dead rat—actually, the more I looked at it, a *nearly* dead rat. I could see it breathing, its body vaguely rising and falling with its last weakened gasps, and occasionally I could make out the tiniest, subtlest movement in an arm or the neck.

This challenge I just did not want to tackle, especially not from below and risk having it tumble down onto my head. Or come magically to life just when I approached at eye level and have it gnaw at my face. I wanted a superior vantage point, so I re-entered the office, bolted the back door, walked through the pine-scented gas chamber, up the stairs, through the dining room, and out onto the street. Coming around the side of the building, I reached the top of the staircase and got a better look at the rat. He was still breathing and yet, the rat looked—corporally, if you will—completely dead, as if it had died at least a full day before. It did not seem biologically possible that it was living, the way its eyes were long ago caved in and dried out, and its mouth was in full rigor. Yet, unmistakably, its long plump body was swollen and vaguely undulating. Then—I had no doubt whatsoever— it started to move, ever so faintly.

The rat started listing heavily to its side, and only at the last second, when it started to slip off the second step, did I realize what I was witnessing. The rat slowly, like a sock filled with coffee beans, slouched over and landed with a pillowy thud on the third step—and then exploded with thousands of maggots teeming inside. What had looked like shallow breathing was the undulence of maggots at a meal. Efrain, the porter, had arrived and was inside sweeping, but I just couldn't foist that onto someone else. I went and got a gallon of bleach.

Not even a week later, I was on *The Martha Stewart Show* demonstrating how to prepare Italian wedding soup. It was a glamorous day. They sent a sleek black car to pick me up. Me! In the backseat of a black Lincoln Town Car all the way up the Hutchinson to her studios in Connecticut. In my sunglasses, on my cell phone—dialing every friend in my phone's address book to narrate to them where I was at that very moment—*in a private Town Car sent expressly for me.*

And then the hair.

And then the makeup.

And then the schlepper who fetches you a bottle of water and a cappuccino and a small plate of fresh cut fruit!

When the adorable production assistant at the studio had offered me a cappuccino, I was totally thrown. After all, that's *my* job; I'm the schlepper.

"Oh no, no, please, thank you, that's so nice of you but really, I can do it myself. Just show me where and I can fix myself a coffee or something and I'll do it myself. Really, thank you, that's so kind of you."

He stared at me a long second and said, "I'll just get it for you. How do you take it?"

"Okay. Um, light no sugar."

I thanked him profusely when he brought it, and he told me a kind of alarming story about a famous chef from Boston who'd been on the show who was, apparently, a great deal more comfortable than I with the whole being-served-by-the-schlepper routine.

"Oooph, that sounds ridiculous," I said.

"Well," he said, clearing the empty fruit plate, "I don't know how you stay so humble."

And I nearly burst out laughing with images of maggoty rats and the stench of human shit so very fresh in my mind.

"Oh, that's not a problem with this line of work," I said.

And then what? The car dumps you back at the restaurant just before service. You swan through the joint in front of all your employees in your heavy for-TV makeup. The waiters and dishwashers and line cooks ooh and aaah appropriately at your general fabulousness and want to know everything about Martha. *How was she? Was she a bitch?* And on you go in minute detail until it's three minutes before six and dinner service must start so everyone scatters back to their positions. And you? Fabulous celebrity chef you? Downstairs you see that the prep sink drain hole is clogged with slimy caul fat trimming that no one has bothered to clean out and you, automatically, like a reflex, thrust your hands into the drain and spend a few good humbling moments digging unknown slimy shit out of the prep sink.

But, there was a brief minute, in the beginning, when I got a little swelled. I got seduced by customers coming up to the pass leading to the open kitchen and heaping praise upon me. I was stunned, glowing, swollen with their attention. Weepy, brimming, beside myself. "This is the best meal I've had in New York City!" they said. "This is better than Gramercy!" they claimed. "You're a genius," they declared.

And then, soon after the "best meal" comment, a woman came walking up to the pass, straight toward me. I was smiling my prepared smile, expecting the praise, thinking, "The sweetbreads *are* amazing." The woman reached across the slate counter to, I thought for a second, warmly touch me, and then I saw it—her empty cocktail glass with her napkin crumpled up in it.

"Can you put this somewhere?" she asked, and as I took the glass from her hand, she grabbed the cuff of my chef's jacket and wiped her shrimp toast fingers on it.

It took me ten full seconds to climb down from my perch, but when I did I smiled at her, warmly, genuinely, and I said, "My pleasure." And I meant it.

10

ARLINDO IS THIS GUY WHO LIVES IN THE BUILDING THAT THE restaurant is in. He's from Brazil, I think, about six-foot-two and weighs a bit too much; so much that he has man titties. The reason I know this is because he likes to stand outside on the sidewalk in front of the wide-open French doors of the restaurant with no shirt on in the summer, in rivulets of his own sweat.

Arlindo came to me very solemnly when we first opened, introduced himself as some sort of officer of the co-op upstairs, and asked if he could speak with me for just a few minutes. Not knowing then (it was October) that he would turn out to be the kind of guy who stands outside on the sidewalk in front of the packed restaurant on a hot day with his naked gut and sagging man titties hanging out, I welcomed him and sat down for what I expected to be some kind of new neighbor chat.

"What's up, Arlindo?" I asked, in a friendly, new-neighbor tone. Arlindo leaned in very gravely, hesitated dramatically, broadcasting to me with the pain on his face that what he had to tell me was so very difficult for him, but persevere he must. For my benefit.

"I am sorry to tell you, to have to be the one to tell you," he started, in his thick accent and deep, beautiful baritone voice, but then broke off, at 240 pounds, no match for the gravity of the job he had to do. He resumed, "I am sorry to have to tell you this but you need to know that your employees are stealing from you."

This was very early on when Prune had just opened, and so far my employees were like, my girlfriend of four years, my best friend from college whom I'd known about ten, and myself. I felt the need to sit back, just an inch or two, in my chair, like when someone casually mentions that they failed to take their bipolar medication that day. "Really?" I asked quietly.

He knitted his brow in such emphatic sympathy, that eight or ten deep lines of woe sprang up and arched over his sad, sad eyes, like seagull's wings. "Yes," he said, solemnly shaking his head.

"Hunh," was all I could manage. And then finally, "What are they stealing?"

"Well, you should see it, behind the building, I am picking up bottles and bottles of Kahlua and so many empty Budweiser cans. They are stealing your liquor and drinking it out back." At this, I actually scraped my chair back several inches from the table, which maybe he perceived as my shock at the profoundly upsetting nature of the news he had dutifully disclosed to me. But Prune didn't yet have a liquor license, and wouldn't get one for six more months, and when we did get one finally I wouldn't be stocking Budweiser in a can or Kahlua either, so the sudden backing up of the chair was more about concern for my own safety when I realized I was alone in my restaurant sitting across the table from this man who had just introduced himself as one of my landlords for the next twenty years, or however long my lease was.

The next time I saw Arlindo was on the sidewalk, in front of the restaurant again, this time in a muscle tee and with his head wrapped in a big bandage like when you dress up for Halloween as a hospital patient and wrap toilet paper around your head a few times. He had just returned from the emergency room to get some stitches because that day, while painting his apartment, he climbed up the ladder to paint the ceiling but had misjudged how far he was from the ceiling fan and got brained by one of the blades, stopping it dead in its tracks with his own head.

The co-op lets him plant flowers out front and out back of the building and pick out the color of paint for the door trim and other "responsibilities" and they give him the title of something like vice-maintenance manager, which makes him, in fact, an officer of the building. The only weird thing about the title is that it is not, we've discovered, an act of charity on the part of the co-op; they are in earnest with this assistant to the vice-maintenance manager office, which I guess, says all it needs to about the business upstairs.

We've been tenants in the building here longer than the past two co-op "presidents." They've been very sincere, earnest people but I don't think they have been particularly qualified for their endeavors. There was one president, a sort of self-styled "ambassador," a guy who seemed to feel his diplomacy skills were such that he could broker peace between nations. He used to walk into Prune in the middle of the crush of Sunday brunch somehow genuinely expecting to take care of a little co-op business—an electric bill, a conversation about the boiler—and stand there stupidly in the middle of the fray, expectantly.

Sunday brunch is like the Indy 500 of services at Prune. There is a roaring thunderous stampede every forty minutes as hordes of hungry, angry, mag-wheeled, tricked-out customers line up at the door, scrape the chairs back, take their seats, blow through their steak and eggs. The line is two full seatings long at nine-thirty even though we don't open the doors until ten. They are waiting for the go flag. Some have physically harmed the hostess as they sprint to get a table. I once worked the host shift on a Sunday brunch at thirty-eight weeks pregnant—and even my huge belly, my chronic shortness of breath, and my clear proprietary aura (you can just tell when I am in the room that I am not an employee; I exude ownership) even that did not stop the stampede that is Sunday brunch.

We do a little over two hundred covers on a Sunday in five hours with only thirty seats, if that tells you anything. We hardly have the space on the tiny dining room floor to accommodate the crush of bodies, the trays full of Bloody Marys and beer backs going to every table, the large plates of eggs, potatoes, toast, and bacon sailing through the room—everything at brunch goes on a large and heavy plate to accommodate all the things a brunch special requires: fat, protein, starch, double starch. You can't fit eggs Benedict with a potato roesti and a side of coiled lamb sausage on a small delicate plate. The staff are like professional drivers, taking the turns on two wheels, screeching around the room getting the tables turned, the bloodies shaken, the eggs delivered, and then the bus tubs hauled back to the kitchen. The hosts program loud, rocking music to keep the pace what it needs to be, music that is otherwise forbidden at dinner and lunch service when we are seeking a more mature, civilized experience.

The kitchen for its part is hunkered down, the two full rails packed with tickets that all look exactly the same because it's all pancakes, eggs, and bacon with no coursing to be done. Sunday is an order fire day. Every ticket comes in and is shouted out and is picked up immediately. We do not wait patiently while the customer enjoys a section of the *New York Times* over a nice bowl of homemade granola before firing up his sour cream and caraway omelette. We do not. We are sometimes laying down omelette pans on the flames by the half-dozen, and delivering that many omelettes in as many minutes. My station, if I am expediting and not working eggs, is at the front of the pass, where I can look out over the dining room while simultaneously keeping my focus on frantically assembling fruit salads, smoked fish platters, youth hostel breakfast plates, and ricotta with pears and figs and pine nuts, and buttering every piece of toast or English muffin that leaves this kitchen, which, on a weekend, is about 192 Thomas's and 1,440 eggs. This is nothing compared to a hotel or even a big restaurant; the only thing that makes it monstrous is that we are doing it in a kitchen the size of a Lincoln Continental.

In the middle of this high-octane frenzy is when Mr. United Nations strolls in wearing cutoff shorts and flip-flops and stands in the middle of what there is to our dining room as bussers, waiters, and customers blow by him on their way to the pass, the bus tub, or the table, with a wrinkled envelope in his hand containing our water bill or some other rather important item. Only to him could this look like the right time to talk to me about co-op business. Invariably, he gets flustered and hands the envelope to the bartender or a waitress who is relentlessly trained to be helpful and friendly no matter what, who shoves the envelope into the cash drawer behind the bar or in their apron pocket along with the dirty napkins and pens they've got accumulating in there, or he hands it to me and I retrieve it with buttery fingers and shove it in the first-aid kit for safekeeping where I forget all about it. All I can think is that if he had been left in charge of brokering the peace in a thousand-year-old tribal nation, the ethnic cleansing would have been complete as he stood there, in flip-flops, totally flummoxed.

The only person from the co-op who's been with us from the beginning and still with us today is a renter; an elderly woman who looks like she's been avoiding animal protein for so long that her skin is now tissue paper and her hair is as brittle as shredded wheat. Annie memorized our phone number the day it was published and calls us every day to tell us to turn down the music. And she's got us on redial. In the first few months, we were energetically neighborly and ultra-accommodating to all of the needs of all of the people in the building upstairs, and the building next door, and the building on the block behind us. And the building on the north side of us, and the west side and so on until we finally realized that when you open a restaurant, you are a magnet for every lonely, angry, unfulfilled New Yorker who can't afford a better apartment, a haircut, or a meal in a decent restaurant. It's like shaking a tree and out fall all the critics, the naysayers, the people with allergies to even the smell of anyone else's success, or with litigious impulses over the sound of silverware in a dish rack being hosed down, or who call the fire department at the suggestion of meat grill smoke. You get all the people who moved from elsewhere to New York in the first place to bask in its nearly assaulting vibrance but who now write letters to councilmen and form committees to make it more like Main Street back home.

Annie's thing was "black music." We could be listening to Joni Mitchell, Cat Stevens, Johnny Cash, and the Talking Heads all night long at a healthy volume, and she wouldn't ever call and as soon as Angie Stone, Stevie Wonder, or Finley Quaye tracks hit the rotation—we could set our watches by it—the phone would ring and Ms. Vegetarian in a faded terry-cloth robe would be shrieking at us to turn it down. She would come down in her robe and nightcap and complain about the bass, with a restaurant full of customers. To spare us both, we got with her and arranged a volume level together—she in her apartment, us downstairs in front of the stereo, both of us on the phone:

"Can you hear it now?"

Okay.

"Can you hear it now?"

Okay.

"How's this, can you hear this?"

Until, mutually, we agreed on a volume and we took white paint and black permanent marker and labeled the level on the volume knob ANNIE with two exclamation points, so that any host of any shift would know what not to go above. But after a while, she would again start to call constantly and when she complained that she was now sleeping in a hammock made of egg crates in her kitchen on a pulley system high above her dish cabinets so that the vibration from our sound system wouldn't keep her up at night, we kind of realized it wasn't us or our music. Our sound system is two shitty speakers from J&R Music World. We're a small bistro, not a rave club with bouncers on headsets.

These people make entertaining characters in your journal or your published essay or your after-work-with-beers bullshit session. But in the main, a six-foot-two, two-hundred-forty-pound guy with no shirt on, wandering around the building while I'm alone in it, can actually feel incredibly menacing. On an average day in my life, I could do without the added "color" they provide. This work is intensely stressful on its own, the hours are already long, the physical demands are significant. The egg shift at Sunday brunch alone could take down an average man. That heat in the egg station at brunch has a formidable physical presence. It moves about, undulating, coming at you in waves, some of them, like when you open the oven door, smacking you forcefully enough to tighten the skin on your face and make your eyes swell shut slightly.

Much has been written about facing the shocking heat of a restaurant's set of burners, and in spite of what it may reveal about me, I am the only one I know who likes it. I always feel like I am a contender in a nicely matched bout every time we meet—especially every Sunday—when I enter that station at seven-thirty in the morning and begin my setup. Every time I step in front of those ten burners, in that egregiously tight space, less than twelve inches between the wall I am backed up against and the burning stovetop in front of me, I feel like we are two small-time boxers—me and the heat—meeting in the center of the ring to tap gloves. The fight begins with a little slap, totally manageable, when I put that first large pot of water on to boil, and then increases in ferocity from there when the large cast-iron skillet starts to vaguely shimmer and smoke and sputter, magnifying the already immense power of my opponent—inching up the temperature—as I start to render the pancetta for the carbonara. When the pig urine stench of that excellent pancetta hits me in the nose I am red-eyed and snotty—your nose runs in the heat and in the cold equally as it attempts to regulate your body temperature—and it's only eight o'clock in the morning. That your eyes are already a little swollen and your nose is running and your skin is tight on your face gives you a Raging Bull kind of feeling—which gets me immediately in the right mindset. The whole crew feels it—that tension before a fight. The customers lined up outside before we have even turned on the lights and had our family meal, the total knowledge of what we know is coming—the relentless, nonstop five-hour beating—and we practically huddle up, poised for the bell, we are scared even, saying in psyched but tense tones, "Here we go!" as Julie unlocks the door and they flood in, scraping the chairs, and that milk foamer on the espresso machine rages its monster roar, and we stand motionless in the kitchen, looking out onto the floor, waiting for the panic of tickets, tickets, tickets.

It's important not to go down early in your shift. And there are things that will bring you down: You start your first ticket of the day and by accident you tip a full gallon of pancake batter over in your reach-in—both wasting a product you desperately need and now creating a jam in your reach-in because you can't work with pancake batter all over everything. The expediter does not stop calling out tickets just because you have a mess in your station. The orders, all of them at least in part your responsibility because every dish at brunch comes with eggs, keep pouring in while you hustle to get that glop cleaned up and your station back on track. The circumstances won't change. You are always, always going to face forces that can bring you to your knees. No matter how well set up you are, how early you came in, how tight and awesome your mise en place is, there will be days, forces, events that just conspire to fuck you and the struggle to stay up—to not sink down into the blackest, meanest hole—to stay psychologically up and committed to the fight, is the hardest, by far, part of the day. The heat, the crush of customers, the special orders and sauces on sides, the blood-sugar crises—none of it is as difficult as the struggle to stay in the game, once you have suffered a setback like dropping a full quart of ranchero sauce, which has cracked open and exploded in your station all over your clogs and the oven doors.

I like to swear the dirtiest, most vulgar swear words I can think of to get me through it. It can be very Tourette's Syndrome back there when I am working that egg station and the expediter has failed to tell me about a sauce on the side or a well-done poached. I always, to be sure, take the moment to apologize to everyone around me, to promise them that I am not serious, that nothing is personal—but then I rip it out, jaw tight, and spewing combinations of the word *fuck* that even David Mamet has not thought to put together. I have fired people who can't suffer their setbacks and petty failures. If they go down early and spend the rest of their five-hour shift that way, it threatens to sink the whole boat and that can't happen just because you burned your first omelette and had to refire it. You've got to get your GI Jane on.

From too many years of going all day without eating—that freakish thing about restaurant work: Water water everywhere and not a drop to drink—I have blood sugar issues. And they can feel serious.

There are a couple of points in that shift—every single time I work it—that I legitimately fear that the entire brunch service will come to a screeching halt if I don't get some orange juice, iced Ovaltine, and a full quart of ice cold Coca-Cola down my throat in seconds, and in that particular order. In a generous light, I am that boxer in his corner, his trainer squirting Gatorade indiscriminately at his face while the boxer keeps his mouth open like a gasping fish, hoping for the jet stream to get to his throat. But I can, in a less generous light, feel like a dirty glue huffer—shoving my head discreetly and desperately into my cool reach-in—sucking, and I mean sucking, down a quart of chocolatey, malty, milky Ovaltine over a quart of ice—like an addict puts that paper bag of paint fumes over his nose and mouth and pulls that shit into his body with a terrifying force—made more terrifying by the utter calm and clarity and complacency that overtakes you once your hit kicks in and reaches the right places. The Coca-Cola so tannic and sweet and achingly cold that it makes my eyes tear up. And then brunch is back on track.

During the eighth round, close to three o'clock, I get dizzy stupid. I don't even know what I'm cooking. By which I mean, I know what each individual item in front of me is, but I don't know what I'm cooking in the larger picture. Is this the eggs Benedict that picks up with the salmon omelette? Or is this the benny that picks up with oatmeal and lamb sausage? This may seem inane to anyone on the outside, but in my industry, which benny is which matters. You don't just cook food indiscriminately, without phrases, without groupings, and carelessly shove it all to the pass to let the expediter sort out. You have to time your food, according to a system, so that you don't produce a benny that sits in the window waiting for five minutes for a lamb sausage from the guy working the grill station. Five minutes in the life of a cooked egg, unlike a nicely resting piece of meat, is the difference between excellent and bullshit. At three o'clock, with the last pummeling of tickets on the board, I need to be told over and over by the expediter, and probably much to his irritation, which benny is this particular benny. I know all of the strategies and I use them—repeating back the ticket after it's called—"echoing" the expediter, and constantly talking in minutes and seconds with my fellow line cooks:

"I'm two out on benny/carbonara."

"Thirty seconds on huevos/pancake."

"Selling benny/oyster!" We break it down to each other from minutes to seconds to sold! But invariably all I can see by the last round through my red, swollen eyes is the pan and the egg in front of me. I'm just punching and hoping I land one on the guy's jaw.

To have a waiter pop back into the kitchen during this beat down and tell you that Arlindo is outside, drilling holes through the sidewalk down into our wine cellar to drain his flower boxes in a way so the water doesn't pool up in front of his front stoop but instead now drains down—where? Into the earth, does he imagine? Into the great sweet clean aquifer. Just below his front stoop? Here, in New York City? No, when his landscaping fever passes and he realizes, at the same time that I realize, that his flower boxes now drain into his own basement, which happens to be where all our wines with their once-pristine labels are stored, I go slack in the neck from exhaustion.

You want to own your own little place? You want to have a tight relationship with your farmer? Surround yourself with poet-philosopher wine merchants? Make your own ricotta and cure your own lardo? You want to be chef/owner? It's not the eighteen-hour days and the hot kitchen that'll get you. It's all that *plus* a half-naked six-foot-two, two-hundred-forty-pound man in front of your restaurant drilling holes into the basement and then watering his ivy.

11

M ELISSA CALLED ONE DAY, WHEN SHE WAS STILL WORKING AS AN editor at *Saveur.*

"Gabs," she says, her voice very, very low, not whispering, but very quiet, "get this, guess who's here," and then, even lower, "Jacques. Pepin."

Top Chef, Iron Chef, The Next Food Network Star? We don't give a shit. Flavor of the month, right place at the right time, big-fish-small-pond? We are not moved. Jacques Pepin breaking down and boning out a whole chicken with a paring knife?

Five phone calls. A play-by-play re-enactment. Later, when we meet for drinks, a physical demonstration. *I stood here. . . . Jacques stood here. . . . He said . . . I said . . .*

She commutes into the city from Jersey. Sleeps on my couch three nights a week while her husband does the role reversal, dad-as-mom thing. Compared to those bleak winter days in that Williamsburg loft, we love being roommates. She's the only one in my family who's held on tight to me, and I will never let go of her.

"What's he doing there?" I ask.

"We're doing a piece on The Greats. The French New York Greats. Soltner. Saihlac. Pepin. You know, Lutèce. Le Cygne. Le Cirque. Before what's going on now with the CO_2 guys, and the Aspen *swanaround*. You know, Alsatian onion tart. Soltner, who missed only five nights in thirty-four years at Lutece . . . Anyway, Pepin; I've invited him for lunch."

"Very cool," I say, understanding perfectly every word of this slightly free-associative answer.

The following week, after Pepin, she invited Soltner. To anyone under thirty he's not famous, and he's not doing a show on the Food Network, not using hydrocolloids or glycerin. For us, however, he is a big deal and the real deal. She was prepared. And called to run it by me. As we do.

"So he's coming for lunch on Tuesday. Nothing big. Just casual. Just a visit. I'm not really even going to cook—that would be stupid. Can you imagine trying to cook for Soltner?"

And I'm on the other end, forty minutes before we open for dinner service, phone on a long curlicue cord up between my ear and my hunched shoulder; I'm blanching beans, finishing anchovy butter, having sign language conversations with the dishwashers about getting these trash bags changed *now, please* before dinner guests arrive, and dodging my fellow cooks who are hustling to get their stations set up, too. I'm just grunting "un-hunh, un-hunh, un-hunh, right, yes, un-hunh," the whole time as she works it out with me on the phone, which is mostly just about her working it out—out loud—with me as a sounding board.

I'm listening but I'm also working. The thing with Melissa is that I fully and completely and 100 percent understand and comprehend what she is saying—to its fullest meaning—within the first fifteen seconds. And unfailingly by the end of the third sentence. I'm not saying I'm that smart. I'm saying I get her that well. We Two Are One.

But her purpose is not to merely convey to me the story or the information until I have comprehended. Her purpose is to take a long luxurious bath in my ear and to disgorge the entire unedited contents of her brain—with sidebars, cul-de-sacs, dead ends, and repetitions—

so that she can examine those contents. She is processing. She long ago abandoned those one-line phone messages and three-sentence notes when we were roommates. When she senses, somehow, that she is running out of time or your patience, she'll say, *okay, a long story short*—and then continue on her winding, circuitous, often amusing way for another several detailed chapters. And I understand every single word of it, every stop for gas, every detour. I think exactly what she thinks. She says, finally: "I am not going to even *try* to cook for Soltner." And I get it. Entirely.

It would be pitiful to try and impress this man with some elaborate meal. I get it. I agree, "un-hunh" into the phone while holding the cord up over my head so the busser can duck under it with a full tub of glasses—like a game of London Bridge.

"Yeah, don't go overboard," I say. "Just a pot roast or soup or something."

"Right?" she says. "I mean I think I'm just gonna make omelettes and a salad."

"WHAT?!!" I involuntarily shriek. Everybody on the line looks over and pauses.

"Yeah, Gabs, omelettes and a salad or something. Ultra simple."

Now I'm raising my voice, incredulous, my setup and my last-minute prep thoroughly halted as I give her my full attention.

"Melissa, you cannot cook omelettes for Soltner. Are you crazy?!"

Andre Soltner is currently a dean at the French Culinary Institute. He's the guy who judges a cook by his omelette, his roast chicken, his vinaigrette. After that, whatever you want to flambé or shove in a ring mold is up to you, but if you can't make a French-style, perfectly yellow omelette, you can't graduate, or something absurd like that. I have heard the legendary tale—exaggerrated I am sure—that the final exam, pass or fail—your six hundred hours of cooking school down the fucking drain if you fail—is to make the perfect ovoid omelette with tiny curds so finely pored that it resembles a baby's butt.

"Hmmm," she said, kind of deflated. "I'm going to have to think about this. Later 'Gator."

"Ciao Mein," I said. "Good luck."

On several different occasions, Melissa and I have tried to piece together where everybody was that summer after the divorce, when Simon and I were left alone. She claims to have been home that summer, but she was definitely not. We both think maybe Jeffrey was around, too, having surely returned from Africa by then to discover an already split-up home that had been intact when he'd left. But we can't place him, and I can verify with total certainty that he was not, that summer at least, in the house. We have had long incredulous conversations with each other about our often starkly different experiences of the very same family. She wants me to be sure to know that our father once took his clean white pocket kerchief and folded it successively over and over onto itself, with the precision of an architect, until it had the sharpest angle imaginable and he kneeled down and dabbed a gnat that had slammed into the inner corner of her eye.

There are only five years between us, but five years is enough time for the geography and topography of a family to change dramatically, for ravines to form, trees to upend, streams to run dry. By the time she is calling me at the restaurant in the hectic minutes before dinner service, excitedly hissing in my ear about this famous French chef on his way over the very next day for lunch, she's the only member of my family that I still know the entire, detailed landscape of.

Soltner arrived and Melissa, in spite of my warnings, said she wanted to prepare him an omelette, if he wouldn't mind, and she was wondering if he wouldn't mind showing her how he makes them. She enlisted the instructor in him. And he was glad to oblige, but asked her to prepare hers first. So she made her omelette the way we do at home, perfectly delicious, dragging the beaten egg in from noon, three, six, and nine o'clock in the pan until all the loose egg had run into the pan and set. She let the omelette get a touch of golden color on the exterior. Then she filled the omelette, turned it in half making a half moon, slid it onto a plate, and kept it warm in the oven.

Andre Soltner picked up one egg and cracked it on the edge of the counter. With two hands, he split the egg open and deposited its contents into a bowl. With each thumb, he reached into each half of the shell and scraped out the remaining albumen that tends to cling to the membrane until he had thoroughly cleaned out the egg.

He said, "When I was growing up, this is how my mother got thirteen eggs out of the dozen." Then he put the shells in the trash.

I acutely remember how badly I wanted to be able to crack and split eggs with one hand when I was coming up. I had seen guys cracking eggs by the crate into large white buckets over a china cap using one hand to do the whole process and then flinging the shell into a trash bin set farther and farther away—which was part of the fun in an otherwise tedious task. That's how I'd seen it at Mother's and that's how Greg and I did it at Jake's, cranking it out to Guns N' Roses. I have become totally competent at this one-handed maneuver, regularly wiping down the streak of watery white that ends up on the fridge door or stove lip with every toss into a remote garbage can. But this story stopped me in my hot speedy tracks. I felt this strange mixture of admiration and contrition. I had lately been fascinated by the deconstructed, dehydrated eggs Benedict at the newest temple of molecular gastronomy. And had even been thinking that I wanted to learn how to copy the sous-vide seventeen-hour egg at the trendiest restaurant downtown where you will never get a reservation. But this story of this seventy-five-year-old man, cracking an egg slowly and accurately with his two hands and using his thumbs to get the thirteenth egg as his mother had done during wartime food shortages, put me right back on track.

He beat the eggs and poured them into the prepared pan and then he agitated the eggs with a fork, constantly, over low heat until the curd was soft and tiny, and when the egg had adequately set, he tapped the pan, with gusto, on the burner to take out any last tiny gasp of air and then—did he flip it in the air, did he set it on fire, did he get out the chemical compounds to make omelette "eggs"? He did not. He grasped the pan in his left hand and tilted it slightly toward the back of the stove. With his right hand, he tapped his left wrist, like a junky searching for a good vein, over and over, causing a little vibration in the pan that pushed the omelette incrementally with every tap up against the lip and then, when cresting, back in over itself until the whole omelette was folded over into thirds, a perfect football shape, absolutely no color on it, just perfectly cooked yellow omelette, and he put the little torpedo onto the plate for lunch. The omelette. As prepared by Soltner with just two hands, a fork, and a sauté pan.

12

I MET MY HUSBAND WHEN HE STARTED COMING TO PRUNE TO EAT. HE was on his way to a popular crappy Italian spot around the corner where, even though it was a nothing place with cheap German "Parmesan" standing in for the real thing and commercial balsamic vinegar in industrial-sized plastic jugs, you had to wait an hour on the sidewalk for a table, naturally.

Michele does everything, no matter what, *in* Italian. He picked our pediatrician because she's Italian, he buys only Italian wine, he roots for Italian soccer teams, reads Italian newspapers, and though he has been in this country for more than twenty years, he has determinedly maintained an Italian accent so thick and a syntax so poor that his English is very often incomprehensible. This is not a provincialism, by any stretch, but rather a point of view.

But he decided to forgo the hour-long wait on the sidewalk at the Italian joint and came to check us out. We had been open less than a year. He looked in and saw all women in the kitchen and mostly women on the floor and, like an Italian, slowed down a minute and took a closer look in through the doors. And then he came in. And then he met and made friends with the hostess and the hostess's girlfriend and then he made friends with my sous chef and her girlfriend, and then he fell for one of our waitresses and then another of our waitresses, and by then he kind of got swept along by the current, possibly unaware of the lesbian drift of things—or simply undeterred— until he washed up on the shores of the kitchen and landed his sights on me.

I was standing at the pass, a little too thin, drawn and pale, cooking the lamb sausages wrapped in caul fat, the rye cracker omelette with fried duck skin, the rabbit legs in vinegar sauce that he was falling truly in love with when he finally sat down to eat at Prune. And he became less casually intrigued and more seriously *innamorato* and came back again, quickly, and then again, and pretty soon he was actually "in love." But with what? With whom? With the place or the person behind the place? I think he was like the teenage girl who falls in love with the drummer in the band—she loves the music, the smoke, the light show, the emotion conjured in her own self, and there at the back of the stage, keeping the whole thing running is the drummer. She decides it's him she wants.

I can understand him. Prune was a juicy place in the beginning. The women were dolls and the wine was freely poured and an Icelandic accountant, let alone an Italian bachelor like Michele, would've been hard-pressed to feel nothing or indifference when eating here. Plus, the food reminded him of his mother's in a way. He was always exclaiming, "Theees eees exactly like my motherrrr used to make."

But I do not believe he was aiming for me at all. He was just pointing his boat toward the twinkling lights on shore. Prune was a place with so much warmth and insouciant female energy that I believe we seduced more than impressed our earliest fans. But eventually, inevitably, he bumped up against me and for some outrageous audacious reason considering we had barely met—maybe it was the monkfish liver, the trippa Milanese, the marrow bones—he lightly scratched me from the shoulder to the wrist, one long, slow, light scratch with his fingernail the long distance of the tender back part of my arm, and I, electrified, turned around to finally take a look at this guy whom I had barely registered until now. It was ballsy and accurate, that scratch; two qualities I find particularly appealing.

The timing of it was rather appealing as well as I was skidding on the rocks with my gold golden girlfriend of goldness. You can't script these things better than they happen in real life. A year of restaurant intensity had done its destructive best on the relationship finally, as I was chronically scurrying home in the middle of service to strip us of a handful of desperately needed forks or a chair, but otherwise gone from eight in the morning until finally hauling my ass home at two the following morning. There was not a single day off, not a single one, and not a single thought not thought about the restaurant in all that time. My girlfriend, still an adamant Michigander almost three years into our city life, personally offended by overt professionalism as if it were showoff-y and self-referential to display some, herself fundamentally and philosophically opposed to vulgar Ambition, found herself widowed by mine, abruptly. Her resentments were palpable and insurmountable.

How utterly perfect, then, to meet up with an equally ambitious, hardworking heterosexual male for whom I would probably never feel much more than warm affection. How unthreatening. That scratch was not his opening gesture. He had started earlier by bringing me food at the restaurant that he himself had made. I was very moved by this, even though the food was mostly unspectacular and lived for long periods decaying back in some unreachable corner of the lowboy until it became so furry it had to be tossed. There was an olive bread that was flat and hard and overworked. It tasted of nothing but the effort. Then he brought incredibly beautiful ravioli that he had made—so thin you could see through them like collected stamps in a cellophane sleeve. One of the completely unanticipated parts of owning a restaurant that I had failed to envision was that people would be so kind to us. I had no idea how many people I would meet, how many friendships I would forge, how much warm feeling and gesture would be passed back and forth between customer and us. I thought we would just be taking care of and serving unknown people. But customers bring us wine, send us postcards, have their birthdays and anniversaries here, and Michele started as one of them, proffering homemade ravioli for our family meal. I have never gotten over it. Maybe some guys open restaurants because they think they're going to meet chicks or drink for free or make a lot of money, which are pleasures not to be underestimated, but there is a subtler gratification in that lovely exchange with the customers that is worth all of the profound anguish and worry and hours clocked in.

But I had a girlfriend at the time and not only did I still love her and live with her; if you turned around from scratching my arm in that most suggestive and sexually charged way, you would see her there behind the bar, polishing some glasses and mixing the cocktails while we stand over here in my open kitchen doing that utterly forbidden thing: shitting where we eat. The warm exchange between customer and restaurateur is not supposed to go quite that far. In the script, though, you and your girlfriend are already on the rocks and filled with resentments and anger and every conversation turns into a fight and you've stopped having sex a long time ago and then of course, like clockwork, someone appears who finds you attractive, who is not yet angry with you, who wants to win your affection. And then it's just a hastening to the inevitable ending.

Michele was that part of the script. Right on time, page 53.

But lesbians are incredible. We take a year to break up when a week would do, and then we like to remain roommates while still toughing it out at couples counseling. It's so *sensible*. Improbably, my affair with the Italian, an intensely overachieving M.D./Ph.D., actually breathed new stamina and energy into my relationship with the bartender because I was now getting some relief, some kindness, and some sexual attention outside of the relationship, which took the heat off the expectation at home. We went off-script and we *didn't* break up. That Michele was male was even better, as far as I was concerned, because I thought I knew certainly it would go absolutely nowhere. I didn't even feel that I needed to disclose this little facet of my life to my girlfriend because, as far as my heart was concerned, there was nothing going on.

As the restaurant moved out of its first year and into its second, and gained its footing, I finally allowed myself a regular day or part of a day off. Michele came to pick me up.

It was a rather chilly afternoon in late fall but he came on the motorcycle anyway.

"Aren't we going to freeze?" I asked. And he pulled out of his messenger bag an extra set of gloves and handed them to me. He drove expertly through Brooklyn and then Queens—boroughs I had rarely even been to in my twenty years in New York—and from the back of the bike I got a tour of the parts of my own city that I never knew. When we saw mansions lining a broad boulevard I yelled through my helmet, tapping him on the shoulder, "Where are we?!"

"Woodside," he easily replied without even needing to think about it.

Soon we started to smell the ocean and we passed through a park land or state preserve, with tall golden grasses lit up by the afternoon sun. We drove through what felt and looked like a village, like an actual village in a small town in a small rural community—and yet, if I looked behind me, I could still see the city. Little Cape Cod–style cottages sat next to each other in a row and almost all had American flags and also Italian flags here and there, proudly displayed in their front yards.

"Now where the hell are we?"

"Broad Channel."

A few minutes later we were at the empty beach, wide and rough and exciting in the off-season, and we were almost the only ones there. Two men fished together close to the surf and seemed not to catch anything. We sat and stared out at the ocean, not really speaking, which is effortless at a dramatic ocean in the off-season. He unpacked from his bag several sandwiches wrapped in aluminum foil that he had made himself. He had used prosciutto and arugula and good bread from Le Pain Quotidien. And then he had dressed the sandwiches with olive oil from his own orchards in Puglia.

"This is your own olive oil?"

"Yeah."

"What do you mean, *your own* olive oil?"

"Eh"—he shrugged—"it's mine. We grow it."

I sat eating my sandwich, deep in my coat and sweater, thinking the oil tasted very good, buttery and acidic at the same time, but wishing there was more meat and maybe a smear of cool waxy butter also. I love the perfection of three fats together—butter, olive oil, and the white fat from prosciutto or lardo.

"These could use one more slice of meat, maybe."

He was silent.

"And maybe a little sweet butter."

And he has made them that way ever since.

That winter, Michele took me to Ducasse for my birthday when it was $1,500 just to walk in the door or something crazy like that. I half panicked in the vestibule.

"This is where you're taking me?" I halted in the lobby, as we entered the hotel and I realized what restaurant was there. "I am so not adequately dressed for this place!"

But he pushed me ahead and the beautiful young woman at the door, more expensively dressed than I, warmly said "good evening" and put me right into one of those chairs at one of those tables with the heavy silverware as if I were welcome. We ate pigeon and an oeuf en cocotte and I got a slight chill—from the actual temperature, not the exalted level of cooking—the pigeon was unfortunately so rare that its juices hadn't even begun to run—and when I asked if I could have my coat back from coat check, they brought over instead a wooden box of pashmina shawls in a dozen colors from which I could pick the one most matching my outfit. I never would have gone there on my own and at that time, with my $423.00 weekly paycheck, I never could have afforded it, but I am still, to this day, more impressed by the sandwiches.

An affair is an exhausting proposition when you are in the restaurant business. The work hours are already rather long, and especially so in the beginning years if you are both the chef and the owner. To pull off an illicit affair within the hours of two a.m. and eight a.m. while living with your girlfriend is not an easy undertaking. At the affair end of things, you just cut to the chase. You are not spending your few hours together having long and deep meaningful conversations getting to know each other. You are not meeting each other's friends and getting to understand the guy through the context of the company he keeps. You aren't taking the time to discover if you even like each other. No. You are doing your thing in every corner and on every surface of that apartment and then eating sandwiches just before hailing that pre-dawn cab back downtown. But somehow, we continued, and our affair took on a little weight without, oddly, depth or dimension.

In the summer we drank negronis. And as things progressed, haltingly, we drank them on a brief vacation in Italy, in the square at Campo di Fiori, at twilight, while my girlfriend stayed home in New York, pulling her bar shifts at Prune, returning to our empty apartment, and she and I prided ourselves on the independence we were able to celebrate in each other. We were not each other's *property,* we delighted in agreeing. There was a great deal of darker hue going on there between us, however. And to be sure, real polyamory is a serious dedication practiced by total pros. We were pure amateur slop. Having an affair, no matter how enlightened and forward-thinking the feminist in you is, is still an act of hostility, usually retaliatory. And requires private real estate. I remember meeting a friend of Michele's some years later, herself married, who said, with a puzzled look on her face, "But why would people who love each other hurt each other?" Possibly forty-five seconds of silence ensued before I erupted in the deepest belly laughter of my life, which lasted for four days.

Suddenly, Michele came to me with green card issues. I was thoroughly unmoved. I couldn't understand how he could have made it here for eighteen years without arranging his visa story properly. He showed me new statistics and articles from the *New York Times* describing how changed the immigration landscape had become and how difficult to navigate. I told him to muster five thousand dollars and pay someone in his lab to marry him, which he was adamantly opposed to. But unless you are a performance artist, nobody, not even an erstwhile lesbian enjoying her midnight liaison with an Italian, wants to get married for pragmatic reasons. And I was not feeling persuaded as yet by any of the other romantic reasons either. I knew every inhale and exhale of my girlfriend, I knew the long pause every morning between sock and shoe on her left foot and sock and shoe on her right foot, as she dressed and contemplated the day to come. I knew her fears and quiet joys and she knew mine.

The Italian and I were still completely unknown to each other. But Michele had been kind to me and he desperately needed a kindness, as he explained to me that all eighteen years of his research on septic shock would now go down the drain as he returned to Italy. My girlfriend had frequently accused me of being unkind, and so in a perfect triangulation, I agreed to marry Michele. As if to prove my kindness. By the time Michele and I were getting married, I had known him for almost three years, but at the City Hall ceremony our friends were meeting one another for the first time, and we were meeting many of each other's friends for the first time, and for years when acquaintances heard I'd gotten married, they'd asked, assuming it was the bartender, if we'd gone to Massachusetts where lesbian marriage is legal!

The negroni is a short and perfect aperitivo made of equal parts bitter Campari, sweet vermouth, and floral gin over a couple of ice cubes with a small slice of fresh orange dropped in it to release its oils. That perfectly Italian presence, which sparks your appetite and brightens your mood, holds in balance the sweet and the bitter, which I can't help but think of metaphorically, as the relationship with the non-threatening Italian continued even after the girlfriend, whom I had come to think of as the great love of my life, finally left, giving me and our many shared years the double bird, that very same double bird I had taught her to use as a parking and driving tactic when she first arrived in New York. She and I have never spoken since.

IT WASN'T CLEAR TO ME that I was really getting married when I got married. I am not sure what I was thinking—not because my thoughts were vague but rather because my thoughts were contradictory. I approached the wedding—and talked it up—like a piece of fun and spontaneous downtown performance art. Yet I rolled the idea of it around in my mind much more than I should have, and with greater investment than someone as ostensibly nonchalant as I was. Nonetheless, in the interest of time, I put my thoughts aside and I treated it as one of those catered weddings of which I'd done a hundred. And I invited my sister by saying, "On the outside chance that this turns out to be my actual wedding, I'd like you to be there." I didn't even mention it to my father, and obviously, not my mother either. To my best friend, an adamant opponent of marriage on political grounds, but a devotee of downtown performance art, I said, brightly, "Bring a camera and take lots of pictures. We're going to need plenty of documentation later!"

In just a few days, I planned a small reception, hired town cars with chauffeurs, stumbled upon a perfect dress at a vintage store, and pulled the whole wedding together for about a thousand dollars. It remains one of the best weddings I have ever been to.

When the day arrived, in the afternoon, all the girls who work at Prune came over and crammed into my apartment for a twenty-minute glass of Billecart-Salmon rosé champagne and to admire me in my dress and hair and makeup. I had to get to City Hall before the last "ceremony" at three-thirty and the girls had to get back to work, so we didn't have much time to drag anything down. They looked exactly like themselves in their aprons and chef jackets, checked pants and clogs, and it felt so much better than if they had been awkwardly stuffed into matching colored bridesmaids' dresses with their flabby pale underarms and "we in the restaurant business eat too many cake and steak scraps to be wearing this dress" kind of tummies. I was working a French twist and a stiletto heel a mile high. I really love an urban wedding. Urban weddings are classy.

And so I arrived with my sister and my best friend, Heidi, in her four-button, narrow-leg Helmut Lang suit at City Hall, and we got in line to go through the metal detectors. If you want to feel like the most glamorous woman in the world on your wedding day, just be the only one dressed in a good heel and a vintage couture dress at City Hall at two-thirty in the afternoon, surrounded by people going about their municipal business of renewing their driver's license or appearing for jury duty or verifying their city marshal bond.

There were a few people ahead of us at the chapel, which was just a tight, ugly room upstairs with a dirty carpet, and cigarette burns on a few of the fiberglass chairs where we sat to await our turn. The small group that we had assembled were all impeccably dressed, with the Italians really understanding how to work a good suit and a good cashmere sweater and an expensive colorful silk tie. Michele was so nervous he had cut himself shaving and so appeared at his own wedding with a Band-Aid on his neck under his ear. In truth, Michele was not marrying ironically. For him this was not a piece of performance art whatsoever. He claimed to love me and to want this marriage. Inasmuch as he was able to know himself at the time and to have insights about his own desires, I trust he was getting married for love. I am sure there are many women who would find it wonderful to hear the man they've just started sleeping with start to make suggestions about living together, and who would thrill to receive a Tiffany box after a few brief months into their affair. But I was annoyed by it and felt erased and unseen by it. "Jesus, slow down," I warned. "You don't even fucking know me." I had flatly refused to even introduce him to people we ran into over the first few years, and I never once entertained his preposterous idea of living together. But he wouldn't for an instant even entertain the idea of marrying someone in his lab just for a green card. He showed up to City Hall at three o'clock in the afternoon to really marry me. At the ceremony, my lesbian friends wore suits, too, which covered up their tattoos, mostly. I've never seen a more disparate group of people in a room for the same occasion before in my life—an Italian Upper East Side doctor eleven years my senior and all of his cohort, and a downtown, pierced and tattooed, recently defrocked lesbian dishwasher and her motley crew—all convened in chapel C on the eighth floor.

And yet our candid black and whites in our wedding album look so genuinely happy and festive and relaxed because we were, in fact, just that—happy and festive and relaxed, unburdened by any sense of a "real" or a "deep and somber purpose."

When we emerged, married, we exited from the building under the huge vaulted arches of the southside doors and there, on the cobblestone, with pigeons all around us and my sister throwing rice—all of it captured in black-and-white photos—it looked an awful lot like an actual, consummated marriage.

I had arranged for a small fleet of black Lincoln Town Cars to wait for us outside City Hall and take us across town to a tiny and excellent wine bar in the West Village. Heidi held the car doors open and helped guests into the cars, shut the doors carefully, and then patted each car on the roof when it was ready to take off, and then the next one would pull up in the queue and she would install a few more of our party, and tap the roof of the car signaling the driver, until she had us all successfully whisked away like visiting foreign dignitaries in sleek black Town Cars that crept through the tiny streets of the deep West Village and spit us out on Carmine at Bedford. We spent the waning afternoon hours having chilled Lambrusco and soppressata tramezzini, all twenty of us packed into that tiny space where Jason, the owner, let us bring in, instead of wedding cake, a large platter of burratta—the soft, custardy fresh cow's milk cheese from Puglia, which Michele had introduced me to—and thirty silver soupspoons, and for our wedding cake moment, amply photographed, we exchanged big killer spoonfuls of soft, creamy burratta.

Starting with our very first morning of a seven-day honeymoon in Paris, Michele changed his hard-driving campaign of "get-the-girl" to "get-away-from-the-girl." I've never seen anyone so abruptly debilitated by the prospect of his own marriage—and the emotional intimacy of it—as he became. We found the neighborhood where we'd arranged to stay, and as we were rolling our luggage along the cobblestones to the little apartment we'd rented, he was half a block ahead of me, where he stayed the rest of the trip. While I strolled the boulevards, looking in all the shop windows, gawking at the precision of the pastries and the gelatines and even the string to tie the little boxes, Michele bolted ahead, looking for a signal on his cell phone, leaving a perpetual half block between us the full seven days of our "honeymoon."

At our meals he overate so nervously and so terribly that each night after dinner, back in our apartment, he moaned on the couch with severe indigestion and I pretended to read in the empty bed, wondering what was exactly going on. I ended up eating our last dinner in Paris alone, after a day neither of us will ever forget, roaming around Père Lachaise cemetery together but apart, where I only sometimes caught a glimpse of his back as he scuttled along a path in urgent search of a particular mausoleum. For the INS wedding album we knew we had to assemble, we stood with our heads leaned in together and held the camera at arm's length, catching a shot of us in front of the Centre Pompidou, the Galleries Lafayette, and *en fin,* in front of la Tour Eiffel. As we boarded the plane home, Michele walked down the aisle holding his three newspapers in three different languages, rather conspicuously I felt, and we flew that long transatlantic flight as we would a dozen times hence—almost without speaking. For someone who had almost cruelly emphasized the green card nature of the wedding, even I was curious about how devastated I felt.

13

So I came to possess, of all things, a husband. This didn't make sense for the longest time, to anyone, myself included, but that was also before I had met his Italian mother. Eighty-year-old Alda Fuortes de Nitto cooks eggplant that satisfies like meat, grows her own olives, peels apricots from her own trees, and sun dries tomatoes to make her own tomato paste. I adore her and our summer visits to her home in Puglia, at the tip of the Italian boot heel.

She drives like a bank robber and calms my babies as only a mother of six can. Every exhale is accompanied by staccato grunts that make it sound as if she is perpetually enjoying a private joke, and hip surgery has not stopped her from cooking delicious meals for the entire family.

Her food is so simple and prepared with such dispatch that it is almost unnecessary to speak of recipes, and wrangling one from her is more of a poetic than a didactic encounter.

How many potatoes? "To the eye," she says. How long should I cook the onions? "Until you put a dent in them," is her answer. What is the melted butter for? "Per la faccia," she says, *for the face.*

The first meal of Alda's I recall was a lunch of simply vegetables, well boiled. The table was set with a cloth, a water and a wine glass, five pieces of good silver per setting. And a cruet of her own golden, buttery olive oil in the center—all this for a spare lunch of zucchini, green beans, and chicory. Left out on her Salentino pottery, covered with netting to keep the flies away until we arrived after a long, intensely hot eight-hour motorcycle ride from Rome. We sat in the cool, dark dining room—eating the most delicious, unapologetic, undressed meal of a lifetime—the harsh glare of the white-hot afternoon shuttered out.

Alda cooks mostly vegetarian in the summer as the meat is of notoriously poor quality in the south. She uses only the limited variety of ingredients that are available, but they are like none you could get here, no matter where you shop.

Many are her own. Pine nuts in the shell that fall out of the tree in the courtyard of her youngest son's summer house—so piney they taste almost mentholated; her own oranges, their juice squeezed over ice crushed in a dish towel with a mallet for a midday snack for the kids; figs that are juicy and cool when picked at ten a.m., warm and jammy at four p.m. Burratta and buffalo mozzarella and giuncata— the fresh cow's milk cheese that sits in giuncata (rush) baskets that impart its flavor and its name—were brought to the house by the local woman who makes them—still warm!—the first time I tried them.

The eggs yolks are as orange as persimmons—making it clear why the Italian word for egg yolk is *rosso di uovo,* "the red of the egg." The zucchini is less porous, less watery, and has smaller seeds than ours. The beans are darker, chewier, and more slender and taste like pure chlorophyll. The eggplant, from vines surrounded by rocky terrain of wild oregano, fennel gone to seed, and sweet garlic, is more flavorful than the eggplant from your local organic farm, grown among clover and corn.

"Poor people's meat," she says of the eggplant. The way she makes it though, using more than a dozen eggs, two whole balls of buffalo mozzarella, and easily a liter of extra virgin olive oil makes me wonder what kind of poor people we are talking about. The kind who own their own olive orchards and industrious chickens, I guess.

To start, she slices the eggplant in her hands without using a cutting board or a table. She holds the vegetable in one hand and slices toward her body with the other—using her one dull knife that she's been using forever, never sharpening it. She salts and drains the eggplant, but then never rinses it. She first flours and bread crumbs each eggplant slice and then dips it in egg before sliding it into hot olive oil to fry. The chef in me longs to sharpen her knife, buy her a new one, use a cutting board to get uniform, perfect eggplant slices and to dip the slices in egg before the bread crumbs. But the daughter-in-law in me follows Alda, who has been making it this way for fifty or more years.

Her pizza rustica comes from a recipe of her own mother-in-law: a thin, enclosed pie of mozzarella with a puff-pastry-like dough. It's equally simple and uses that very Italian way of measuring for a dough—you go by the quantity of eggs you are starting with to determine how much flour is used. She only ever measures anything for my benefit, so I can write it down and make a recipe, but I'm glad every time to see her dump the car keys and daily mail that sit in the pan of the old balance scale and weigh out flour—from her own wheat!—throwing little brass weights into the other pan.

When she pulls her old sawed-off broom handle out of the kitchen drawer to roll out the dough I sigh happily to be so far away, literally and conceptually, from my stainless steel restaurant kitchen where the freezers all freeze to precise Department of Health standards, and there's a knife for turning, for boning, for filleting; there's a wet stone, and a dry stone and the need for improvisation arises rarely. I sip my negroni and contemplate my new, unexpected circumstances.

She and I do not speak the same language, and because of that our relationship really thrives. Even my twenty words of Italian—all of them in the present tense—don't work with her because she speaks formally and sometimes in a Leccesi dialect.

So we just hug and cook a lot. Which can seem, at times, like a greater intimacy than the one I have with her son, and a very compelling reason to stay married to him.

14

WHEN I WAS PREGNANT WITH OUR FIRST SON, I SUCCUMBED FOR a brief period to large ponderous reflections about the big stuff: Family. Motherhood. Lineage. Heritage. For a short time, I frequently thought about contacting my mother, whom I hadn't seen in twenty years, but then I never got around to it. And then, very suddenly, my brother Todd died, and ten days later my own son was born and because of the inverted parallel of that, I wrote her a note. It was a clean, straight condolence note with appropriate compassion, and at the end I offered to arrange my family for a visit to Vermont, where she lives and rarely, if ever, leaves. After twenty or so years of being asked, when it comes up in casual conversation, why I don't speak to my mother, I can still barely even cogently explain, because there was, wasn't there, all that sitting in the lap and the wine going down her throat and the fun games in the pantry and the honeysuckle beads—and we were not, were we, burned with cigarette tips or made to sleep on dog mats leashed to a radiator. She was, wasn't she, the very heartbeat of the most cherished period of my life? So what is there to make of the simplistic thing I've come to utter in explanation, which is so drab, so monochromatic, so water on top of ice even though it's the most direct, most distilled path from my heart to my mouth: I feel better without her.

I don't know if she considered declining, but, in spite of the twenty years, she accepted.

So in October that year, I rented a car, gathered my infant son, my husband of two years, and my milky self and all of our shit into the Volvo wagon and hit the road for the eight-hour drive to her home in the Northeast Kingdom, where she lives, just an hour short of Montreal. Michele loaded the car with a case of very good Italian wines. He figured out the rear-facing car seat. He was ready only thirty minutes late instead of his more customary hour when I arrived to pick him up at his apartment. We were still then living separately. He had figured out our route on the computer and printed out the directions. He was really stretching himself.

By contrast, on the day that I went into labor I called him first thing in the morning when I realized that the cramps I had been having all night were accompanied by some sharp contractions at the end of each one and that there was a little bit of blood in my urine. He was not yet awake when I called at seven-thirty and had that funny sleeper's defense where you pretend that you are wide awake in spite of having just been roused and you want to sound like you know exactly where is where, who is who, and what is what when in fact you are still wearing a narcotic brain helmet of cement and foam.

" 'llo?" he grunts.

"Hey. It's happening. Here we go."

"Okay."

"So, I'm going to shower and then take a cab to your house. I'll be there shortly. This feels like it's really moving," I said.

"Okay. Okay. Ciao."

But when I arrived at his apartment with my sister in tow and all of my phone calls to the pertinent people—including the doctor—already made, and my little bag all packed just so, he was just turning on the shower, letting the water run to get hot. He was standing there in his boxers and a T-shirt. Melissa looked around the apartment, saw the crib in a box in the corner, and said, "Hey, Michele, you've got to get a move on here, guy. She's having a baby, like, right now. This is it. This is real. You're having a baby, Michele."

"Okay, okay," he said, making that very Italian gesture of shrugging his shoulders high up to his long, low-hanging Italian ears and holding open both of his hands as if to say: *What can I do?*

"Take your shower, man, and let's go," Melissa directed.

He got in the shower and meanwhile my labor came on hard and fast. Major contractions, five minutes apart. I was on the couch clenching my teeth and mooing like an angry cow every five minutes. Melissa paced around, cleaned up the espresso cups and grounds in his sink, wiped down the counters, and tried to straighten up his apartment a little bit to make it look ready to receive a newborn. Finally the shower water stopped and the sink faucet was turned on and I knew that sound to mean he had now begun shaving, in a nice steamy room with his pores open, the water running the whole time in the sink while he lathered and razored and blew air into each cheek and meticulously drew the razor over the ballooned skin coming up from under the chin and working up toward the cheekbone. And then the chimpanzee face as he tightened his lip and blew air up under his top lip to get all the moustache and nose hairs. My labor, which would unbelievably continue a further thirty-six hours, appeared to be getting more acute by the thirty-second interval, making both me and my sister kind of agitated and antsy to get going to the hospital. Michele finally emerged from the bathroom and went into his bedroom to get dressed so Melissa and I gathered our bags and moved to the foyer, thinking we were now just a minute or a minute and a half from leaving. Michele reappeared in socks and pants and a shirt, unbuttoned, with a tie in each hand and asked, "Which tie?"

This was kind of a good, validating moment for me, in spite of the urgency of the situation. Melissa went gently off the planet and said all of the things to Michele that I long to hear someone else besides me say. Her tone was exceptionally polite.

"Hey, Michele," she said. "Let's get go—ing, my friend. Your tie doesn't mat—ter," and she split up *go-ing* and *mat-ter* in a way that sounded overarticulated, like you might speak to a child or a foreign person. I loved her ten times more than I already did for this. It is exactly how I feel in that moment but I am too doubled over in cramp hell to say so, and I felt so taken care of, so relieved that she was acting like me for me. Proxy me.

But on the day that we were leaving for Vermont to meet my mother, Michele was actually making an effort to get the lead out.

In spite of that effort, on both of our parts, we didn't get on the road until close to noon, when we really should have left around nine, to be safe and leisurely. Poor Michele had been primed. I had been coaching him for weeks.

"Five-minute showers, Michele. Five minutes. Don't shave and let the water run."

"Don't sit around like you do here, Michele. Don't sit around at all. Do chores. Offer to do chores constantly."

"Don't be late. We can't be late. She goes to bed at seven-thirty or something and her blood sugar falls at five. She eats *early*. She'll be pissed and trembly if we're late. We cannot be late."

I remembered short showers and chores and punctuality and blood sugar crashes from when I knew her twenty years before. But Melissa, who had just recently made a trip up there herself, had called and generously guided me around a few potential snags that I never would have thought to anticipate on my own, which she had, unfortunately, navigated alone and unsuccessfully.

"Arrive with a full tank of gas, Gabs, or you'll never get off the property. She won't want to drive her car because she doesn't want to buy gas. She'll suggest going for a walk or something instead of letting you off the property."

"That's ridiculous," I said. "I'll buy her a fucking tank of gas."

"I'm just telling you how it was. And don't forget to wash your hair before you go."

I didn't get the meaning of this. "What are you talking about?" I asked.

"The shower takes longer—more water—when you have to also wash your hair and not just your body."

I had to laugh it was so unbelievable.

"I'm sure she was in full rigor over that," I said.

Melissa exhaled deeply over the phone. "My biggest mistake," she continued, "was in trying to make up time. I left a little late, as usual, and so I decided to skip the stop into White River Junction to get a bottle of gin or something for my little cocktail."

"Oh no!" I groaned. "You arrived without anything to take the edge off?" My poor sister, because she, too, was running late, like all of us with the multiple demands of kids and families and jobs, like all of us who are not unemployed and living alone on a hundred acres in the woods of Vermont are prone to be, my poor sister arrived after an eight-hour drive with unwashed hair and nothing to sand down the edges.

I made Michele wash his hair and shave twice, consecutively, before we left. I couldn't possibly ask this man who sometimes showers twice a day, and who hand-blends his own cologne every morning before knotting his silk tie, to go a whole weekend without showering, but at least I got him into the mindset of a five-minute shower. My mother's frugality can be so acute that it takes on an actual hostility, and I was trying urgently to protect Michele from catching the sharpest edge of it.

Between constant nursing and trying to run the restaurant with a baby attached to my boob, I had managed only a small case of Asian cooking ingredients for my mother's pantry. Which he also packed securely into the back of the wagon. Michele drove and I sat in the back with Marco.

We inched up through New York and Connecticut, practically wordless. This was not uncommon for us, but I'd always hated it. I really like to talk. I thought those wordlessly shared sandwiches on wintery beaches were just the appropriately remote closeness of two people catching a quick deceit at three in the morning, but I'd since caught on that that was as much as we could find with each other. We were still living apart in our separate homes as we always had, discovering, harshly, all of the ways in which a new child can really stress out an already fragile relationship, even though we had enthusiastically intended the pregnancy. But I think he felt complimented that I would introduce him to my mother. I think he saw it as a *privilege*. I, of course, for twenty years, had been more or less successfully sparing those I loved from the experience. But Michele, following his own internal logic, viewed it, I believe, as an honor. How close we must be getting, he and I, if he alone made it to the inner sanctum: my mother.

No sooner had we crossed out of the state of Massachusetts than I started to feel a certain lack of enthusiasm. I was not gladdened by the Vermont Welcomes You sign. Even though we were only minutes over the Massachusetts border, still hours from her house, still surrounded by fellow travelers, people like us who enjoy other human contact and human activity and who don't need to be secluded on a hundred acres without even a house pet, we were nonetheless in the state of Vermont where she lives, and I started to feel like I was standing too close to someone phlegmy and contagious. After only an hour in Vermont, the last of the daylight disappeared and a crushing darkness fell, by four-thirty, nearly denting the metal panels of the safest car in the world, it felt, and buckling the hood and roof, and threatening to seep in around the closed windows. Marco slept, nursed, then slept again. And I envied him.

Driving in this pure pitch, with nothing to talk about with Michele and nothing but the back of his head and the surrounding blackness to see, it's possible that I've never since known such isolation, save for maybe that one time when I couldn't bring myself to get out of my car. Even a vaguely picturesque barn in the far far distance, with one light at the top of the phone pole to light up the yard and the tractors, where I could have imagined a taciturn family having dinner after a long and healthy day of outdoor work, only served to emphasize how much pasture, darkness, and solitude there was between *them* and *there* and us and here. I listened, apprehensively, to the thinning radio station, wondering how many more miles before we would lose the signal entirely. When another car traveling south, across the unnecessarily wide median, approached in the distance, my spirit lifted and I never took my eyes off it as it came over the top of the hill into sight and its headlights intersected with ours, but then it passed behind us—and my reticence re-descended, now in the distinct shape of dread.

We were left alone, abandoned by the southbound car, us speeding north, to emptiness. Black emptiness. The southbound car that had just passed us would soon enough be encountering lights, city limits, people, art, commerce, poetry, citizens living actual, messy fantastic delicious Life. But we drove on at impossibly harrowing speeds, toward the sticky netting of my mother—a black widow spider at the center of her one-hundred-acre web—and my certain poisoning. I am thirteen all over again.

Suddenly Michele swerved terrifyingly to avoid a possum in the middle of the road. I was in the backseat nursing Marco, without a seat belt, because I can't nurse a baby while being so confined. Michele had been driving one hundred ten miles an hour, without even realizing it. The wagon of the car left the asphalt for a second and I lost my mind. A hot red ore of rage poured out of me in the shape of an unpunctuated curse of Michele, of my mother, of Italians, of dying brothers, lazy line cooks, crazy co-op officers, self-absorbed fathers, Vermont farmers, possums, raccoons, and deerflies. In just the two seconds of the tires leaving the asphalt we all discover, in a most colorful way, that I am an intensely stressed new mother with a new infant and a dead brother, a busy restaurant, an incompatible husband, and an uptight, ferociously rigid mother. Who is just a few exits away.

Duly catharted, we all drive on in silence. Twenty deathlike minutes later, Michele says, in his thick Italian accent, his shoulders up to his ears as usual, "But, Gabrielle. It was only one hundred eighty kilometers per hour."

As we take our exit, I ready myself. From here on in, we are on dirt roads, deep in the dark, under a canopy of trees. I mentally leave my body, swept and neat, exactly as I would leave my home before a journey of several days. I crawl deeper and deeper back into my impenetrable mind, until I am lodged so far back that I can see the periphery of my body as I peer out from it, like being inside an open, dry shed while it storms outside. I set a placid indecipherable half-smile on my lips and visualize what it will look and feel like to pause as long as I need to between anything my mother or my husband might say to me, no matter what, and anything I might say in response.

I vow to pause as long as it takes before answering to even a benign and harmless, "Do you want coffee?" let alone an incomprehensible European metric system defense of egregious speeding as if somehow, *in Italian,* if you translate it into Italian, it is not, any longer, one hundred ten miles an hour. I will let long minutes pass if necessary.

I will smile. Do what is expected of me. Unhook myself quickly from any disagreeableness. And fortunately, I have an infant that I can attend to. I will be absolutely fluid, pliable, malleable. If they want one thing I will want that, too. And if I need time, I will step away and pretend to nurse or nap or change a diaper. We get lost, now, on these country roads, and lost again, even on the road where she lives because I remember and recognize none of it, it's been so long, but I feel cool and calm. If we are late we are late; I am in my mental shed.

Of course when we arrive, travel-worn and weary, our long journey executed with intense adrenaline at the end of already profoundly stressful and taxing workweeks fully dispensed, my mother is nothing as I've described her. We open the doors of the car and the crisp air hits us; it's so clean it's difficult to recognize as air. She emerges from the softly glowing house where wood smoke puffs from the chimneys, and she comes to the car, all wide grins, a soft sweater, soft brushed denim jeans, her apron, as always, around her waist. She is totally disarming. Even so, I notice her Kleenex tissue crumpled up and stowed under the cuff of her sleeve for reuse, where she used to make us as kids keep ours, too, until every single corner of that tissue was snotty and spent.

She greets us warmly, big kisses on both cheeks for Michele, whom she is meeting for the first time. She throws him a few words of Italian, nicely pronounced and in the right gender and syntax. He appreciates the friendly gesture. She gurgles appropriately at Marco in his little Moses basket. We also, without awkwardness, kiss on both cheeks as if we'd seen each other last week. It means nothing; it's just a greeting. One we've been taught to use since we were able to stand up on two feet and greet any stranger, guest, or friend who would arrive at our house. Her posture is still, at seventy-four years old, erect as a ballet dancer's.

She leads us into the house and we are hit immediately by the luscious scent of our meal. She has prepared a delicious dinner, with meat—which is way out of her budget—and she has stayed up way past her usual bedtime to eat it with us at the well-set table. She makes apologies to me, her chef daughter, in advance of the meal even though I am certain we both know that I learned to cook, exclusively, from her. There are two chickens. She has splurged. She uses a shallow, oval, glazed clay baking dish that she has had the entire time I have known her. It is cracked in several places and glued back together in those same places. It now has the beauty of an antique. Its edges are black and thickened with accumulated cooked-on crust and its surface is bumpy and textured now from so many years of use. The chicken is perfectly roasted with garlic and rosemary and Dijon mustard and lemons; it's the same chicken I roast at the restaurant and at my own home.

I have washed that baking dish carefully and dried it and put it away, properly nested in its pile, not casually and sloppily set down in an indiscrimate tower in the cabinet, probably thirty times in my life. Considering I haven't lived with her since I was a twelve-year-old, when our family imploded from divorce and relocation, that is a lot of young handling of this platter. I am sure I am responsible for at least one of those glued and reglued cracks.

"There are no accidents," she'd say, sternly looking down at the eight-year-old offender with the two broken pieces of some dish in her soapy hands. "Only carelessness."

I admit I have said the same thing to young cooks at my restaurant.

I look around the house and see many things from my childhood that I haven't seen in so long and that it feels good and sad at the same time to see. It's a marvel to see the things themselves but I am also stunned by how far back in time I have to carry myself to when these things were routinely in sight. She keeps her dish soap—pearly white Ivory Liquid, the only kind we ever used in our house—in a good-looking old clear bottle on the sink ledge. Her burnt orange Le Creuset pot is on the back burner of the six-burner Garland stove.

She keeps her coarse kosher salt in a wooden spice mortar next to the stove. She has beautiful red enameled tin cooking spoons that she has been using to stir food in pots with for the full thirty-nine years that I have known her. My childhood is a lot further away and harder to recollect, I notice, than it used to be. Everything in the room seems to illuminate just how many intervening years there have been since the dish soap, the ticking and winding of the clock, the clay oval baking dish in the soapy water, and the kosher salt in the wooden bowl were all backdrop to my daily life.

Her home looks warm and generous, picturesque, aglow with soft lighting, interesting old brass reliquaries from Greek churches, a wood fire burning in a cast-iron stove, dried hay and grasses hanging in artful but not cutesy-craftsy arrangements from the open rafters of her wooden-beamed kitchen. The old windup clock that we had in the house when I was a child, a heavy, warped black steel box with a white-enameled face and black-enameled Roman numerals kept ticking by a hammered brass disc that looks like the sun—the whole contraption looking like an instrument that Picasso might have made when he devoted himself to sculpture—chimes nine times, and she doesn't even hasten us from the table. Michele raises his eyebrow at me as if to say: This? This is the snaggle-toothed, fire-breathing dragon you've been cutting off?

And he turns back to my mother, determined to enjoy himself, because he knows just exactly how to abandon me.

My most relieving, comforting experiences surrounding my mother are when strangers meet her and later say to me, "Wow. She is one piece of work." I never feel embarrassed or defensive on her behalf; I feel, rather, relieved to have my impressions of her confirmed by outsiders, not by friends whom I have persuaded to agree with me. But Michele, naturally, sees nothing but the soft sweater, the nicely seasoned crispy roast chicken, the obvious taste in the large open room we are sitting in. Being Italian, he also sees, if nothing else, a woman. And his tribal code requires him to charm and be charmed by anything female, regardless of the poisons they may carry. Besides, it would be unnatural by this point in the unraveling of our carelessly knit relationship for him to be my ally. He is already always my opponent.

"Yes, I do eat at five o'clock!" she says, and Michele nods, appearing to be interested in their conversation. I excuse myself to check on Marco and as I am walking to the next room, I hear her say, "As a matter of fact, I listen to the *Canadian* radio station!"

At last we get in our beds under deep piles of blankets and click off the reading lamp and with a little Italian wine in our stomachs, hit deep, deep, narcotic sleep, like Hansel and Gretel.

Those trees the state is so famous for greet us, like a calamity, when we wake in the morning. Peak fall foliage—alarming yellows and rusts and browns and hazard oranges—roils on all sides of us and makes me panic as soon as I open my eyes. I lie still for a few minutes, checking everything out. I listen for the location of everybody. Of her. I did this when I was little. I would lie still and silent in my room, listening for a clue about where she was in the house. She had some blood sugar and rage issues of her own, and it was always a good idea to know exactly where she was as the combination often turned suddenly violent. And then finally, a rustle of the *New York Times* downstairs or a clank of a wooden spoon or her whistling along with the classical radio station and I had my answers. She was always home.

My inventory on this morning tallies Michele still asleep in the next bed, Marco still asleep in the Moses basket on the floor between us, and outside, cerulean sky and peak fall foliage. I cautiously lift my head up from the pillow, and glance out the windows on the far side of the room and there, there in the flowerbeds bordering the house, her face pressed up against our window, shielded only by a thin lace curtain, there she is! I remain motionless. My mother, my actual fucking mother, is outside our room in the lily beds peering in through the lace curtains to see if we have stirred, she herself having been awake, and rubbing her six hairy legs together with hungry impatience, for hours.

Michele and I are in two separate tiny twin beds, the beds my siblings and I had as children, with the same blankets and sheets, washed in the machine but hung outside in the air—which costs no money—

to dry. Our feet hang over the ends but she would never throw away those "perfectly good beds" to replace them with something more suitable for visitors who have, in the intervening decades that have passed since we last slept in them, grown by at least thirty inches. Nobody visits enough to be worth it. Across the gap between the two short beds separated by a tiny bedside table with a reading lamp, I hiss quietly to Michele, "She's right outside. She's at the window! Don't move!"

Part of my strategy for making the weekend go faster is to go to sleep early and wake up late, thus shortening the days. Marco is, like us, wrapped head to toe in fleece and blankets because my mother turns the thermostat off at night or just down to the legal limit, if there is such a regulation, to the temperature where your lungs are still able to achieve shallow breathing but you have not yet died of exposure. You walk around the house all weekend, fully dressed in many layers and still your shoulders are hunched up around your ears as if you stepped outside without your coat to check the mail and got latched out by accident.

Michele peeks out from under the covers and confirms that my mother is, in fact, peering into our room from outside through the lace curtains to try to discreetly ascertain if we have risen. He looks across at me with something vaguely resembling friendship for the first time in what feels like five years. She doesn't even have to confess it; I know, for a fact, no matter how friendly and easygoing she presented herself to us when we arrived the night before, that she has already been to our door several times this morning, to press her ear to the rough-hewn wood, listening for sounds of movement. Finding none, she forced herself outdoors to do her chores, apprehensive that she might miss a moment of us. She has me in her clutches for only forty-eight hours and she is, like me, counting them. Though we are counting for very different ends. And if more hours than she can stand are being spent on sleep, she will start to hum and whistle louder and rattle the cooking pots a little more vigorously until she has made herself perfectly clear.

But even she knows that seven-thirty is an unacceptable hour to wake the guests, and she exhibits this restraint, I am certain, in order to continue giving Michele the impression that she is benign and woefully misrepresented by her sullen and ungenerous daughter. So she mustered the discipline to let us continue sleeping and she pushed herself outside to pop the dead heads off the lily bulbs bordering the house, which is how she managed to spy on us from outside our window while just innocently "gardening." She is wearing her prescription glasses under her wraparound sunglasses. My mother. My outrageously chic French mother who warmed the end of a wax kohl pencil every morning to apply her eyeliner is standing outside my bedroom window, thirty years later, wearing two pairs of glasses on her face at the same time.

We remain still and wait her out. I decide to nurse Marco both boobs, until they are fully drained and my arm hurts from holding my body up for so long. I would rather have cramps and temporary paralysis of the upper body than get out of bed and face the day. We hear the front door open and close and now we know she is somewhere inside the house.

Sure enough, Michele gets up finally to pee and shower, and when he opens the door of our room to cross the hallway to the bathroom, she is already there, alive with joyous over-friendly greetings from the state of Vermont, from her heart, from the Weather Service.

"Can you pick 'em? Did you really pick 'em?"

Her face, which normally has several discernible features, has become one giant, fantastically eager smile, ecstatic that the state of Vermont has provided us with peak fall foliage and the most beautiful day in all Octobers in memory. She is severely caffeinated on black currant tea, I can tell by the pitch and volume of her voice, not to mention the content of her sentiments, as she escorts him the scant three yards from the door of our bedroom to the door of the bathroom. I vow not to follow my immediate impulse to become heavy and silent and scowl like a furious teenager, clinging to the ground for dear life so as not to be hurled skyward by her ebullient, ballistic, nearly manic effervescence. I try to mimic some healthy, good-natured Vermont ski school instructor who might respond to this freakish bloodsucking life force with a hearty "good morning" and a total nod of full-fledged agreement at what a beautiful day it is. I only manage, in spite of my best efforts, a quiet "un-hunh," and a deadly "very beautiful."

Holding Marco defensively in front of me, I try to head directly for the coffeepot. But she bends at the waist and proffers both of her cheeks for me to kiss. It's an excruciating habit she's had ever since we all—all of her kids—achieved parent-child separation more than thirty years ago. Instead of honoring our "oogey-meter," which would buzz and wail and flash wildly when she sought these kisses, she bulldozed right over it and insisted on receiving compulsory, desultory kisses on both cheeks from children who felt they needed a Silkwood shower after the whole transaction.

When my dead brother Todd—who became a voracious, virile Wall Streeter, a vice president at Goldman Sachs by the time he was twenty-eight or something unheard of, and where he was, in a certain way, running the entire world—he still, even at forty years old on his annual obligatory visit, would have to kiss the cheeks of our mother who would bend at the waist and mewl like a kitten, tapping her fleshy finger against her fleshy cheek. Todd, who was accustomed to holding two phones up to his two ears at the same time and altering the Fates by spitting no more than four staccato words through his unsmiling lips alternately into both of them, really used to grimace through that one.

I was hoping, in vain, that glorious, fall foliage morning standing in the mere nine feet of hallway between the bedroom and the bathroom with my son and my husband and my mother, that the past twenty years of cutting her off might have sent a certain signal to her. I was hoping she would observe that I had become something of a full-fledged, self-possessed adult with rights and wishes regarding her affections, that I had become something other than her issue over whom she seemed to believe she had total proprietary access to bodily privileges.

But with Todd dead, I realized, as she nuzzled up to me and made me kiss her on both cheeks while she made her little kitten noises, she had some capital—an unexpected windfall—with which to work.

She was The Bereft Mother of a Recently Dead Son. It was just the license she needed to be maudlin and to leverage greater physical closeness than she had inspired. I was not strong enough or gracious enough to allow her this; she had, in fact, just lost a child. But somehow, that did not, as it might in a made-for-TV movie, suddenly sew up the twenty-year gap. Instead, I just felt physically trespassed upon, snared in her sticky web at eight o'clock in the morning, with a hairy spider bestowing and demanding indiscriminate wet affection.

But now, as I'm trying to get away from her, and to endure the compulsory cheek-kissing, I notice her shoes, sensible sand-colored crepe-soled shoes from Payless. Made in China. And she's wearing oatmeal-colored socks on which the elastic has worn out, which she is holding up at each knee with rubber bands. I'm so taken aback, I point at them. Mistaking me, she proudly sticks out her leg to model the shoe, with an insouciant little twist of her still outrageously elegant dancer's ankle, which I recall my entire life seeing in a good Dior heel.

"*Pas mal,* eh?" she boasts, about this ugly, sensible number that is one step up from a Velcro-closing sneaker.

"Twelve bucks!" she continues, delighted, vainglorious, the cat who ate the canary.

I observe, with not a little discomfort, that this is just the kind of thing I also do. When one of the twenty-year-old waiter girls at work admires my jacket, skirt, or shoes, I say: "Hey, twenty bucks at the Salvation Army in Buffalo!"

When you have some style and taste, but you don't have the cash, you brag about your "finds" from the thrift store. You sit in your chair with great satisfaction when you pull off a delicious dinner for ten people for only forty bucks, the same way my mother fed a family of seven on tails and carcasses and marrow bones. But seeing her now and how uncannily similar we are, I fear that it won't be long before I, too, am so obsessed with thrift that I have manifested my own poverty and am holding my socks up with rubber bands, living alone in the middle of nowhere, estranged in varying degrees from all of my children who would rather not kiss me, given their druthers. How far down the path am I already if I make Prune's dishwashers nest the bowls properly after they are washed and if I stop a cook from throwing away the onion tops because "these are perfectly good, and someone had to grow it, pick it, wash it, and then get it here and that someone wasn't you and now you, you're just going to throw half of it away?" I ask, incredulous, peeved, like a freaking lunatic who may as well wear two pairs of glasses at the same time, and who, I fear, will be working that same fashion statement before long. How can it be, after all this concentrated effort and separation, how can it be that I still resemble, so very closely, my own detestable mother?

But what is there to detest? I am scrutinizing her, now seventy-something years old, alone on her hill. What is so detestable? She has splurged and generously bought half-and-half for our morning coffee. She roasted two birds for dinner when one would've stretched. She fetches and splits and stacks the wood by herself. If a bat flies in she chases it out. She is holding her socks up with rubber bands but she has her living will, her health-care proxy, and her estate and final years totally taken care of in a way that will never saddle her children with awkward and difficult decisions. And now, in the daylight, we go through the wines that Michele packed and the hard-to-find Asian ingredients that I packed, and we spend the morning talking, neutrally, about food and wine. It is unclear if either of us is going to mention the past twenty years. I am prepared to skip it because that's not why I've come. She seems just as inclined. So we discuss the best way to store and cook Vietnamese rice stick. I see pinned above her little desk a cartoon torn from the *New Yorker,* in which a piece of rigatoni pasta answers the phone and exclaims, "Fusilli, you crazy bastard, how the hell have you been?!" and she and I laugh solidly three minutes over that one. Even Michele joins in.

She speaks a little Italian that she has learned over the years to Michele but he answers in English, so mostly she goes on in an English heavily peppered with French. My mom grew up in a French-speaking home and spoke French to her parents until the days they died. Michele tries to answer her in the little French he knows but in an Italian accent so thick, he is just impossible to understand. I recognize this simply as the need that two people in a room who speak more than one language always seem to have—they need to demonstrate their ability to speak more than one language—but somehow it makes me want to inch back a little further toward the deepest wall of my mental shed while this little patch of rain falls. I am drawn to Marco's simplicity. He just needs to eat and sleep.

"Well, Pruney, how do you use this jar of Asian soup paste?" She is squinting at it, perplexed.

It seems odd to be showing my mother a jar of tom yum paste and explaining its potential in soup and noodle dishes when she is the woman who taught me everything I know, pretty much, about eating, cooking, and cleaning. But she seems to be doing what everybody does when they age—becoming incrementally less and less competent. I expect this with her in terms of technology—the stunning rigamarole around an answering machine and cordless phone in the 1980s made it exceptionally clear that she was not going to join us in the computer age. But I am kind of taken aback by this confusion with the food.

And now it's me who's staring at her sternly, like she's an imbecile, much as she looked at me when I was ten, trying to understand what she was saying about slicing a corned beef across the grain. I remember being baffled by what the "grain" of a hunk of meat meant, but she was relentless in her expectation and unyielding in an explanation and so I figured it out in spite of her menacing gaze. And I began slicing clean thin planks of corned beef by sawing back and forth across the grain and noticing how it stopped shredding now that I had turned the meat. But I just cannot believe she doesn't know how to stir a little paste into chicken stock or coconut milk or both. Is it possible that I now know more than she does about food and cooking? Have I surpassed her?

I consider for a moment that it's the "foreign" part of the jar that defies her. But this is the most sophisticated, snobbish woman in the world. Traveled. Exposed. She regularly read the *New York Times* and the *New Yorker.* Listened exclusively to classical music in our house. Danced in the corps of The New York City Ballet. Saw Balanchine in the corridors. Blew past the overweight tourists in our town as they trudged along the cobblestones in their white sneakers enjoying the quaint "historical" markers and the gas lanterns while licking ice-cream cones, and she'd snarl out the window of her antique Benz, "Gros cochon." She gave us all Champagne at Christmas and taught us to flip the savoiarde ladyfinger biscuits from the edge of the table up high into the air and have them land—with a festive splash—in the flute. This same woman unable to navigate a jar of Vietnamese soup paste? *Pas possible.*

At last, the afternoon has passed and it has gotten dark. Michele opens an aglianico, a real beauty, but my mom declines. She is accustomed to a little cocktail, she says, that she really prefers to anything else anymore. I watch as she pours some blackberry schnapps, white jug wine, and a tablespoon of brandy into a jelly jar over ice cubes. I am stunned. My mother is drinking some sort of shitty wine cooler. Torpedo Juice! My snobbish, superior mother. The woman who taught me everything I know—delectable and odious alike—has been shed and here before me is a new woman. A woman that anyone meeting for the first time would find perfectly lovely.

I am suddenly wondering what I've been so afraid of and what I've so diligently kept my distance from these past twenty years. A quiet internal frenzy starts in which I try to recall and to catalogue all of the reasons I might have ended my relationship with this perfectly nice woman who has roasted chickens, built a fire, and who is now casually fixing herself a disgusting wine cooler that would've been way beneath her when last I knew her. To be clear, all of our "differentness" when we were growing up was not merrily enjoyed in a live-and-let-live, *chacon à son goût* kind of benevolence. Something in our household was being arduously protected. Our shit was fiercely defended and prioritized. Everybody around us went to the Jersey Shore for vacation but my mother would *never.* All of our school friends lived in plain houses with a swing set in the backyard, but we lived in the burned-out ruins of a nineteenth-century silk mill with pigeons and bats, and said unkind things about the cookie-cutter developments called Sunset Drive and Village Two. Most people ate Mrs. Paul's frozen fish sticks and Kraft macaroni and cheese and Oscar Mayer bologna, but we ate coq au vin, sesame bread sticks, and le Puy lentils for less money than the store-bought stuff. Other people had rec rooms and television, but we were forced to entertain ourselves outdoors, even in the rain, from waking to bedtime. Other people threw all of their garbage into one big bin, but we composted, recycled, and separated, and drove it all to the center. Other kids got Partridge Family lunch-boxes with Snack Pack puddings, but we got ratatouille sandwiches on homemade bread in oily brown paper lunch bags. And we were taught by her to see ourselves as infinitely better for our dedication to high culture.

I've been trying for twenty years to rid myself of this Gallic snobbism. When I see my now seventy-something-year-old mom pour herself a tumbler of wine cooler, the oppressive heavy wet burden of snow slides off the roof of my soul in one giant thawing chunk and suddenly I feel clear, light, and permissive. Marco is asleep in the basket, but I risk waking him and get down and give him a long, soft kiss on the head. *This fucking bitch,* I think, but without any of the electric adrenaline I felt when I first thought this sentiment thirty years earlier. *This is a bait and switch.*

I quietly understand. I have developed deep rigid grooves and stonelike calluses around these perfectionisms, elitisms, excellences, and impeccablenesses—these high standards of nothingness to which we were held—that she no longer even cares about or holds herself to. In the intervening years since I last knew this woman, she has softened and changed. Casually, idly, by happenstance, I discover that my mother now drinks blackberry schnapps mixed with jug wine and isn't even embarrassed or apologetic, and suddenly I ache with a retrospective shame. I send one blanket megaton apology out into the universe, smoothing my lips against Marco's forehead. I feel like I could have been so much kinder to so many people if I had just known this earlier about her.

When Michele and Marco and I leave the following morning, there is thankfully no mention of the future. I don't promise to return and she doesn't ask me to. She holds my hand and tugs me outside behind her house and weepily shows me the tree she has planted for Todd, and I try to take my hand back because I still feel uncomfortable when she touches me. I hold Marco so close to my chest I can feel him swallow and breathe as I kiss my mother good-bye on both cheeks.

15

EVERY TIME I GET PREGNANT, AT FIRST, IT'S JUST FUN NEWS FOR THE staff of my restaurant to gossip about. There is no inkling of the reality attached to the announcement: "Hey guys, I'm pregnant." And then as I grow and waddle, I'm just an amusement for the crew; an excuse for a betting pool—gender and birth date—and a great entertainment as I try to bend over to pick some vegetable peel off the floor when I can't even touch my own toes. But when I started to really get close to the reality of my first son, Marco, and out to *here* with a belly, my sous chef at the time, Matt, a thirty-seven-year-old former Marine, fell apart in my arms with an anxiety attack so severe I had to rush him to the VA hospital. Hustling him to the ER entrance on Twenty-third Street as best as I was able in my condition—huge and breathless—we soon, fortunately, were reassured that his EKG was absolutely normal and his psychosomatic heart attack was all in his head. I left him on the hospital gurney to rest and recover, in the capable hands of the VA nurses, and walked back to work.

It is true that he would soon be under a lot of pressure to keep the restaurant in order while I was away having my baby and nursing for the first few weeks, and it is also true that his much respected and loved mother had just died. Equally true is that within days of his mother's passing, my own brother Todd died suddenly, of a rare and massive stroke, and it is true, as well, that I was just ten days away from giving birth for my first time. Either way, in the end, it was me who worked the egg station at brunch that weekend. When I found myself down on all fours after that pummeling brunch service, cleaning pancake batter off the reach-in fridge with a green scrubby while my belly grazed the mats and my staff seemed calm and assured that the ship still had a captain, I wondered, uneasily, about who I'd become.

At the time, I was proud of my capableness, my strength, my dry-eyed and clinical receipt of the news of Todd, not to mention my handily earned boasting rights over Matt, which I later flaunted, kind of behind his back, with a studied nonchalance.

Whatever. Matt went down. Fake heart attack. But I worked eggs at thirty-nine weeks pregnant. I shrugged, as if it were nothing to speak of. I sounded like one of those defensive eternal line cooks, with nowhere to ever go from there, who still pulls back his sleeves to proudly show off his burns, when all of us who have deepened our focus and pushed through to greater accomplishments know that a little experience and a finessed game could keep your arms relatively free of burns.

In the week preceding the birth of my second child, Leone, twenty-one months later, a line cook responsible for five shifts a week quit unexpectedly. Connor, a kind of bland and amiable *dude,* came to the office and said, "Umm, listen, I've been made an offer I can't refuse."

I had been fantasizing about a modest and crazily spontaneous three-day getaway to a beach place, just to get a tiny break before the onslaught of a new infant and the constant suckling that makes me feel cannibalized, and the unhinge-ing I experience from sleep deprivation when I never hit REM sleep for the better part of a year.

In my mind, if I could book it online and find a maternity bathing suit fast enough, I would ignore the doctor's no-air travel rule and score a lightning breakaway to one of those all-inclusive resorts in Turks and Caicos, with a swim-up bar where you don't need to carry any money. I knew it was a fantasy but still, in it, my little Marco could have breakfast with Big Bird and make cookies in the afternoon with Cookie Monster while Mamma spent the afternoon at the maternal massage spa, the sun-soaked beach, and the virgin rum drink lounge.

But with Connor standing in my basement office giving notice on this cold and rainy April afternoon, I knew, realistically, where my next three days would be spent.

"Hmm," I said, looking up from the schedule I was just finishing, which outlined the next six weeks and which had Connor featured in at five shifts a week, as we had just confirmed and talked about, at length, merely days before. "Tell me more."

"Well,"—he sighed—"it's like hardly any hours and it's like triple the pay."

This is exactly as much as I need to hear. He is dead to me. There are more words, about fifteen minutes' worth, but I hear nothing. I loathe the way he offers this line of reasoning—triple the pay and hardly any work!—to *me,* to me who has thrived her whole life on triple the work for hardly any pay, obliviously expecting it to be the salient point that cements my opinion of him as a decent guy who— as if fatally—has an opportunity that cannot be resisted.

"How can I turn that down?" he asks, holding out his hands palms up. "You know?"

"You know" is that horrible interrogative at the end of a sentence that demands your complicity in the story. But I'm staring at the guy, days away from my due date, thinking: *Well, of course you can turn it down, bonehead. You say: I'm sorry, I am not available for that job at this time as I just made a commitment to my employer for another six months. Would you please consider me again in six months' time?*

But I say nothing. I listen to his earnest and apologetic speech, which he has rehearsed on the subway, and feel his hot air blow over me as if it were the Caribbean breeze I am being deprived of.

Without even flinching, I say, "Okay, so, can you give me two weeks? Is this a standard two weeks?"

He looks down at his hands, "Um, well, I wanted to tell you last

Monday but you seemed so busy so it's almost two weeks but not totally. My last day will be not this but the coming Sunday."

I look back at the calendar. That leaves me eight days to have a baby and fill Connor's shifts.

While I can do kind of extraordinary things with my own body under some pretty intense pressure, even I can't cover a line cook from a hospital bed with four stitches freshly sewn into my perineum.

"Okay, Connor. Sunday, then. Thanks."

I can generally punt—pretty painlessly—with one man down, but in this case, it was supposed to be me who was the one man down. Connor put us at two down. That made me nervous. The weekend passed, and on Sunday night, I discussed this with my sous chef, Alexis. She said, about Connor, "Ugh. Good riddance to that tool." Practically spitting on my clogs.

"Okay, I agree with you philosophically, but pragmatically, that will mean seven days straight for you and six shifts in a row for one of the others. At least until I hear back from some of the calls I placed."

"Whatever," she said. "We can handle it."

I am calmed somewhat by her reassurance that she can handle the seven-day week and wrangling the rest of the cooks into a six-day week and the lag until we find a replacement quickly. These things are harder in a small restaurant where we can't carry any excess payroll; it's not like a huge operation with unpaid cooking school externs all over the place and all you have to do is move them around and promote a few of the salad girls. It would be made a little easier, obviously, if I were just the male chef husband of a wife who was about to be having a baby and not the actual female chef about to be having the actual baby, because he could just take a few days or a week off and then get back into the game. And it would be better still if I had one of those rock-solid marriages where both working parents living in the same harmonious home take on the responsibilities of parenting equally, but we were still living apart and parenting alone, in a kind of pass-the-baton relay and thanking the stars for the full-time babysitter who was the true third parent in our little off-kilter arrangement.

On Monday afternoon, possibly three days away from my due date but none of us knowing for sure, as it was just an educated guess on the obstetrician's part, Annabel, a skilled line cook with a good palate, arrived for work, late and breathless. I was at my cutting board at the downstairs prep table, making a family meal for the evening shift. I was so profoundly out of breath with the baby's foot so far up into my guts that there was no room for my lungs to expand to full capacity, and I was winded just standing still. My apron string was tied up under my breasts like an empire waistline but I walked to the sink and back like a mailed and mounted soldier who has just had a long tough match on the jousting field—and not like a maiden in the palace. I said, in three or four breaths, across the prep table, where Annabel had set up her board and put out her knives, "Hey, Annabel . . . did you . . . hear . . . Connor's news?"

And she said, across the prep table, as casually as we might say, "I'll blanche the beans, guys," she said, "Oh yes. And I've got news, too."

I looked up and stopped working on the birds I was deboning.

I said, "You mean, news? Like, you're-giving-notice news?"

"Yup, that's what I mean," she said, matter-of-factly.

"Do you mean, like, giving notice as in two weeks' news, right here across the prep table, in front of everybody, like it's nothing?" I managed in a miraculous single breath.

And she said, "Yes."

The room came to a painful halt. I stood there with two other cooks and the pastry chef, and there was such a surge of stunned electricity in the room that the lightbulbs practically flashed. Before I could stop myself, I burst out laughing, and then said, as if it were just a mere fact, "You fucking suck so much."

In the throbbing silence, I put down my knife and walked out. I went to my office and with the door closed stared futilely at the schedule. Then I called my obstetrician and scheduled my labor for Leone.

He may have naturally been born on the twenty-seventh or the twenty-fifth or the twenty-ninth—I was healthy and there were no complications, and Dr. Kalish was going to give me two weeks on either side of the estimated due date for Leone's arrival. But I got so unraveled by the announcements of these two line cooks just days apart, coupled with so many other unknowns and things out of my control—like, for example, how I would chef a jammed, brimming restaurant and take care of a twenty-month-old and a nursing infant—that I felt, in the moment, like the only thing I *could* control was the birth of my second son. "Okay, come in at six a.m. and we'll get you checked in and then we'll start to induce. I'll be there no later than eight-thirty." My obstetrician was matter-of-fact; I felt like I was placing my meat order with the butcher, over the phone. I am often slow in catching up to the times, but even so, I still cannot even grip this idea: With nothing more than pitocin in your IV drip, you can sooner control the date and time of the birth of a human being—the gushing entry into the great blue world of a whole new person—than you can the scheduling of a few line cooks in your operation. Leone Tommaso Fuortes would be born on April twenty-fourth. By appointment. Like getting your hair cut or your dog groomed.

I hung up the phone and sat at my desk a few seconds, staring at the schedule in front of me, realizing abruptly how passed-over Annabel felt when she didn't get promoted to sous a few weeks before, and thinking about some of the tricks I have for these kinds of occasional, egregious cook shortages. I can limit the menu, run a two-person line, call in a freelance catering cook to punt for a week or two. I grabbed a black Sharpie and wrote myself a To-Do list for all of it. In twenty years of chronic, compulsive list making I had authored some that have been downright Beckettian in their sequencing, and it is exactly the anomaly in that sequencing—the non sequitur—that makes some of those To-Do lists earn a spot in your box of keepsakes. One of my recent favorites had been:

Doctor aioli
Find pH strips for dish machine
Why is meringue weeping?
Braise rabbit
Tell Dad I'm pregnant
Clean out shellfish tags
Tweak gremolata ratio

But this one, written in a calm and steady hand, surpassed and out-surrealed all other To-Do lists in my life thus far lived.

> Get w/AT and limit menu
> Train CR on a 2-man line
> Call Roode for fill-in?
> Have baby
> Tell brunch crew vinaigrette too acidic
> Pick up white platters
> Change filters in hoods
> Figure out pomegranate syrup

And I did, in fact, do all of that, and the syrup got figured out and the platters got picked up and the hood filters got changed and the baby was born and the ship sailed, with a diminished crew and a severely handicapped captain. But most urgently, besides listing what to do and when to do it, alone in that office with the door closed, I sat trying to figure out how to leave my office and re-enter a room full of keenly watching cooks, and get back to my cutting board and family meal, without appearing devastated or even dented. The staff does not want to see you fall apart. It unnerves them. You can let it go in the privacy of your office, you can weep in the walk-in, but at the bench, you must pick up your knife and finish boning out those chickens.

It's possible that working that brunch egg shift at thirty-nine weeks pregnant is badass. And also possible that biting the bullet and scheduling your own labor is badass. Keeping your shit together in front of your crew, no matter what, is badass. Maybe even driving out to IKEA to pick up thirty white china platters and get back by dinner service the day before you are going to give birth is badass. But badass is the last thing I am interested in being. Badass is a juvenile aspiration.

At thirteen, when I was stealing cars and smoking cigarettes I wanted to be badass. I was cultivating badass. At sixteen, coked out of my head and slinging chili at the Lone Star Café, I was the understudy to badass, and I knew all her lines and cues. At twenty-five, blow-torching my way through warehouse catering kitchens, cranking out back-to-back doubles, and napping in between on the office floor with my head on a pile of aprons and checked pants, I was authentically badass. But at thirty-eight years old, hugely pregnant with my future tiny, pure, precious son, I don't want anything to do with badass. I want to be J. Crew catalogue-clean. I don't want to be that woman who can—and did—get down on all fours and scrape the pancake batter off the oven door after having just cooked three hundred eggs with a near-constant monologue of *fucking fuck of a fuck* issuing from her lips. That disgusts me. While I would never want or hope to be the type of pregnant woman who would doze languidly in the afternoons while playing Mozart tapes to her womb, being down on the mats with a soapy green scrubby and rattling my unborn fetus with a string of expletives to make a trucker blush . . . well, that is certainly not the woman I meant to grow up to be, either.

When you are the one throwing the party every night, emptying the ashtrays, making sure the tonic is cold, the limes fresh, the shifts covered, the meat perfectly cooked and adequately rested, the customers carefree and the employees calm and confident, it will leave its marks. Someone has to stay in the kitchen and do the bones of the thing, to make sure it stands up, and if it's you, so be it.

16

I WAS INVITED TO BE A PANELIST AT A CONFERENCE HELD AT THE PRES-tigious Culinary Institute of America in Hyde Park, New York. The conference was called "Where Are the Women?" and the student chapter of Women Chefs and Restaurateurs had gathered a pretty decent roster of women chefs from around the country to come to the campus for the full day and evening and to participate in discussions, both formal and casual, with all the young women cooking students. Incredibly, it never goes away, this question about women.

My relationship to women is exhaustively researched. I am one, for starters. Not quite as clean and polished as I'd like, but nonetheless . . . I'm a daughter and a daughter-in-law. I am a sister and have a sister. I've got a mother. There've been a lot of women in my life. I've had sex with them. I've hired them. And fired them. Worked side-by-side with them and under them; several bosses come to mind. Women have brought me to the deepest bitterest tears of my existence. And some, equally, have made me feel like brand-new money. And not to rely on that old tired credential, but, some of my best friends are women. Still, what an impossible group to have to represent and presumably, speak on behalf of.

On the early morning train ride up, bleary-eyed, short on sleep by a critical several hours, I was thinking about what a particularly hard time I have had with women in my industry. When I was coming up in kitchens I was not the first or only woman in the kitchen. I was frequently the second woman; the "other" woman. There is nothing worse, I think, than being in an all-male kitchen with only one other female. Invariably, with so much territory at stake, she will treat you worse than any of the men. When I am asked to wax rhapsodic about the virtues of women in a kitchen, I feel claustrophobic and hemmed in by the task. But that was so many years ago.

Now, I imagined what a bust the conference would be. Letting my mind roll over my own payroll, female after female after female—from general manager to bar manager to sous chef to pastry chef to owner to server—I couldn't imagine that we were still having this conversation, this draining, polarizing conversation about where the women are in the industry. When I opened my own restaurant, nearly ten years ago, I finally put to bed that whole business about being a woman in a male-dominated profession. I was so obviously in charge that I didn't even need to say it. I unlocked the gate and the office in the morning and brewed the coffee. I wrote the menu, cut the checks, posted the prep list, cooked the food, and locked the door at the end of the night. Men who came to work at Prune understood at the threshold that there was a woman in charge, and all of them worked each shift, virility intact, without needing to challenge that. I received five resumes a week from young women entering the field, evidently not deterred by the reputation of the industry. Surely this stuff is over, I thought, finding my seat on the train. *This topic's a dinosaur.* Was it really necessary to get a chef who had worked late in her kitchen the night before out of her bed at such an hour in order to get to the upstate New York campus to talk about this all day long starting at nine a.m.?

Chefs work late and chef/owners work later. There's always more to do after the food is cooked. It was around one-thirty in the morning when I finally was in my pajamas, and setting the alarm for five. I had stopped nursing my youngest son only a few months before, so the idea and practice of getting very little sleep, in increments, was still completely routine. When I saw the alarm clock digitally glowing its 1:33 a.m. message as I was setting it to wake me up in just a few hours, I strategically coaxed my mind away from thinking ruefully about a pitiful night's sleep and redirected it to thinking deliciously about a long, full, luxurious nap. Somewhere between kid number one and kid number two and chef and owner and nursing and prepping and line cooking and worker's comp and commercial refrigeration, I learned to re-envision the amount of time I have available to sleep as an excellent nap instead of a paltry night's worth.

In the morning, by the still weak light of day—I could not distinguish between the color of oatmeal and the color of yellow, it was still so dim—I dressed with the same grim determination as one about to take her vaccination shots. I packed a small bag, took deep, intoxicating lungfuls of my babies while lightly kissing them as they slept, and slipped out of the house into the dawn. The Peruvian pan-pipe player who sets up at my subway station was unbelievably lively and already hard at work even that early in the morning. He's five-foot-two and "playful." He kind of darts and dances around the waiting passengers while he pipes along to the *Titanic* soundtrack and some Simon and Garfunkel tunes. Someone, I am sure, finds his qualities charming. I have murderous feelings about him and regularly fantasize his violent death on the tracks and imagine how much better off the world would be without him and his Peruvian pan-piping version of "My Heart Will Go On."

To be assaulted by this little nuisance ten minutes after living through the agony, the unmitigated heartache of leaving my two guys in their beds asleep without one moment of being with them on this day—out before they wake and home well after they've gone to sleep—was more than I could take on less than four hours of sleep. When Mr. Pan Pipes segued into "El Condor Pasa," I stood at the farthest end of the platform cursing both him and these cooking school girls who could even think to drag me from my barely warmed-up bed, from my two boys with their soft tubbied faces mushed up in perfect sleep, their diapered asses up in the air.

Grand Central was fully alive with commuters clogging the escalators and shops and the concourses. I stood in a long but fast-moving line at a coffee place where the women in front and back of me ordered—with straight faces—drinks called double-skim half-decaf vanilla latte—and the young caffeinated baristas called thesé very same words back to the customer when putting up her drink without a single hint of scorn or derision in their voices, and I marveled, genuinely, at their generosity. I hate hating women but double-skim half-decaf vanilla latte embarrasses me. I ordered a plain filtered coffee, as if I were apologizing on behalf of my gender, and when I dug through my heavy purse to pay for it I discovered in my bag a diaper, a resealable jar of apricot puree, and one of Marco's socks, which had somehow in the general loss of boundary and private real estate that is Motherhood, made its way in there.

Once on the train, I sipped the coffee and read the prepared questions for the panel and the agenda for the day. I felt a small nervousness set in. What would I possibly have to say that could help these young women? I had never had a television show on the Food Network, had never hired a PR firm in my life; I had never chosen this career formally and had no experience climbing a ladder. I had just jumped into the fire and opened a restaurant of my own without ever having cheffed in one. The questions all seemed largely aimed at discovering how to attain recognition for oneself and on this particular morning, lovesick for my own children, terrifically backlogged on work at my own restaurant, I wondered uncomfortably why I was making the journey to Poughkeepsie just for that. Just to end up carping bitchily at the girls about the most obvious of all obviousnesses: *Put your head down and do your job and let the recognition end of things sort itself out.* When I stepped onto the platform in Poughkeepsie, I was afraid of my own mood.

I expected to fall into the company of my fellow female chefs and immediately, comfortably, be grousing with my sister panelists about these young, entitled students who know nothing of hard work and who just wanted to instantly have a cooking show on the Food Network so that they can be "famous." I thought we women chefs would be allied against this obsession among the young with Recognition and Fame above Merit and Talent. I was not interested in answering this tired question: *Where are the women?* Especially when we know perfectly well where the women are. They jumped to publishing, and are now busy with idolizing the male chefs who made it impossible for them to continue cooking in restaurants and they are so busy writing features and articles about them that they don't have time left—or column inches—for the female chefs who actually toughed it out. Women have self-selected out of the chef life, which can grind you to a powder, and have become happily married recipe testers and magazine editors, or private chefs, working moderate hours for good pay and benefits while successfully raising several small children whom they do not damage. I was sure my peers would feel equally disinclined. What was there left to say, really? *Get in the kitchen; cook well; and the rest will take care of itself. You can't be a recognized woman chef if you are working at a magazine.*

My phone rang and it was Carlos, my sous chef, calling from the restaurant to check in. When I had left the night before, I wrote a long note for the day crew, but couldn't explain everything for a new dish we'd been running that nobody else had prepped but me. So he was calling for that most frustrating of experiences—the chef-by-phone-tutorial.

"Hi, boss!"

"Good morning. How's it going?"

"We're fine. I'm going to start this rabbit project now. I think I've got it. I've read your notes."

"Yeah," I said. "I'm sure you'll be fine. Just take care not to over-brown or to brown too fast the legs—you know how it really toughens the flesh as there is no 'skin,' like on a piece of poultry or whatever."

"So, don't brown the rabbit?" he asked.

"No. Yes. Brown the rabbit, yes, I'm just saying take care not to over-brown it or to use too high a heat. It can make the meat have a stringy, tough quality even after the braise."

"Okay, I got it," he said, with a little unsettling tone that makes me, on the platform in Poughkeepsie, feel useless and not confident in Table 7's experience with the rabbit later this evening.

"Okay, and then, Carlos?"

"Yes, Boss?"

"It's not fatty, you know, and the bones are quite small. You can't just leave it to braise and forget about it. It can only braise about twenty-five minutes and then it's done. So, when the joints are loose but not falling apart. It's finished."

"What joints?" he asks.

Now I'm pacing on the platform, dodging the few people who have exited the train and are filing toward the station.

"The joint between the thigh and the leg. It's got to have give and motion but if it separates, you've gone too far. If it's too underdone, it won't recover in the pickup. It has to be braised properly in the prep, otherwise it's just hot but not adequately cooked through when they pick it up at service." As I'm trying to explain this, the platform has completely emptied and I am the last one standing on it. A train employee with a rolling garbage can enters the empty train to collect discarded newspapers, coffee cups, and breakfast wrappers.

"Okay, boss, I got it. Have fun up there. See you tomorrow!"

I took a taxi from the train station to the campus and stood for a moment where the driver dumped me at the bottom of the circular drive. I felt like I was at an Ivy League college in New England that I would have been rejected from had I applied. There were big brick buildings and sweeping views of the surrounding valley. Students were flocking across campus in every direction, in a hurry, but instead of low-cut jeans and cashmere sweaters and backpacks, all were dressed in checks and whites and carrying their knife rolls. *Ivy-covered brick buildings in which to learn the five mother sauces!*

In the lobby of the building I met up with the other women chefs who were also just arriving, and Cat Cora came in behind me, looking so fresh and excited and pretty. I immediately got caught up in her good energy and natural kindness, and the dangerous mood that had started to take hold of me on the train quickly evaporated. I shook hands with the few panelists I had never met, and I warmly hugged the women I already knew. It's not that uncommon, after a very short while, to feel like you know all of the other women in your industry, as the pool gets small fast. If there's an event for women, we are all trotted out sooner or later, and we meet each other with some frequency.

That should have made me think, then, while greeting my co-panelists, that maybe there was some validity to the conference after all. If there were so few of us visible in the industry that we kept seeing each other at so many events, there must still be a problem with employing female chefs. I suddenly recalled running into a male colleague on the street in New York one summer. He's not a chef, but he owns some restaurants and has an excellent female chef at the helm of his places. He was walking down the sunny street with his tall, elegant mother, who was visiting from San Diego. "Hey!" we exclaimed to each other. "Hello there!" He introduced me to his mother as *one of the top, one of the best female chefs in New York City.*

I laughed. "Well, there are only four of us in New York, so I don't know about that."

We all laughed. And then, without even thinking about it, I said, "Now, if we could just get that word 'female' out of the sentence." And suddenly, this dead cheerlessness came over the sidewalk, and all of us felt awkward, taking that moment to reimagine the same sentence without the qualifying word *female.* "Mom, this is one of the top, one of the best chefs in New York." I wished I hadn't mentioned it. But on this morning in Hyde Park, I was fixed on dismissing the validity of the conference. Even though I can't understand for one second what the difference is between a male chef and a female chef—the food has to be cooked and we all just cook it. Even though I simultaneously soar and cringe to be called one of New York City's top *female* chefs. Somehow I had set my mind to it, that this conference would be a bust, even as I was palpably buoyed by the sudden shift in power, that infectious energizing feeling, while standing together in the reception hall with this bunch of smart, strong women.

There was a brief awkward moment in the coat-check area, where we were asked to don our chef coats for the rest of our time on campus and I didn't want to—whenever I see a chef outside of his kitchen in the civilian world, dressed in his whites, I think he looks like a dipshit with an insecurity issue. But the organizers wanted to make a statement, with the visual cue of ten women in starched monogrammed chef coats walking from building to building, from lecture to cocktail reception, to dinner to evening panel in the audi-torium. I couldn't decide if I wanted to emphasize my femaleness or my chef-ness. If I were emphasizing my chef-ness, I would have worn the jacket. But if I was emphasizing my femaleness and my confidence in my equal abilities and talents, I wouldn't want to wear the jacket. I would want to say, sartorially, that I am so confident and secure in my role that I don't need the costume to prop me up.

At every single event with women chefs that I participate in, I can see the women struggling, on some level, with this very basic question of what to wear. The woman in shiny pink patent leather clogs has decided one thing. The woman in a black shirt and apron but no jacket has decided another. The woman who dresses exactly like Thomas Keller has decided yet another. Even this question of dressing for your work is exhausting. Would a guy have gone through this kind of soul-searching? I think he would have just worn the coat. He may even have arrived wearing it. If there'd been a toque requested, he probably would have thrown that on too without hesitation.

When we got to the auditorium it was packed to the gills and humming with the excitement of hundreds of young women. They were sitting in every seat and spilling into the aisles. We took our seats at the table on stage facing them, and I felt nervous and looked down at my own stomach and noticed that in the dim light of early morn-ing, I had not seen the dried, crusty oatmeal on my yellow sweater that Marco must have rubbed there with his little fingers some or other morning ago. For some reason, I worry terribly about appear-ing dirty and ill-put-together. In the same way that I don't want to be taken care of in a hospital by a pale, chain-smoking doctor, I feel like the people who prepare your food should look healthy and robust and tidy. I scraped at the oatmeal with my fingernail and pushed my open handbag farther under the table so no one would see the sock, and the diaper, and the apricot puree tucked in with the wallet and the keys and the travel toothbrush.

There were a bunch of young men in the audience as well. We were introduced by the moderator, and I thought our chiding would start right then and there about how you should put your head down and do your job and stop worrying about fame and fortune, but the first question came to the panel from a young woman high up in the balcony on the right and my heart broke in the first five seconds. She stood up and in a thin voice that she managed to project all the way down to the stage, she asked her pressing question.

"Is it okay to cry?"

I do almost $2 million a year in sales. I know that is nothing compared to my colleagues who have hundred-seat restaurants and four branches, but for an independent, thirty-seat "joint," with no single wine over $89, I am very proud of this volume. We have never accomplished the standard industry ideal of 10 percent profit, but I love the revenue number nonetheless. I think it's an accomplishment. More important, I decide who our purveyors are, what sodas and beers we carry, what linen service we use, what garbage removal service we use, the glassware, tableware, the wine and liquor, the cheese, the meat, the vegetables. I mention this only because if I'm going to spend $100,000 a year on produce, or linen, or printing, you can't send a sales rep who calls me "Hon." You can't be a potential produce vendor seeking my business by addressing your query letter "Dear Sir." I will drop that purveyor's list in the trash can unread—right on top of my bloody tampon—as soon as I see that out-of-date salutation at the top of the page. But I won't cry.

Equally, someone seeking employment can't fax in a resume to "Sir" because I won't hire him if that is his default point of view. I won't cry; I just won't hire him. You don't have to fight or argue or bitch or cry at all; I just quietly spend my money with another company that I perceive has caught up to the times and I hire people I can enjoy working with. This genuine power makes you gentle.

Many of the students were concerned about the constant negotiating one does, internally and externally, to get by in the male kitchen and asked the panel how to navigate that. Melissa said she used to just do her work and quietly shine. But Helene said, "No way! I roared through the kitchen, I 'bested' the men at every turn. When I got promoted and they didn't, I turned around sweetly and said, 'Bye Guys!' "

I had tried smoking filterless cigarettes, swearing like a sailor, pissing in bottles, and banging out twice as much as my male cohorts. And I'd also given lipstick and giggling a try, even claiming to not be able to lift a stockpot so that the guys would help me. Neither strategy is better than the other.

It was not until I opened my own place that I realized how present and ongoing the struggle to be female in a professional kitchen had been. It's like the hood during service. Everybody talks about the heat in a kitchen, and the heat, without doubt, is formidable. It's a powerful opponent. But for me the real punisher is the exhaust hood, with the suction so powerful that it sucks up all the metal bound filters from their spots and bangs them against the lip of the hood. The big mechanic kick of the fan belt starting up, the unified clank of the filters rising—like a Rockettes kick, all in unison—then followed by eighteen draining hours of heavy-duty vacuum hum, over which orders are barked, dishes are clanked, pots are slammed around, and the stereo blasts. Then finally at midnight or one, after the disher has turned off the fryer, someone turns off the hood and a profound silence descends. I never realize how much space the noise of the hood takes up in my mind and head—that heavy vacuum sound—until I shut it off, and total bliss and relief set in.

In the same way, when I opened my own restaurant, I enjoyed such an absence of boy-girl jostling that I only then understood that, all through my entire work life, I had been working a double shift. I had been working the same shift as my peers, with all of its heat and heft and long hours on your feet. But I had been doing a second job all along, as well—that of constantly, vigilantly figuring out and calibrating my place in that kitchen with those guys to make a space for myself that was bearable and viable. Should I wear pink clogs or black steel-toe work shoes? Lipstick or Chapstick? Work double hard, double fast, double strong, or keep pace with the average Joe? Swear like a line cook or giggle like a girl?

Meanwhile, the parsley needs to be chopped, and the veal chops seared off. There is, still, the work itself to do.

Someone on the panel to my right said, out loud into the microphone, "Women are more clever than men."

And then, as if inspired, the woman to my left said, "Women are smarter than men."

I was feeling hot and insecure about the oatmeal on my sweater to begin with, and was still reeling and deep in thought about the crying question, so I had said only a few words so far into the microphone, and I felt like while I had withdrawn for those few minutes, this group of women, my sister panelists, had set up camp and staked out the territory in a very different place than I wanted to be. This was not double-skim half-decaf vanilla latte embarrassing, but a different kind of bothersome.

Ann said, "Women don't like to come out from behind the stove and be a presence on the floor of their restaurants."

Helene said, "Women have better palates than men."

Odessa said, "Women are more nurturing than men."

Nora said, "Women are not competitive. They shy away from the limelight."

I slumped in my chair, dying.

We attract and hire a lot of female cooks at Prune because word got out in the industry that if you wanted a nice place to work without the feel of hostile male colleagues, you should come here—Prune likes women. That is not technically true—we like anybody who gets the job done—and that happens to be the profile of many hard-working and qualified women who have passed through my kitchen over the years. And it is sure that if you work at Prune, you will be handling the meat and the fish as much as the guy next to you; you will not be shoved into the pastry or the salad station in perpetuity. And you will probably enjoy the way that being in the company of many women renders your own femaleness almost inconsequential, such a non-issue that it is never a distraction from the work itself. But I could never truthfully, or proudly, utter the sentences these women were letting fly out of their mouths. If anything, I have come to love the men who also feel that the kitchen is a better place when women are allowed to work in it, the men who feel that if any part of society is abused, that it demeans the rest of the society. Those are the men and women I want to spend eighteen hours a day with over a hot stove under a relentless humming hood.

Identity politics never ends up going the distance for me. The categories tend to fall apart on me when I rely on them too heavily—gay people, women, whatever. Every time I think I can rely on a group or a category—like my sister women in the industry or my sister lesbians or whatever—Ruth Reichl frosts me at an event, for the seventh time, or the women on my panel say ridiculous things about women's superiority or the lesbians go out and start voting Republican—and the whole thing caves in for me, and I start to mistrust my own kind. Especially when they start saying things like "Women are better than men."

I had really checked out of the panel. I was so caught up in a livid confusion deep in my own mind that I wasn't even listening to the panel anymore. I get adrenaline rushes sometimes that are so thick I feel as if I've blacked out. When I could hear again, I heard a young woman ask, "How do you manage family and career? I want to get married and have kids but I am afraid I won't be hired as a chef if I say that to an employer, and I'm worried I won't even have a boyfriend anymore if I have to work the hours I've heard about."

To her question, my sister panelists gave peppy, cheerful "You can do it!!" kind of crap answers—completely generic, unspecific answers—

And before I knew it, I had reversed my own allegiances and was now in love with all of the CIA students and totally dismayed by almost half of my peers on the panel. I wanted to hang out with the students and gripe about women panelists. I now wanted to answer all of their good, valid questions and I suddenly felt that the conference was highly pertinent and overdue!

I really started itching when this sixty-year-old woman droned on into the mic to her twenty-year-old audience about the joys of building relationships with local, sustainable farmers, as if these young cooks were about to enter jobs that would put them anywhere near to the sourcing of the restaurant's ingredients. I was thinking about the pleasure, the sheer pleasure of killing the line on a busy night, setting those tickets up and knocking them down, of the knives laid out neatly on the magnet, the worn wooden cutting boards, the feel of the cool, silky flour every time you dip in with the measuring cup, of sitting down with everybody after work and drinking cocktails telling grossly distorted tales of your own heroics on the line that night. I felt I had to testify to this pleasure, to speak about the total satisfaction of killing the line, the way scrubbing down your station afterward puts your mind right, about "the third shift," the drinks after work. I wanted to say that we are all not sitting around in our naturally woven fibers eating our organic quinoa salads and thinking up our next sustainable charity project. Some of us are actually cooking. And enjoying cooking. But I had shut down and couldn't muster for this part of the panel, where my supposed peers were gassing on about themselves, giving these young women the impression that each day in a kitchen is like going to some priggish church.

They were speaking as women who were thirty years into an industry, and the young women we were meant to address had yet to experience even their first day of it.

Why didn't a single one of us mention cooking? Why didn't we say, If you want your cooking career to be recognized, be a good cook! Cook, ladies, cook.

Defeated, I thought about what I had had to do to arrange getting to the conference that day in the first place. If I had just told them about that small journey, from my apartment with two sleeping children to their campus, as the chef and owner of a restaurant and the mother of two little kids, wouldn't just that answer all of their questions about family and career and motherhood?

If I told them about the pan-pipe player and the full day in which I would never see my boys awake. If I told them how I joke that I now pity the women who start families who have *not* been chefs. How I wonder earnestly, how does the office worker woman who is so accustomed to her forty-hour workweek, her daily lunch hour, her inbox, and her out-box, handle all the pain and the physical contortions, and the mayhem of suckling, crying, ear infections, and working if she has never had to skin a live eel, placate the angry patron at Table 7 who finds his rabbit a bit stringy, and carry an epileptic line cook off the mats who has suffered a grand mal seizure during service? How will the woman who is accustomed to great personal and bodily integrity suffer the cannibalizing feeling that nursing constantly can leave you with, as if you were being eaten alive, not in huge monster-gore chunks, but like a legion of soft, benign caterpillars makes lace of a leaf?

I thought of telling them how changing a diaper reminds me, every time, of trussing a chicken. How sleepless nights and long grueling hours under intense physical discomfort were already part of my daily routine long before I had children. How labeling every school lunch bag, granola bar, juice box, extra sweater, and nap blanket with permanent Sharpie is like what we've been doing every day for thirty years, labeling the foods in our walk-ins. How being the chef and owner of a restaurant means you have already, by definition, mastered the idea of "systems," "routines," and "protocols" so that everyone who works for you can work smart-hard rather than work stupid-hard. So that by the time you are setting up your household and preparing yourself for adding children, you have a tendency toward this kind of order, logic, and efficiency.

Multitasking—answering questions on the phone, cooking something, and trying to monitor a line cook, while hearing your name repeated possibly six or seven hundred times in less than eight hours—is exactly like trying to run a family and a business. A choking patron, a grease fire, a badly cut employee—once you have been through that, figuring out how you will get your injured child to the emergency room of a hospital in the nearest Italian town where you are alone on vacation should come a little easier to you.

Not to give the impression that if you've been a chef, then adding parenthood to your day is just as easy as running a lamb shank special on your menu. Days go very badly and there is never balance. Everybody gets shorted, everybody gets hurt, and you, the mom, not the least. But it does give you a leg up, I often think, because the restaurant family is a perfect starter family. It's such an accurate in-flight simulator that I have grown to feel sorry for anybody who enters parenthood and a domestic project without having first run a restaurant. From the earliest stages of family life when you are pregnant and uncomfortable and not sleeping well at night, the parallels to running a restaurant are almost over-obvious and all of that work you've done on your feet all day, with back problems from lifting so much heavy stuff or standing in one place for so long, with sometimes no time to eat or even to pee, and not sleeping much at all because of your commitment to your restaurant will all feel incredibly familiar and doable. And then when the suckling critter arrives, you will just fold that into your day like you have all the other leaking, sticky, oozy fluids you've been handling for the past decade. Every time you have to change the diaper of a noncompliant kid you will be reminded of every chicken you've ever trussed and every eel you've ever had to wrangle. Petulant adolescents who just want to borrow money, raid the refrigerator, and talk on the phone with their friends about what a bitch you are? That will be a piece of cake once you have managed a front-of-house staff, denied the bartender her vacation request, and uneasily loaned the new line cook her first and last months rent deposit on her new West Village apartment, knowing well you will never see that money again.

I wanted to interrupt my fellow panelists now going on about how women cook better than men, and how they're faster and cleaner and smarter, and just tell this story to the young woman in the fifteenth row. But their essentialist drone drove me to silence. And I saved my tears for the train ride home.

Butter

17

CARMELUCCIA CAME ONE AFTERNOON TO PAY A VISIT. WE HAD ARrived in Leuca just a few days before, Michele and I and our two kids; the new one, Leone, while only a couple of months old, lavishly adored. We were just settling in, like butter on toast, to our annual July vacation. I unpacked our suitcases and stored them under the antique iron bed; Michele walked into town to get *il giornale* and *i cornetti*. Carmeluccia arrived with eight of her own eggs, biscotti she had made, a little hooded bath towel for Leone, and about a kilo of homemade *orecchiette,* "little ears," and *minchiareddhi,* "little penises," still damp and warm from her hands. Carmeluccia, in Michele's family's history of "help," came before Rosaria and after Pasqualina. There has always been The Woman. The Woman who comes each day and helps with the cooking and the cleaning and the ironing. I have known only Rosaria in the years that I've been coming here, but I met Pasqualina, now in her seventies, one year when Michele took us all to pay a visit. She was, even in the depth of summer, all in widow's black with heavy stockings and a woolen cardigan, and she showed us a couple of her own rabbits in her freezer, killed and skinned with her own hands.

I vowed to start my long arduous application for Italian citizenship by marriage as soon as I got back to the States when I saw those rabbits. In my vision of my own old age, I too, want to be shelling fava beans and skinning rabbits and having the people I have cared for stop by for a glass of cold tea. I want to grow old in Italy.

Carmeluccia, in her sixties now, the woman between Pasqualina and Rosaria, arrived to pay us a visit in the late afternoon.

She is stout and red in the face with good meaty hands and round hips and ankles so sturdy that they looked kind of wrong in the dressy heeled shoe that she was wearing. She was in a clean simple dress without earrings or makeup and wore only a gold chain that had a cross and a saint's medallion and her wedding band. There was much kissing and hugging when she arrived and great koochy koo-ing with Leone and an extravagant display of amazement at how big Marco had grown since we were here last year. Every single Italian woman I have ever met is perfect with children, and Carmeluccia is more perfect than them all.

We all sat in the parlor, on the good chairs, kind of pleasantly staring at each other. Michele disappeared to the kitchen to spoon out pink and white ice cream into four glass bowls, place them on a tray with the real silver spoons, and as if he were again the thirteen-year-old boy in short pants that Carmeluccia cleaned up after, who was forced to comb his hair and kiss the ladies' hands and to serve the visiting guests, he came around to each of us and politely served us the ice cream from a tray.

And there we sat, three women accustomed to work from the moment we wake until the moment we lay down our heads, not quite seamlessly transformed into gentle ladies by a tray, a cushioned chair, and the polite sharing of a hot afternoon's bowl of ice cream with silver spoons. Marco splashed around on the terrace in his little blow-up swimming pool, Leone snoozed in the linen basket, and Alda and I sat with Carmeluccia and they made conversation while I just listened and tried to decipher the Italian. I couldn't understand but a few words of it and I wondered if they were speaking to each other in local dialect, but even so, or especially so without language, I could see that we were all kind of stiff and uncomfortable, with not that much to say once children and various family members had been asked about. During a pretty significant lull, I admired Carmeluccia's orec-chiette, and asked her a few questions about how she made them, while we finished up the last bites of our ice cream.

"Do you want me to show you? I can show you! It's nothing, Signora, flour and water! Come, let me show you!"

And within a few minutes we have escaped the parlor and are all back in the kitchen where we are all most comfortable, rolling up our sleeves, forming a little circle around her while she prepares to make pasta at the kitchen table.

"Donna Alda," she said, "where are you keeping your flour now? Where is the flour? We need the durum flour, only the durum flour."

I smiled to think that she believed it possible that the location of the flour could possibly have changed since she was with the family. The flour, as it had been for decades, was kept in The Cabinet, and I retrieved it for her.

Without even removing her wedding band, she dumped a small pile of the flour directly onto the table, made a well in the center, and added water. There was nothing to measure. She began to knead the dough as familiarly as you or I might pet the family dog. The dough stuck to her fingers at first and she scraped it off and worked it back into the greater mass of dough. Alda found an apron, and from be-hind, like a tailor draping a client for a custom suit, tied it around Carmeluccia's waist, barely disrupting the kneading. I don't know what they are saying, but conversation has really picked up, and now Rosaria is with us, holding baby Leone and offering advice on texture and humidity of dough, and Alda, of course, has her own advice and opinions. Even Michele, who is so far removed from the time when he made pasta like an Italian, the fifty-two-year-old doctor who's lived in America for the past nearly thirty years and who now shops exclusively and with great American enthusiasm for discounts and bargains at Home Depot, The Gap, and Costco, even he wants to weigh in. Through the great din of opinions, without oil or salt or eggs, Carmeluccia produces a soft, pliable, elastic dough. It is simply flour and water.

I have never been able to identify or understand my class. I think we were raised as bourgeoisie but I am not even sure what the term means—shop owners?—and I remember it being spit out in the most derogatory way in the books that I loved most when I was in college. I think it's considered loathsome. I'm comfortable upstairs and downstairs. I do low-paying manual labor and always have but I'm educated and came to own my own business when I was thirty-four years old. We owned our house growing up but tenuously, so tenuously that we jokingly referred to the bank man who carried my father through a lot of dark valleys as "Uncle" Bill. But we traveled in the summers and drank champagne at holidays. I know which fork to use with which course because I have set and cleared so many tables, not because I have sat at so many. I employ a full-time babysitter in New York but I'm so awkward about it, it's so new for me, that I get the skillet onto the stovetop and cook the chicken nuggets, and finish all the dinner dishes and clean out the bathtub of tubby toys and soap scum and sweep the floors, so that she can spend the day watching cartoons with the kids. I have even done all of those things one-handed while using my other hand to hold my nursing infant like a football. Cooking dinner, sweeping the floor, and nursing an infant simultaneously? I have done it. A lot. So that when the babysitter arrives, I have erased any inconvenience for the woman because I'm so uncomfortable with the whole scenario. Americans are raised to be uncomfortable with the scenario and we do it all wrong—we confuse the whole thing with class and status and money, and we pay shitty wages, under the table, without insurance or job security and way too frequently with disrespect for the people who do this work. Or we go the opposite direction and act our noblesse oblige, and when we empty our closets we offer our hand-me-downs, and we inquire after the health and well-being of the nanny's own children, who are usually back in Honduras and being raised by their grandmothers.

We did not have help in our house growing up. My mother

cooked and cleaned and kept the house with five children by herself. There was June, a seamstress, who mended all of our clothes and shortened and lengthened the hems on all the hand-me-downs as they were handed down among the five children. And there was an occasional babysitter I remember, an Italian-American woman, Alice Narducci, and sometimes I was dropped at her house. She ate dinner from a tray in the living room watching *The Lawrence Welk Show,* and she let me have red gelatin with whipped cream for dessert, both after lunch and after dinner. Two desserts in the same day.

The new status of the chef as celebrity further confuses me. I used to be "the help," arriving by the back service elevator, respecting your wishes for well-done beef, dressing on the side, one cube only in your glass of Smirnoff. When I finished cooking and cleaning up, I swept and mopped the floors, put two dish towels under my shoes and skated—printless—to the back door. I called the service elevator and exited your building through the basement warren of hallways with Dumpsters, never having been seen by you or your guests. Now, the Food and Wine Festival organizers arrange my airfare, install me in suites on high floors of exquisite hotels I could never afford on my own income, and you eat my food as I've envisioned it and prepared it—as heavily sauced, salted, or rare as *I* like. Once in South Beach, at the Food and Wine Festival, we were picked up at the hotel and driven to the venue in a black Cadillac Escalade with black tinted windows, the driver in a crisp suit with oiled hair, gold rings, a fresh stick of gum in his mouth. I felt giddy with transgression. We rode a full two feet taller than anyone around us, like military brass. I was giggling, tapping my clogs on the floor, turning around in my seat to share conspiratorial tee-hee's with my sous chef. At a red light, a ruined guy in a wheelchair with his legs sawed off rolled up to the gleaming black machine and begged at my black expressionless window. I quickly imagined myself as a bystander on the sidewalk, watching the electric window whisper down, a disembodied white hand spit out a few bills, and retreat as the tinted glass rose up and resealed the fortress. Then I imagined the opposite scenario—the one in which the guy in the wheelchair faces the impenetrable, black window of the towering SUV and nothing happens, he is simply ignored, facing his own widened reflection in the high gleam. Paralyzed by the hideousness of both scenarios, I turn to Carlos and say, "Well. I feel really good about myself right now!"

But in Italy, I can't understand anyone's class, let alone my own. The Woman comes for a few hours each day in the mornings and helps with laundry and ironing and cooking and cleaning. She owns her own house; her husband runs his own business. This only describes the summertime, vacation help. But when the Fuortes kids were young and their father was still alive, during the school years in the city, there were *two* full-time live-ins plus a third part-timer who came in the mornings to keep the family machinery running. There's something that feels so uncomplicated and without subjugation about it even though I see perfectly well that Alda is the one with the heavy sack of keys. Not one of us seems to prefer sitting down in the parlor being served ice cream. Alda's tone when speaking to these women sounds, to my ear, totally equal and not for a moment proprietary. There seems to be absolutely no money, at all, and nothing coming in, really, from all the land they own, and most of the house seems to be in serious disrepair. But there is no confusing this: They call Alda "Donna Alda," they call me "Signora," they call Michele "Dottore," and when the sun finally sets over the impluvium, we sleep in the big villa on the big street called Via Tommaso Fuortes. Leone's full name, to be clear, is Leone Tommaso Fuortes. He is three months old and already has international travel stamped into his passport. He has a passport.

He will grow up to inherit this house with Marco, or what's left of it by then. This is so far removed from my own experience that I am made breathless by it.

Carmeluccia rolls out a small rope of pasta dough and then cuts little pellets about the length and diameter of a squeeze of toothpaste. From these she makes the orecchiette by smudging them with her thumb until they look like little flat coins on the table which she picks up, turns inside out to become concave and sets to dry on a tray. They look exactly like small delicate ears. The "little penises" she makes by pressing a common knitting needle down into the pellet and using it like a rolling pin until the dough has closed into a tube around the needle. Americans would never recognize the shape as a penis, because of our obsession with circumcision, but anyone familiar with the un-maimed ones—in their unaroused state—will see it in an instant. She slides each minchiareddo off the needle and lets it dry, also, on the tray. These two shapes, she explains, are typically made together and served together because they share a cooking time. This starts a loud friendly argument among them all in rapid Italian—with accompanying hand gestures—about correct cooking times.

I practice my orecchiette.

I ruin my first dozen but then finally get it and suddenly there I am making perfect little ears right alongside these three Italian women—Rosaria, Carmeluccia, and Alda. With more than forty years between our ages, Alda who owns the house, Carmeluccia who has kept the house, and I who have married into the house, we are all at the kitchen table making orecchiette like we are the same.

Later, in the evening, I am sitting outside in the front, having an al fresco dinner with Marco at his "restaurant," a small wooden chair pulled up to the massive granite front stoop of this villa. He's blond and tan and in nothing but a diaper, trying to manage tortellini with prosciutto and butter with his own fork and he is explicit in wanting no help from me. A battered Volkswagen Rabbit slowly pulls in at the end of the drive and comes to a stop; the driver cranks the hand brake and turns the car off, but leaves the headlights on. He gets out of the car, stands at a respectful distance from the house—not to presume.

"C'è Donna Alda?" he inquires.

"Aspetta," I call to him.

I get Michele, Michele gets his mother, and suddenly we are un-loading gorgeous Gallia melons and red plum tomatoes out of this gentleman's dusty car. This has happened a dozen times over the years that I've been coming here. A woman at the end of the driveway with giuncata in her bicycle basket. A farmer with a three-wheeled motor-ized wagon unloading olive oil and eggplant and bringing it into the storage room next to the kitchen. This man, tall and slender, bringing melons and tomatoes. He stands inside the house without touching anything, and will not allow himself to lean against the wall or the door frame even. He is tan.

Who are all these people who approach the big house and stand at a respectful distance until warmly welcomed into the magnificence by Alda herself, once she squints and adjusts her old eyes and then lights up with immense warmth and recognition? Who are all these people of the local countryside who bring her things and to whom she has Rosaria bring out a couple of beers at eleven a.m. when they are taking a break from chainsawing the dead branches? There was the woman who made burratta and giuncata and she used to bring it to the house, still warm, in the basket of her bicycle until she died a few years ago. This man with the VW and the melons, his name is Cosimino—Alda buys a lot of fertilizer from him for her wheat fields, and he in turn, buys a lot of wheat from her, which he then sells for a profit. Along the way, he brings her nice things from his garden. Antonio brings the olive oil and cuts down the branches. Carmeluccia brings the eggs and her homemade pastas. The transactions and interactions seem so genuine and affectionate—and even without speaking Italian, I can see that these people hold Alda in great esteem with respect and kindness and she, I feel certain of it, regards them equally.

I study her. I need to know. I need to teach Marco and Leone.

I can't tell if I am just learning how to make orecchiette, or if I am learning how to be the woman who keeps the sack of keys, but somehow, July with Alda and the Fuortes family has become the most important and anticipated month of my year.

18

WHEN MICHELE WAS FIRST TRYING TO GET WITH ME, HE MADE me some profoundly beautiful ravioli. He got up early on a weekend morning and made his dough. And he went to the gym and did two spinning classes *in a row*—while his pasta dough rested under a towel at home and became smooth as flesh and tender as lettuce. He then rode his bicycle all the way down to Greenwich Village to get his ricotta from Joe's Dairy on Sullivan Street and his pancetta from Pino's across the way and he rode all the way back up to his apartment on the Upper East Side—the whole thing at least an hour's excursion for just the right ingredients to fill his ravioli. Not to mention three hours of strenuous exercise to coerce his forty-six-year-old body into nail-the-thirty-five-year-old-girl shape.

They were small and delicate and a beautiful yellow from the yolks in the pasta dough and you could see the herbs and the ricotta through the dough, like a woman behind a shower curtain.

For the ravioli, he rolled out his pasta with a rolling pin, like his mother uses, not even availing himself of the relative ease and short-cutting of those stainless steel crank jobs that roll dough on graduated thinnesses until you get to nine and you can read the newspaper through the dough. He did that instead by hand on a galley kitchen counter the size of a standard ironing board, between the toaster oven and the dish drying rack. He cut out each round with a paring knife, not even a cookie cutter, and filled each one by placing the ricotta and pancetta mixture in the center of the round, draping another disc of dough on top and then sealing the edges with a damp fingertip. He made dozens this painstaking way. I could imagine him in his lab at the medical college where he both teaches and does research—his technician's/researcher's skills totally utilized—where he gets close up on his task—preparing the Western Blot experiment in which he puts a drop of each "ingredient"—antibodies, saline, dry nonfat milk—onto the gel apparatus using a pipette, a ballpoint penlike tool that holds liquids and you click the top to dispense the drop as if you were clicking open your pen to sign important documents.

He brought Alda into things early on. I met her the first time, when I flew to Italy and met up with Michele on the annual summer month that he spends at home every year. I arrived in Rome, where Michele's family is from, and Alda, his mother, hugged me in the first three minutes of setting eyes on me. Michele took me on a motorcycle around Rome all night, very fast, and gave me a tour of his city in the dark with the fountains and piazzas and cathedrals and statues high high up of winged horses pulling chariots across the sky made even more luminous and more amazing because of their being lit in golden floods against the orange-scented black night, the oppressive heat of the day diminished, the throngs of summer tourists asleep in their hotels. It was just like that.

I have loved making my way, imperfectly, around a foreign city on my own. I have loved walking endlessly and getting lost and arriving at the museum or restaurant or store I wanted to go to just as it was closing. Missing the point of my excursion has forced me, on so many occasions, to find the secondary smaller points: the old woman sweeping out her front yard and putting water out for the cats, the baker cleaning out his ovens for the afternoon, the two kids refilling their shoe shine boxes with polish and clean rags—all of these small moments found only by wandering down a side street behind whichever museum I have failed to get to during its operating hours, or on the one day of the year it is closed for some local holiday I've never heard of. I have loved the feeling of being pummeled by the intricacies of a city. And also loved the feeling of conquering, in small ways, a city by myself, not speaking the language but eventually finding the right place to get coffee the way I want it, a good dinner, the train station, the bookstore. I have fallen apart on many train station platforms in many foreign cities, alone and unable to figure out why the scheduled train isn't running. And I have been helped, finally, by some kind person who can see what shit I am in and who has a handful of English words to offer. I have made "friends" with the man at the kiosk who sells the *International Herald Tribune* and the street maps in his neighborhood, his city. I have even loved, on a certain level, being the tongue-tied patron in the restaurant who so badly wants to eat what the natives all around me are eating over on their tables but being too afraid or unwilling to ask. I have loved being the woman who studies the menu so hard and tries to decode the language digging deep for her four years of advanced Latin, hoping this is a romance language and that that tedious academic effort will pay off as the mother of all languages must have children I recognize, and that will help me discern, linguistically at least, fish from hamburger. I have loved learning a city the hard way.

But I've got nothing bad to say about being introduced to Rome by an extremely capable Roman in a good silk tie who wants, for whatever unclear reasons, nothing less than my heart. So while we rode around Rome at night, eating at tiny perfect trattorie high up in the no-cars cobbled streets of Trastevere—marinated white anchovies, Parmesan omelette, fried cod with zucchini and almonds and buttered bread—and walked across the bridges and made out in public like I would *never* consent to in New York, his eighty-year-old mother, Alda, stuffed and baked tomatoes, cooked turkey leg with oranges, sent her vegetarian daughter out for the best prosciutto, and laid everything out each day at lunch on the dining room table with linen that had been hand sewn by the convent sisters of the Marcelline order, and with little cruets of her own olive oil from her own olive orchards in Puglia. She squeezed my hands in her arthritic ones with powerful emphasis, while sitting on the terrace trying to stay cool in the late afternoon, for no particular reason, just affection, not in greeting or salutation. And I was hooked; hard and fast. The only words we could say to each other were *Ciao* and *Ciao,* coming and going. I didn't speak *any* Italian.

And Michele took care of me in such a way that I didn't need to.

I arrived just in time for the family's trip south, which they make every year, to spend the hot summer months at the house in Puglia. Cousin Chiara and Giuliano and their daughter go down to their house in May, sometimes even earlier for Easter. Sister Gloria did away with the trip altogether a few years ago and just moved there into her own house, permanently, winter and summer. Brother Giovanni drives down when he can to help with the opening of the main house and readying it for Alda's arrival. Sister Manuela waits for her sixteen-year-old son's finishing of school, before loading up the dog and her stack of books of summer reading and Ando, and maybe one of his teenage friends, before making the eight-hour drive which she usually achieves in something over ten hours as she is a "steady" driver. Brother Carlo, wife Anna, their daughters Agnese and Maria, Anna's sister, Carlo's best friend and workmate Paolone and his girlfriend Angela as well as their cat, make the trip in June and stay, more or less, the entire season. Alda takes the train with her youngest son, Giulio, who at forty still lives at home because he is Italian and this is what Italians do if they haven't married.

On that first long trip, on the motorcycle—when we left Rome early in the morning—Michele brought me a cold apricot juice and a hot coffee as soon as I woke up. He did the difficult work of driving through that relentless, excruciating hot afternoon on the shimmering asphalt of the autostrada while I sat on the back, lost in the cushion of my helmet, enjoying that exquisite feeling of being totally surrendered, relinquished from all of my responsibilities, even for taking care of my own heartbeat. He drove with care and expertise. He drove fast and assertively. I never felt doubtful. I locked my arms around his chest, leaned into the turns as he had instructed me, and for the rest of the journey spent all those hours on the road gazing out at the rolling hills, and remnants of aqueduct, and skinny tall cypress trees, and centuries old stone barns and let my mind wander further and further away from the kitchen, the hot stove, the chronic necessity of meeting payroll, until I had wandered so far away from my life in New York that I began to think of books, and foreign countries, and I had silvery little fantasies in which I had lived my life as a singer in a small choir and not as a cook in a kitchen.

Michele, meanwhile, paid for the gas and had Italian money already in his wallet before I had even woken up to the fact that I was in another country and needed another currency. He had mortadella sandwiches that he had made—with just the right butter-to-meat ratio—in the saddlebags for our roadside snack under a tree. While I took it all in—the phlegmy diesel rattle of the trucks with whom we shared the lanes, also heading south, their beds empty, while across the median, they teemed north in a militarylike procession loaded to the top of their canvas flaps with San Marzano tomatoes. I knew that we had crossed from Campagna into Puglia, that we had definitively reached the south, not by reading a road sign, but by the tiny Fiat we passed packed to the gills with luggage and in the front seat, the man driving with his suntanned arm out the window while his ample wife rode in the passenger seat with her bare feet up on the dash and white cream bleach on her moustache. Both of them were smoking.

When we stopped for gas outside of Bari, Michele phoned ahead and had cold rosé wine waiting for us at the house when we arrived.

His mother had taken the train. She arrived from Rome at the train station in Lecce and was met by Giovanni, her second oldest son. Alda packs very little for herself. She has one old worn leather satchel that has her few housedresses—that uniform of widowed women all over Europe who wear the same simple smock dress every day, and all of those women, every widow in Europe, has one drying on the clothesline under the oleander trees while the other is on her body. Beyond that, Alda packs not much more than a comb and her toothbrush and a few photos of her decades-deceased husband, Tommaso Fuortes, who died in 1970, at fifty-eight years old, from complications due to malaria he'd contracted when he was a kid. The rest of Alda's luggage—an arsenal of crumpled plastic bags leftover from grocery shopping and tied at the neck with twine and rubber bands—are bulging with things she "needs" that she shuffles back and forth between the house in Rome and the house in Leuca: her pressure cooker, some jars of jam, a kind of biscuit that she likes, and the whole set of good silverware, rolled up in chamois sacks and polished for so many years that it looks white more than silver.

Giovanni, with his quiet, patient, and unflappable demeanor, is waiting for her at the station and carries all the bags to the car. She walks faster than he does, in spite of her pronounced limp from her hip surgery, and her eighty years, forty of them spent keeping afloat a family with six children without a husband. Giovanni drives her to the house, and no sooner has she set her handbag down on the soft, almost powdery stone floors, than she is noticing every detail of the condition of it.

She pulls the yellow leaves from a plant and sticks her finger without shyness deep in the soil to check its moisture. She peers into the waist-high green glass canteens of olive oil, props open the creaky door to inventory the storeroom where the plum tomatoes are stacked in crates next to the laundry machine amid the drying heads and necks of garlic and the clean empty bottles for tomato sauce, and by dinner time has already, with Rosaria's help, put fried eggplant and boiled beans and boiled zucchini and giuncata cheese on the table.

The house is truly impressive. When Michele and I pulled up to the gate at the end of the driveway, I just shook my head. Unbelievable. There before us sat a Pompeiian villa, with a large room smack in the center of the house that has no ceiling. It's called an impluvium, meaning where the rain is gathered, and I have often noticed that my son Marco gets as excited about this room as I do when we get to the house every year. What could be more fun, more impractical, more romantic than walking in your pajamas through the room in the center of the house which has no ceiling, and looking up at the sun, sky, stars, or even—as we experienced last year in the middle of the night as we were frantically moving the dinner table and the chairs and the reading lamps—warlike lightning, thunder, and extraordinary wet winds?

Though completely different from the house that I grew up in, I nonetheless also grew up in an impressive house, and so I was immediately comfortable and felt an odd and unexpected familiarity as soon as we arrived. While it is in every respect a true villa, with frescoes and bas relief and tiled mosaic in the entryway and the soft stone floors called "pelle d'uovo," which describes perfectly the feel of the floors on your bare feet—like the "skin of the egg," that thin film of skin that lines the eggshell, I can't help but say "villa" every time out loud with quotation marks around it and as if it had four "Ls." Because it's just so crazy and over the top that this guy with whom I was casually starting an affair would have given me nocturnal, glittery motorcycle tours of Rome and then delivered me to his "villa" in the south where his loving mother had prepared a simple, beautiful meal of mostly vegetables for our arrival. The only way the story could get more enviable is if I embellished and described Michele as tall, with bee-stung lips and a thick head of dark hair. Or if I said that we slept outside by a fire in dew-soaked sleeping bags.

Even though we were in this villa facing the sea, with a wide terrace for watching the sunset, and rooms with twenty-five-foot-high domed ceilings surrounding the room with no ceiling, I was seduced only by the meal Alda had prepared. The dense, almost purple beans I'd never seen before. The fresh bone-white cheese with undeniably herbal flavor. I couldn't wait to cook with her. I wanted to work side by side with her in her kitchen. At first I needed Michele nearby to translate, but very shortly it became obvious that cooking itself was a way of if not exactly speaking, at least a way of being together in a room doing something that felt comfortable and interactive. Like hunting mushrooms on damp opportune mornings with your own mother. We both soon grasped that we had that as a "language," and I could understand everything she was doing and she could understand me, too. And for all of the years since, we have cooked together in place of talking.

That first morning of my first visit to the summer house, I walked into the big open airy kitchen to have coffee and Alda was at the table, already up for hours, shouting into the telephone—only because the phones are weak and because her hearing is going—arranging her affairs for the day. She checked on the bank, the lawyer, the gardener, the wheat, the olive oil, the hairdresser. Shouting in Leccese dialect into the phone the whole time, often the same question over and over, while Michele leisurely showered and shaved meticulously on the other side of the house, she arranged for more oil to arrive, for the trees to be pruned, for a haircut from her favorite girl in the nearby town of Giuliano.

"Twice as good and half as expensive as the girl in Rome!" She laughs, delighted.

A woman arrived on her motorino, a bicycle with a small motor the size of a hairdryer you have to pedal to ignite, and pulled from the handlebar's basket giuncata and mozzarella cheese, still warm, that she had made herself using seawater, though no one could explain if this was from a parsimony—too poor to buy salt—or an aesthetic impulse to create the perfect balance of salination in the cheese using water she collected from the sea each morning.

In the beginning that first year, I felt awkward and tried to feign an appearance of relaxed casualness, as if I were just sipping my morning coffee in the room with this guy's mother with whom I could not share one word in the same language, like it was the most fluid, easily metabolized thing in my entire day. Really, I was hoping for her to stay on the phone. To receive another food-bearing visitor. To make another call quickly, because even the pause between phone conversations was awkward as she sat there at the table with me, both of us unable to make conversation, she squinting heavily at her handwritten phone/address book trying to make the numbers come into focus so she could dial another piece of her business. Me, bluffing my way through a relaxed contemplative morning coffee.

But then she opened the old refrigerator that rarely cooled below fifty degrees and threw a plastic shopping bag in front of me, opening it up and showing me what she had bought early that morning at the market while Michele and I were still in the hand-tatted, lace-trimmed, heavy white linen sheets, barely awake, listening to the Mediterranean breeze flap the flags and cables of the sailboats anchored right out front in the harbor, with a hypnotic thin *clank clank clank,* and the occasional wasp's angry hum of a passing Vespa under our shuttered window. In the bag were half a dozen wild, unruly heads of Italian puntarelle, a kind of bitter dandelion green different in so many ways from our dandelion here. The stalks were hollow and satiny white, and the tops looked like juicy marijuana buds. And suddenly, with this one bag of humble dandelion—*weeds*—she and I started "talking."

I held the puntarelle and looked at her questioningly. It was not like what I had seen and known sold as puntarelle in the States. She started snapping the buds off the tops where they break naturally, exactly like you would do with an asparagus spear that will naturally snap where the wood ends and the succulent part begins. I understood what she was doing and started to do the same with the other heads in front of me until we had cleaned the entire bag. She got up and soaked the puntarelle "buds" in water and then dumped a few cubes of ice in there as well to really crisp it up. I made a very fatty vinaigrette, like I would have for a dandelion salad at home—with both anchovy and pancetta and hard-boiled eggs and lots of garlic, and I fried some bread cubes in her olive oil. And together, wordlessly, we made lunch. I understand only later, years later, that she will do this almost every morning of every summer vacation we take to see her. She will toss me an ingredient she found at that morning's market in Tricase and look at me, expecting me to know what to do with it: a whole fish, an octopus, a piece of hard-to-find meat. Hard-dried land snails, *lumache.* Whole wheat grains. Pickled lily bulbs, *lampascioni,* a rhizome that looks a great deal like pearl onions. She is always doing this. She tosses an ingredient at me and asks what we should do with it. I am honored that she thinks I am familiar with all of these ingredients but even on the few occasions that I am, I am dying to learn what *she* does with them.

The next morning I arrived in my robe for coffee and she and her daughter Manuela were separating the wheat grains at the kitchen table, like two women playing a quiet, thoughtful game of Scrabble might do. The two women sat at the table in their housedresses, Manuela with her eyeglasses down at the end of her nose, a pile of grains in front of each of them, and quietly, speaking only occasionally, they sat there and separated the husks from the grains. I understood the task immediately—I'd done this in Turkey when I was "politely disappearing"—and so took my coffee and joined them. Quietly, I insinuated myself into their silent "conversation" around wheat—now we all three were sharing an experience. It's not dramatic or significant. It's just a way of communicating. But for me it is everything. I'm trying to show them that I am a worker. That I wash dishes. That I can help clean the wheat. That I am not some useless burden of a houseguest. And it stands in amazingly well for language that we just don't have. Manuela reads and writes and speaks English perfectly, but hesitates, and will do so only when my struggle for a word or to communicate an idea becomes too great, and then she bails me out. And this is how I have come to know Alda, my future mother-in-law, for the first weeks, and then subsequent years of my relationship with her son.

And then we went to a family dinner. As if the motorcycle tours and the villa and the incredible mother weren't enough, I met strangers who came up to me and hugged me, who gave me kisses on both cheeks—but real kisses with actual cheek-to-lip contact as if they truly meant it. I met sisters and cousins and wives and best friends who smiled at me as warmly as if I were a cherished daughter. I met old medical school friends of Michele's whose eyes lit up with unmistakable joy and pleasure when meeting me. It was immediately obvious how much these people cared about Michele, and how the Italian idea of hospitality is automatically and unconditionally extended to anyone someone they already love loves. Alberto and Rosie, within twenty minutes of meeting me, said, "We love you as we love Michele." It's from Rosie, years later, that I learned to put a peeled potato in the pasta cooking water for extra starch. Meanwhile, the olive trees swayed in the gentle breeze, and handmade orecchiette were passed around, and the wine flowed, and someone handed me my first sgropino—that lively dessert drink of prosecco and vodka and lemon ice cream which is so named because it describes the sneezelike sound a horse makes when she's shaking the flies from her nostrils. Because it makes you shudder just like that.

And that's just how it felt to be introduced to Michele's family.

At some extra-low point, some years after we were married, Michele and I went to a marriage counselor in New York and we sat down on the couch in her nice office on our first visit and we introduced ourselves. As soon as Michele started speaking, as soon as she heard his voice, the therapist lit up and smiled and said: "Oh. You're Italian! Are you Italian? I LOVE Italians!" And I slouched down on the couch a little—watching the therapist's face aglow with her own memories of orecchiette and sgropino and olive oil—and I thought: *Oh no you don't honey; you love* Italy.

What did I love? The man? The country? I loved folding myself into Michele's family and loved how much time they could all spend together, happily it seemed, without running out of conversation. We could have been with the cousins and sisters and husbands all day at the pool or the beach, gone home for showers, aperitivi and a costume change, but then at eight forty-five, when we have all reconvened around the dinner table at one or another's house or the local restaurant dining al fresco, everybody—everybody—is talking a mile a minute and gesticulating animatedly as if we hadn't just seen each other over the five long, hot languorous afternoon hours in the shade of the umbrella poolside. As if we had just arrived from the airport fifteen minutes before for the first time since last year. At least that is how it appears to me as a non-Italian speaker. It's possible, even likely, that nobody is saying anything but bullshit, but it can feel very satisfying, like a good sneeze, to be enveloped by it.

It was a feeling that I wished would continue year-round but that we—Michele and I—never managed to get a long run on once back in New York. There was something about being in Italy that made it so possible, and I feasted on it in those early years. The scenery was first-rate—a villa by the sea, a constant blue sky, a countryside dotted with white *trulli*. Michele's whole family effortlessly received us exactly as we presented ourselves, and we were never inconvenienced by any reference to or inquiry about how we had managed to pass each year's preceding eleven, often difficult months of our strange and ill-founded marriage, and so it was almost possible to forget them.

When we decided to have Leone, I realized that I no longer wanted to be some girl passing through on the back of Michele's motorcycle, married as a performance art prank. Now I wanted to stay, to be the mother of many children, to be a member of a family, the Fuortes family. And I wanted it year-round, not just for this wonderful but heartbreakingly ephemeral month after which I would not see or speak with or hear from any of the Italians—including Michele, in a way—for the next eleven months. My ambivalent relationship to Michele had not changed with the arrival of Leone, but my attachment to family had. I thought a great deal of that empty house that my parents had left Simon and me alone in, and understood that no matter what disappointment I felt in Michele, I would never, ever, leave.

But for now, at this time, I am still only a guest. A familiar July visitor, who happens to bring with her every time she comes a new baby with the Fuortes surname, but a guest, nonetheless, for just the month in Puglia. And I was wide awake, prepared even, for the fact. I got my shit together. I knew that we would need cash, sandwiches for the trip, cold rosé at the house when we arrived. I arranged for those things myself even. I bought the plane tickets. I rented the station wagon and remembered to ask for a rear-facing infant seat and a forward facing child's booster seat. I knew that the Lire was out and the Euro was in. I got Leone a passport two weeks after he was born and signed it for him, writing *Mother* in parentheses. I took Italian lessons. And as we were packing the leased station wagon for that trip from Rome to Leuca, with our double stroller and our diaper bag filled with diapers in two sizes, and the bottles, and the wipes, I laughed to Michele, "Look at us now, Mr. Motorcycle!"

We arrived in Leuca after dark and, uncharacteristically, a day ahead of Alda. Her train from Rome was scheduled to arrive the following evening. Before we'd left Rome, she pressed the small heavy sack of keys in my hand, the keys to the house in Puglia, and laughed, kindly.

"Now *I'm* the guest!" she said, smiling.

I carefully packed the keys in my bag and felt an uneasy buzz of responsibility the whole eight-hour drive to the south. We passed the same remnants of aqueduct, and the tall skinny cypress trees, and the huge windmills at Tavoliere and the trucks heading north filled with just-harvested tomatoes, but now I was inside an air-conditioned diesel station wagon reading *Green Eggs and Ham* to Marco and nursing Leone the whole time, taking advantage of their naps to eke out any daydreamy thoughts about paths not taken and lives not lived. Still, Michele and I have nothing much to say to each other and the long drive passes almost wordlessly between us.

We drove Michele's customary quick circle of the lighthouse that looks down upon the whole port before continuing to the house on Via Tommaso Fuortes. I fished out the sack of keys and opened the tall, heavy door, and Michele put all of our things inside, piling up our luggage in the center of the impluvium. Marco said, in two-year-old talk, "Hey! Where's the ceiling?" And we laughed. I turned on the lights in the kitchen and in the storeroom off the kitchen and checked to see what there was: tomatoes, oil, garlic, melon, eggplant. Exactly as it was every year. Rosaria had been there earlier and kindly left us a meal under dish towels in the cabinet, per Alda's phoned-ahead instructions, surely. Michele opened his suitcases and within five minutes exploded like a dandelion gone to seed, his shit floating all over the house and landing wherever it may, wherever he drops it. His eyeglasses, shoes, wallet, keys, camera, a glass of iced tea with a sticky ring left on the desk next to the computer, his cell phone, his newspapers and magazines all over the kitchen table. I got in bed and nursed Leone to sleep and heard Michele in the next room with Marco, having a bedtime story.

"Owa doze ay dinosaurrrrrr saya good night?" And I fell asleep at "Doze ee thrrrrow eez teddee barrrre," noticing how impossibly thick his already thick accent gets as soon as we get to Italy every year.

I rose early the following morning, quickly dressed, and went out on my own, with Leone, just three months old, strapped into the pouch. I stopped for an espresso and a cold apricot juice at the nearby bar on my way up to the market in the square. I used my accumulated Italian gathered during these now half-dozen consecutive years of summer visits, and I had money in the right currency in my wallet gotten from the local ATM machine.

In the square, I found my ideal kind of man. Missing most of his teeth, with his zipper gaping open, he was selling zucchini blossoms under the shade of a large tree. Guys like this are getting hard to come by anymore, even here in this little Italian town. He pulled back the burlap that covered the wagon of his three-wheeled motor cart and showed me, with shaking arthritic hands, his fresh black-eyed peas in the shell, his dark purple green beans, his zucchini flowers. He had a little crate of imperfect prune plums and small dark green watermelons no bigger than a regulation softball. I take some of everything he's got. I know that when he dies he's the last, and this—this—the pants held up with a piece of twine, his work shoes dusty and curling up at the toes, and the simple way he has tossed his wares into the bed of the wagon next to the jug of gasoline and the coil of thin rope and the cracked plastic pails, covering them with a light sheet of burlap—a grain sack split open to make a sheet—this all goes when he goes.

When I asked him how much for the zucchini flowers he said, "One euro the handful" and began filling a crumpled up recycled plastic bag that he dug out of the front seat of his little *ape,* the three-wheeled motor scooter made by the same company that invented the Vespa. Called the ape—bee—because it makes that noise with its fifty cubic centimeter lawnmower engine. He ended up giving me handfuls as big as we would call armfuls of the bright yellow-orange blossoms with powdery dark amber centers.

There are no more donkeys with wooden saddles, no more community ovens where all the women in the village bring their breads and casseroles, no more tinkling of goat bells in the oregano-scented breeze from a small herd and their herder coming down the mountain—him carrying a tall stick and smoking a filterless cigarette, looking like he's in his eighties. They are all but gone, these kinds of people who make and grow food. Here in this average daily market that sets up each morning in the square next to the bocce courts and the permanent butcher and fish monger, my *vecchio* boyfriend here with his fly gaping open and his posture bent in half is unique. His companions are here in state-of-the-art mobile stalls—clean, electrified dromedaries that carry their own source of running water. Traveling stores whose windows pop open on the sides and "eccola!" there you are having your cured meats sliced on the spot, imported from Germany, or even if imported from Emiglia-Romana it's all the same because we are not in Emiglia-Romana, we are in Puglia. There is smoked scamorza and bread from the hard durum wheat, salted capers in three sizes from the size of a lentil to the size of a fat green English pea. And there are big bouquets of dried oregano, alongside vats of brined things, mostly olives. But the vendors themselves are intermediaries, just merchants. The produce guy wears a T-shirt emblazoned with a currently hip rock band and a huge pair of counterfeit Gucci sunglasses with white, diamond-crusted frames. His teeth are gleaming, his ass is packed into his stonewashed jeans. His hands are clean. He didn't grow it, pick it, water it, or even pack it.

It's the toothless vecchio who makes my pants pound, not Alfonso over here with the hair gel. He has his American counterparts, Mr. Gucci sunglasses does. The "chicks" and "dudes" who drove me from the farmer's market years ago. I love the vegetables but I can't go near the place. There's always the girl with the bicycle, wandering along from stall to stall with two apples, a bouquet of lavender, and one bell pepper in the basket of her bicycle. A teeming throng of New Yorkers tries to push past her to get to the vegetables for sale, but she shifts her ass from side to side, admiring the way her purchases are artfully arranged for all to see in the basket of her bike, and she holds up the whole process. And I struggle, as well, with the self-referential new kind of farmer, aglow with his own righteousness, setting up his cute booth at the market each morning, with a bouquet of wildflowers and a few artfully stacked boxes of honeycomb and a fifteen-dollar jar of bee pollen. And from what I've seen, that guy behind the table, with his checkered tablecloth and his boutique line of pickled artichoke hearts in their jar with their prissy label packed just so, he *wants* to talk to Miss Bicycle, to Miss I've-spent-four-hours-here-this-morning-to-buy-these-three-cucumbers. He gets off on it. I stopped going to the farmer's market years ago when some hipster chick in sparkly barrettes and perfectly styled "farmer" clothes came screeching at me "DON'T TOUCH THE PEAS!" After that, we just ordered directly from the farm and had it delivered to the restaurant. Of course, I'm in love with the toothless guy with the gaping trousers. He's everything I grew up with, he's the end of an era, he's the last of what it was like to just be a good eater and a good grower. A time when we just grew it and cooked it and ate it and didn't talk so much about it. When we didn't crow all over town about our artisanal, local, organic fwa fwa. We just went to the farm and bought the milk. I bought everything I could from that old guy.

There was a dinner party planned, at the Masseria, where the whole summer congregation of family would assemble, and I realized I could put everything—puntarelle, beans, black-eyed peas, all of it—to use for that meal. None of it would be wasted.

At these incredible family dinners, there can be up to forty-six immediate cousins, uncles and brothers, aunts, wives, and kids. Everybody brings a dish and usually the host supplies the wine. I've tried ardently to get Michele to agree to host one over the years, and every time we start to do the count—what about cousin Mercedes? And Beppe? And don't forget Massimo and Antonella!—he falls apart when we get into the high forties and in danger of breaking the fifty mark. "Massimo and Antonella are friends not family," he'll argue, vainly trying to get the numbers down, knowing full well without my even having to say it in my impatient and frustrated tone, that they are as close and cherished as any cousin or blood relative.

The Italians even have a way of counting that works perfectly for these kinds of family dinners that I wish we had in English. If you ask how many we are expecting for dinner this evening, they'll answer "un trentina"—a little thirty—or "una quarantina"—a little forty. It's like saying "roughly twenty," so we know that we can expect anywhere from thirty-five to forty-five when someone answers "una quarantina." I want this vague yet perfectly precise way of counting in so many contexts of my life. I always want to say everything was twenty years ago. Or you cook it for twenty minutes. Or I've been a cook for twenty years. Or I haven't spoken to my mother in twenty years. But exactly twenty? Not for an Italian minute. Exactly a "ventina."

I am built for this kind of dinner party. It's in my blood—all those childhood lamb roasts for hundreds. It's in my bones—those decades of catering sit-down dinners for 1,500, 250, 900. I really ache to host one, a real one, where no one has to "bring a dish." It's possible that everybody, just like that marriage counselor, thinks that everything, once translated into Italian, is just simply better, even a potluck dinner. And, in some ways it is. The food at an Italian potluck is probably a little better than the food at an average American potluck. But there are no two more heartbreaking, soul-deadening words to me in any language than "pot" and "luck" put together. The idea of seven variations on a lentil salad and one bottle of lemon-lime seltzer sinks me. And even the one guest who was thoughtful enough to prepare something expensive and complex and warm—like curried shrimp— even that person has no idea how to cook for a potluck, and so eighteen people stand around the little quart container of the only dish that has any protein and any flavor and try to get a tablespoonful before it's all gone.

I dream, with fervor, all summer long of putting that villa to work. I secretly write menus in my journal that I would prepare if I was allowed to have a party there. And then I even write out the prep lists, the equipment and ingredient lists. I draw little sketches on paper towels. I lie awake in bed at night in a mosquito coil haze visualizing the dinners I would host there—the concrete order *and* the watercolor image—the way I would bring that house to life. How I would rake the property of all the dead oleander leaves that have fallen, and trim back the trees themselves so that fifty guests could stand on the terrace and actually see, and not just hear, all the boats anchored right there in the harbor with their twinkly little lights winking, and the shimmering rings of gold that surround each boat in the black night-time sea it floats in. I long to put a perfect crimson negroni with a half moon of orange into the hand of each and every one of those cinquantina. Wondering if it might not go totally unnoticed that the color of the aperitivo echoes, ever so subtly, the color of the sunset.

I long to clean out the broken bicycles and abandoned bedsprings and sagging towers of twine-bound mildewed newspapers and women's magazines that now clutter the "summer kitchen"—that warren of outrageously handsome whitewashed cool rooms under-neath the house where meals used to be prepared in the summer months to avoid the punishing heat. I wish I could store all the toma-toes, figs, melons, and eggplants down there, and hang some home-made sausages from the rafters, and tie some bunches of the wild garlic to dry from the big rings that still remain from where people used to tie their horses so many lifetimes ago. I wish I could pull out every piece of Alda's old Salentino pottery and wash it and use it and rescue it from its dark hibernation in the heavy wooden credenza. I want to wash all of her charming old crystal glasses and drink from them, instead of admiring them every year as I do, shuttered up in their beveled-glass cabinet. I want to throw away the harsh lamp with the over-bright bare bulb in the impluvium that Giovanni has been repairing for thirty years with more and more, and then more, black electrician's tape and let the open sky above us have less to compete with. I want to gather all the trim from the olive trees and burn an im-mense fire outside over whose coals I would grill forty whole fish stuffed with wild fennel fronds picked from the surrounding fields. And dress those fish with the olive oil from the olives of the branches that fueled the fire. And I want to set out lanterns all over the prop-erty, so that people could wander after dinner. I want to replace the ripped and sagging hammock with a fresh, softly woven one in which people could canoodle if the negroni and the grilled fish and the fresh figs happened to inspire them to want to go lie in a hammock and get tangled up in the soft arms of their *amore*.

But as soon as I start to paint that little picture for Michele, before I've even dipped my brush into the can of scenic paint even, all I have to say is, "Could we please host one of the dinners this year?" and Michele gets his black dark face, his pinched eyes, his wrinkled forehead like I've just told him he has incurable blood cancer instead of that I want to feed people delicious food and pour delicious wine and fry dozens of the local eggs in brown butter and sit outside all summer night long and have utter pleasure. Every year he tells me it would be too much for his mother. And that is the conversation ender, every time. If there's anyone I totally respect and don't want to burden or tax or upset in any way; it's Donna Alda, Nonna to my kids, suocera mia, Senora Alda Fuortes de Nitto.

But even when I swear to Michele that I will do all the work myself, or get help from Chiara and Giuliano—who have been known to shove sausages they've made up their own chimney to air dry and who, I am sure, would help me host a big dinner out in *gli olivi or sta villa Fuortes*—he doesn't yield. On a small excursion in his wooden boat, cousin Giuliano once packed in a small woven chest the twice-baked hard biscuits of the region, a few tomatoes, some chili flakes, and a few basil leaves from their garden. And Chiara taught me to hold the biscuit over the edge of the boat and soak it in the seawater for one "Ave Maria" to soften and season it slightly. And then onto the biscuit we put the tomato, warm from the sun, and the leaves of basil and ate an impromptu lunch with vaguely cold beers right there in our bathing suits. They would certainly help me with a party, I am sure of it. Michele stands between me and everything he has introduced me to, everything I now want, all of it sprawled out in plain delectable view just behind him. All of it unattainable without him, and oddly, impossible with him. He Will. Not. Budge. We will not be hosting a dinner party.

"What about a nice Sunday lunch?" I suggested one year, thinking that if I switched up the hour of the day I would sneak one past him. But I believe he knows exactly what to say no to to be sure he is breaking the very heart that has never quite convincingly felt him all these years. He's nothing if not smart, Mr. M.D./Ph.D. Without him, I don't get the family. Without the party, without the building of the fire, the lighting of the candles, the rushed and hectic preparation all day of the food, without the *hiss hiss hiss* of the blood hitting hot coals, I will never find consolation.

Alda arrived in Lecce the following evening and was retrieved from the train station by Gloria, her third oldest child. Gloria is a radiant beauty who dresses in flowing colorful fabrics and long dangly jewelry and kind of floats through the house with a perpetual beatific smile on her lips and a bemused twinkle in her eye. Gloria seems unburdened, happy, and physically healthy. She is quick to light up with laughter, and while I have never once seen the family "darkness" shadow her eyes, turning them black and impenetrable as I have seen in the other siblings and even in Alda, she does kind of fabulously wilt in the heat and dramatically heads off for "rests" and afternoon repose like Blanche DuBois. She arrived with Alda and helped her into the house. Alda immediately, even at eight o'clock at night, went from room to room—the clack of her heel on the floor from her uneven gait from the hip surgery and her staccato little exhale echoing in the twenty-five-foot ceilings in all of the rooms as she passed through them—checking on the olive oil, the tomatoes, the potted plants, the bedding. Gloria cooed at the babies and her pleasure in seeing them permeated the house. Yet another Italian woman perfect with children. Alda pressed a large tray of homemade biscotti wrapped in paper on to Gloria to take with her back to her house and a disproportionately wild frenzy ensued, in part I understand, because Italians do it this way—even the most simple transactions have to become wildly gesticulated and vociferously argued. And in this family particularly so. How many cookies should Gloria take with her?! Not all of the cookies, Mamma!! Take the cookies, amore mio!! Gesticulations! Raised voices! Overlapping shouting!

The decision? *Leave us a few and take the rest.* We all at last said good night and amid much Italian gesticulating and urgent tones, confirmed that we would all reconvene the next evening at the Masseria for a family dinner with everybody.

It's true, when we had the family dinner at the Masseria that year—the renovated farmhouse in the olive orchards where Carlo lives in the summer with his family—Alda did run out of steam—sort of validating Michele's resistance to a party of our own—but honestly, not until the very end of the race and not more than a yard short, frankly. And certainly, it had been my fault.

Alda, rising early the next morning, before the heat of the day had taken its rank, had cooked all morning with Rosaria, and when she had finished her mozzarella pizza and her eggplant parmigiana with hard-boiled eggs, she went to take her little late-morning nap. With the kitchen now free, I started prepping the treasures from my old farmer man.

Nursing an infant, in the first few months, really sucks up the day. I never get over and am always totally taken aback by the amount of time in a day it takes to nurse a baby. When you are all and solely what they eat in the beginning of their lives, which I am in the habit of being for about the first year—Marco a little longer, Leone a little less—it could be, if you were a less driven and energetic person than myself, about the only thing you accomplished in a day. Certainly in a vacation day. But I imagine the total sensory pleasure for the kid— to pass out at the tap, belly full of that rich, sweet good stuff, and then he is in a little incomparable sleep coma with his cheeks still smashed up against the warm boob firmly and securely held in the arms of his mother—and so I tend to give my kids their twenty minutes of nursing and then their twenty minutes of post-hookup nap, undisturbed, in the very position they fell into it in, regardless of my own discomfort, arm cramps or list of shit to do that day. If you do the math of that, in pure forty-minute increments, factoring that an infant needs to be fed every couple of hours . . . well, an eight-hour day can really fly by, and what I used to accomplish in that time gets reduced to a maddening fraction. A whisper more than zilch.

And on this day I aimed to cook four separate dishes—the puntarelle, the Leccese beans, the black-eyed peas, the zucchini flowers—each to feed twenty-five people. I cooked all day, all after-noon, in between lunch and siesta, after siesta, even during the siesta in that still, empty, depressing part of the day when everything is closed and no one is outdoors and the houses are shuttered, and I cooked in between a half-dozen nursing bouts with Leone until I was still assembling the platters at the last minute, right up until we were leaving for the party at eight o'clock that night.

Alda, in spite of doing her own cooking for the party in the early morning, had helped me all day. After her nap, she sat at that kitchen table, trooping through with me, corroborating my ambition. She cleaned the puntarelle, shelled the black-eyed peas, tipped the green beans. She'd held the fussy baby, entertained Marco, made me a coffee!—as if I were a guest!—and I'd had this feeling all day that we were working together toward the very same end, that my mother-in-law and I were busily and mutually engaged in our goal: generating enough delicious food for our contribution to the large dinner party we would be going to later that evening, where we would finally sit in the cool comfort of the olive trees, drinking excellent wine, watch-ing the kids run around, being enveloped by the comforting din of Italian bullshit.

Michele—and I live for this kind of old-world genius—took a stack of large clean dish towels out of the drawer and opened each one, set a finished platter on it, and then by drawing the four corners of the towel in and knotting them he created a built-in carrying han-dle and a way of keeping the food wrapped to carry it to the car. No Saran, no foil, no Tupperware. Beautiful Salentino pottery wrapped in heavy, clean dish towels. This is one of those old-world anachronisms, like when your mother would hard-boil eggs in the morning and pop them in your coat pockets, piping hot, to keep your hands warm on winter mornings as you walked to school, and then you had part of your lunch ready in your pocket when they cooled by midday—that retains such beauty and efficiency and clever simple invention that you never let it go, even with the advent of plastic cling wrap and the microwave oven.

While Michele—with cute "help" from two-year-old Marco—

carried the many platters to the car and packed them neatly and snug in the trunk, I rinsed off, combed my hair, and put on my dress. As I was hastily heading through the house to get to where everyone was waiting in the driveway, turning off the lights in some of the rooms on my way, looking up at the purplish- and pink-streaked evening sky as I crossed through the impluvium, I saw the light on in the clean empty kitchen. I breezed to the doorway and reached in to turn off the light and there sat Alda, in her nightgown, at the kitchen table under the harsh light, eating a bowl of cold cereal with milk for dinner.

An unspeakable sadness overwhelmed me. I felt inexplicably abandoned. I ran to get Michele. *Alda's in the kitchen, in her nightgown, pouring a bowl of cold cereal.*

"Your mom's not coming?" I asked Michele, my eyes stinging. "What the fuck?"

I couldn't help welling up and needing to look away. Michele came inside with me and we went to see his mother, sitting happily and peacefully in the kitchen with her cereal.

"Che c'è?" Michele asked, and his mom rattled on in cheerful, but exhausted, tones.

Michele turned to me. "It's too much for her. She doesn't want to go—all those people." At this I laughed out loud, as if "all those people" were some large group of tedious work colleagues from some other floor or department in your company, and not her own sons and daughters and grandchildren.

And Alda reiterated, confirmed, from her chair, "E troppo per me. Troppo, Gabrielle. Vai. Vai—amore mio, divertiti." *Go. Go. Have fun. It's too much for me.*

Suddenly I saw that she had aged. Alda was getting to be old, old like a grandmother, exhausted at the end of a day, ready to sleep alone, in the lumpy comfort of her horsehair bed, surrounded by her heavy old furniture. It's got to be something, that kind of tired, where you are not simply tired from that day, but an accumulated fatigue from the past 29,000 days. Where even the dinner meal with a crowd seems like too much, and just a cold bowl of cereal at the kitchen table alone is what you can or are willing to muster. In the time it takes to switch off a kitchen light and notice a figure at the table, I saw that I was going to lose her, sooner than later.

During the hottest hour of that day, while Leone slept and Marco went to the pool with Michele, I had sat with Alda, wordlessly shelling the black-eyed peas that I'd bought from the hundred-year-old farmer. They were so tender and young that their "black eyes" were actually pinkish purple and their bodies were still the palest green, not yet dried into a chalky, withered, tea-stained white. Some were as small as grains of Arborio rice. They reminded me of that amusement park memento where they paint your full name in black ink on a grain of rice and then put it in a tiny glass bottle of mineral oil and string it onto a necklace. We split the pods open with our thumbnails and slid each pea out into a colander set in between us. What I have loved about cooking my entire life, especially prep cooking, is the way that it keeps your hands occupied but your mind free to sort everything out. I have never once finished an eight-hour prep shift without something from my life—mundane or profound—sorted out. A new way to organize the walk-in. An opening and closing line for an essay. A way to prepare the zucchini. A likely reason I came to long for my green card marriage to an Italian man eleven years my senior to become something other, deeper than a piece of performance art, and why it never quite became that thing.

Not two handfuls into the black-eyed peas, it started. *What am I still doing here this many years later? What am I still doing in this marriage with someone I don't know and who doesn't know me? This was all so intoxicating my first year. The simply boiled vegetables, the meatlike eggplant parmigiana so charming that I wrote an essay about it for the* New York Times *my third year. And now this, my fifth year? My sixth?*

Oh yes, I remember, it's only our fifth visit, but it's our sixth year fooling around. There was a year when we were fighting excessively. And Michele canceled the trip after I'd already bought the tickets because he didn't want to "subject his family" to our domestic frost. I said, "Really? You think the family won't be able to handle our garden-variety marital shit? Can't we just do one of the very few things we do well together and take the lousy trip to Italy this summer?"

"No."

And that's how we've been here together only five, and not six, times.

I am sure he was right. We would have fought and I am prone to fighting big and cathartic. The marriage counselors in their tidy offices tried to teach us the therapeutic tune of the moment, a horrible song of constant restraint in which you may speak only of your own feelings—which I experienced as having a constantly full bladder but never being allowed to let it out, but for a tablespoon at a time—with nil relief. We tried it, the concessions, the conscientiously held tongues, the supposedly edifying reiteration of those catch-phrases that all ill-suited couples resort to, mantralike: Marriage is *hard work*. Marriage is a *compromise*. But I like to break the furniture, throttle the bastard's neck, hurl epithets across the room and narrate the exaggerated story with myself as the innocent. All of which I will cheerfully apologize for in the morning, but not until I have drained all the poisons, every last drop. In hindsight, I can see how it's good that we skipped that year's annual July visit. Michele, by contrast, was raised to see anger as vulgar and unintelligent, so his, unexpressed, steadily seeped into our life like lead leeching into the public drinking water, which, I've heard, is what brought down Rome.

I have no way, it occurs to me looking over at Alda while we shell peas, to canvass her to know how she would have felt if we'd come anyway, in spite of our marital discord. Over the years, I've picked up some Italian, but with her it doesn't work. To her I remain incomprehensible. Michele says that he thinks the reason I have become relatively able to communicate with almost everyone else over the years but not with her is that she has become more and more deaf. So just as I've become vaguely conversational, she's tuned me out. But I sense from the way she is about everything—so extremely patient, so good-natured, the way she addresses all of her children as "amore mio" when they enter the room or call on the telephone—that she would be able to metabolize anything we would have brought with us, no matter how flulike.

We shell the rest of the peas and start tipping the beans. Alda offers me something to eat from a platter of something unidentifiable she's had stowed away for two full July days in the dish cabinet. I was seduced that first year by her boiled vegetables. And totally enamored with her dish cabinet with corks and espresso plates and leftover fried eggplant all jumbled in with the mosquito coils and the bottle caps and the fifteen-year-old dried dead herbs in jars.

But as she's proferring that plate of something I believe to be fried béchamel that has sat, uncovered, next to and on top of the mismatched espresso cups, the bags of dried pasta, among the moth-infested polenta meal, and the jars full of soda bottle screw caps. I start to unravel a bit, without letting on. A little spider of disappointment crawls down my back as she's handing me the plate of undercooked béchamel still tasting of raw flour, rolled in bread crumbs and fried. It's her great-grandmother's recipe. *But I need a meal, a full meal, a hot meal. I need fresh food that hasn't sat in the propane oven and then in the dish cabinet all day. I need a steak. I need something I can't name. I need to take all of the shit off this table—this beautiful old granite-topped table—and put it where it belongs. I need to be a wicked American, a total Italian failure and put the ironing in the laundry room and the cookies in the cookie tin and the scrap paper in the scrap paper drawer and the diaper cream in the diaper bag and the keys in her key pouch in her purse and the batteries for the camera into the camera so that here on the kitchen table we can just shell black-eyed peas.*

"No, grazie," I say, and continue tipping the beans. She returns the béchamel balls to the cabinet for day three.

Of course it's not her; she still holds my hand sometimes and cuts open sea urchins for lunch and fills my suitcase with linens and silver for the children as we pack to leave each year. Of course it's Michele. He would never break a chair, but we will never throw a dinner party together in Leuca, I am sure of it. Over the years, he has never once raised his voice to me; rather, he has quietly and steadily, item by item, withheld the glitter, the motorcycle rides, the silk tie, the sandwiches, the spinning classes back-to-back, the sunset negronis, the cold apricot juice and hot coffee in the mornings, and now, like that long ago plate of courtship ravioli, I am left with the inedible contents of those gorgeous little packets. Undernourished.

I should have known from those ravioli. Those many years ago when he was so heavily courting me, and he painstakingly made those ravioli, and presented them on a paper tray—so tender and translucent and beautiful. When we cooked them for family meal at the restaurant the next day, we took special care to use a slotted spoon to remove them from the water and we browned a little butter with a few leaves of rubbed sage and we all took our first bites and had to spit them out immediately they were so inedibly salty. Michele had failed to blanche the pancetta and additionally had overseasoned the ravioli filling and so those several dozen handmade gorgeous little beauties, which looked so enticing and appealing from the outside, went to waste as we opened them up and took out the filling and ate only the few bites we could salvage of the empty pasta alone with the butter and sage. *I should have paid attention to that.*

19

O N A SUNDAY AT THE BROOKLYN CHILDREN'S MUSEUM I STARTED to get hungry, just as Marco was beginning to fully appreciate the twelve types of drums that he was allowed and encouraged to bang on with different mallets and sticks. I said to Michele, who was holding Leone, now eight months old, "We'd better start to make our move. I'm going to need to eat soon."

People who know me well understand fully what I am saying when I suggest that I am working an appetite and that we'd best be making our move. This means it is time to hit the road before my blood sugar—what's left of it—crashes to that point where I'm going to *ruin your fucking day*. My friends dive into their pockets, backpacks, and purses and proffer any peanut, energy bar, lint-covered M&M that they can lay their paws on, because friends are great like that. They can see what's happening, from where they are standing, before you can. Even though I'd done a decent job of recognizing my hunger signs at their earliest appearance and duly notified the family that it would now be a good time to start "making our move," making our move from the African Drum Room to the Volvo station wagon with the stroller, the umbrella, the boots, the coats retrieved from coat check, the bathroom pit stop, and two small children still in diapers buckled into their safety seats doesn't happen as fast as my appetite comes on.

But once they were all buckled in and I had the forest green wagon in reverse out of our parking spot, I had a burst of ambition. "Hey, Michele," I asked, "wanna try for a real lunch? Like, with wine and silverware? Like, in a restaurant?" Like we used to do, which I didn't say out loud.

Michele looks at me for just the few seconds he needs to assess where I am in the hunger scheme of things—like a tree scientist who can tell exactly how old a redwood or an Adirondack spruce is by the rings in its flesh—and he takes a look at both kids, estimating them both close to falling into a nap, and says, "Sure."

We were still well out of the extreme danger zone. Chris Grill, the friendliest man on the planet who was Prune's daytime sous chef for five solid years, knew the danger zone at every shade of yellow, orange, burnt umber, and into full Code Red, and he would gently suggest a peanut butter sandwich just from reading my tone at a kitchen meeting.

But we're still out of the danger zone, comfortably in a pale yellow mood and I'm driving, feeling a-okay. I catch Michele in the rearview mirror and say, "Hey, a real lunch. With wine and stuff. This sounds awesome!"

You know, we don't do this kind of thing anymore. We have become, to each other, all parents all the time. We eat plain buttered pasta at dinner every night, and even that we don't eat together, because the way we have worked out our childcare and career schedule requires that one or the other of us is home alone with the kids while the other is enjoying his or her "late" night at work. We sleep in separate beds in separate rooms, each with a kid or more usually, me with two kids, him snoring alone for the few hours before his alarm goes off while its still dark, when he has to get up in order to get to and teach his eight a.m. lecture on the liver or the nervous system or the structure of the cell. We look at each other as units of labor to be bartered, traded, and assigned. *If you take Wednesday night I can work that private dinner party, but then I'll take Thursday night so you can go to that lab meeting, but Sunday I need to check on brunch for a few hours, okay?*

We are not really in these days seeing in each other much of a lunch partner. More like a relay race partner. This is kind of a tragedy, since there are only a few things we really have in common—food, an exorbitant love of and attachment to his mother, and the thing Italians I think are kind of known for—the luscious business—which we no longer very often have the energy or the inclination to seek out in each other. We still call Nonna on Saturdays. But aside from that, all the good stuff—the wine, the food, the deed—the stuff that cushions you against the central loneliness—has been triaged to the urgent and utterly consuming demands of parenting two children under the age of three while maintaining full-fledged careers.

So, in some burst of energy, for me to suggest an actual lunch, braved with two children, gets us both . . . excited. But it's about three in the afternoon on a Sunday in the dead of winter and we are deep in Brooklyn. Not the section of Brooklyn where white people push strollers around, but deep in the section of Brooklyn where we now live, Bed-Stuy, where there is no such casual Italian place where we could have a late three p.m. lunch with wine and cutlery and a tablecloth. Or if there is, we have not yet found it. Michele and I had just a few months earlier, upon our return from our Italian vacation, begun the experiment of living together, which we had, in spite of our seven years, two children, and a City Hall wedding, never done. But the kind of space we thought we would need, if we wanted the experiment to stand a chance, was only to be found—in a comfortably impermanent two-year sublet—far out in a section of Brooklyn that, while it had 3000-square-foot homes with generous backyards and many shuttable doors, did not have any restaurants. We could have gotten some excellent curried goat probably or some not excellent fried chicken for sure—there was a Bojangle's or Popeye's on every corner—but we didn't really know our way around yet and besides, I wanted old times, nostalgia, our past. A tablecloth.

I started to drive not knowing where I was heading, and at first the excitement and good cheer kept my hunger at bay; I knew something good, real, and adult was coming. I could wait.

But there immediately appeared some signs of resistance to our

brilliant European lunch idea. Every place I called on my cell phone
in every neighborhood in Brooklyn where I could think of a place at
which I wanted to eat all said the same thing: *Not open until six p.m. for
dinner service.* I called a little-known decent neighborhood place called
Locanda Vini e Olio in Fort Greene and the excellent Al di Là in Park
Slope and was turned away, so I then even called Peter Luger, the famous steakhouse in Williamsburg, reasoning that I would happily sink
into a burger and a gin martini, even if it was not exactly the broccoli
rabe with pepperoncini and braised rabbit that I was craving. A burger
would work. But the woman who answered just laughed me off the
phone—*No chance of a burger, honey!* I start to get a little orange and
less yellow; not yet red, no, but still, one ring closer to the danger zone.
Michele's got me in the rearview mirror, keeping an eye on me the
way you might keep yourself aware of where the scorpion is in your
room when you check into the hacienda you booked in Tijuana. You
are game for an adventure, but best to know where the scorpion is at
all times.

Now we are heading toward the Slope and looking for Mary's
Fish Camp—I've decided I will, at this point, happily sink into an ex-
cellent lobster roll and a beer at a counter with plain paper table mats.
I make the call and they also won't reopen until six p.m. for dinner
service. Brunch until three. Dinner at six, said the outgoing message.
So now it's done. I am tanked.

And just at that moment, Leone started to cry his pitiful not-so-
little falling asleep cry. I have never understood the heartless Ferber
people who let their kids "cry it out." If you are inclined to view
your three-month-old infant's cries as "manipulative," as a means of
discovering if she can get you to come into the room and pick her
up "on command," then you should rethink parenthood in the first
place. I don't think you are mature enough, frankly. An infant, to be
sure, can't haul herself downstairs and help herself to a glass of water,
can't call upon a good friend at two in the morning to discuss the
finer points of her fears and anxieties. I feel compelled—involuntarily
compelled—to pick up and try to comfort my child when I hear
him wailing. My hormones shake like a passing tank when I hear

children—children on an airplane not even my own—wailing in distress. I long to just pick them up and comfort the little guys. After all, they are crying. I'm going to assume they are crying for a good reason—even if it's just an infant's run-of-the-mill: *Pick me up and hold me because I'm afraid of falling asleep because sleep is like death.* For me, that is a good enough reason to pick up and hold my kid, so that he may feel—at a minimum—accompanied to his perceived death by someone who gives a shit.

Michele doesn't feel as I do, unfortunately. So there I am, stuck in the driver's seat driving, cell-phoning, and having a blood sugar crisis while my eight-month-old expresses his perfectly good reasons for wanting comfort to his totally unpersuaded father, who is able, some-how, to sit through the tears completely nonplussed, while giving me friendly suggestions about some $8.99 brunch place he used to eat at with his old girlfriend twenty years ago. "And you get a frrrree mi-mosa," he tells me from the backseat.

Meanwhile, I don't eat $8.99 brunch with a free mimosa. I have rules. Standards.

I do not get vague or generic appetite, which will be satisfied, more or less, with just anything that is handy. I will skip a meal rather than eat the corner joint's interpretation of eggs Benedict with spinach, button mushrooms, and "blood orange" hollandaise sauce. I don't eat that kind of shit. Michele, from the backseat, kept saying, "I rrrreeeeemember a place, verrrrry good brrrrunch, up here on the left." But when we approach and I see the chalkboard on the sidewalk advertising free mimosa, I speed up and drive on.

Free mimosa is the kind of signal I rely on to stay away from a place. Why is the mimosa free? What is wrong with a place that it needs to provide the customer with an incentive to eat the food? On the other hand, things are now kind of urgent and a mimosa would really soothe and refresh. I'm saying things I don't mean, that I will later regret, and that Marco is sure to repeat as soon as he can think up a way to work them into a sentence. I'm saying things like: *Maybe if I just order poached eggs and toast it won't be so bad up here at The Red Po-tato Bistro.*

Four o'clock or so is a diner's wasteland. Nothing's open, it's between services, and those few places that do stay open continuously go through shift change so you spend countless minutes being ignored while the bartender restocks his wine for the evening service and a busboy resets tables and you can hear a dishwasher on the intercom in the kitchen yelling down to the cooks: Here is a ticket! Here is a ticket! But this is my favorite time of day to eat, to eat well, to eat long luxurious meals with high-end wines. I have eaten staff meal in restaurants at odd hours my whole life and now I am geared to have my main meal at four-thirty. It's the new eight-thirty as far as I'm concerned. Every week or so an outraged woman or somebody's grim personal assistant trying to get an eight-thirty reservation at Prune scoffs at our offer of six p.m., which we more generally have available, saying: *Who eats at six o'clock? Amateurs! Amateurs eat at six!*

It may be amateur, but a restaurant at an early hour is my kind of joint. Maybe especially with Michele, as we were always just leaving the beach around then and we would ride the motorcycle to Astoria and have a late lunch of grilled fish, octopus, skordalia, and a bottle of retsina. Or at four o'clock, we were scratching at the door of Bar Veloce for two sweet salami tramezzini and two hot speck panini and a bottle of gruner veltliner. After, there was still time for an eight o'clock movie. This was all during courtship, though, and I think my attachment to a four o'clock lunch is about clinging to a past, a deep nostalgia for a time when we rode motorcycles, drank negronis, and smoked cigarettes.

But here we are in a Volvo station wagon fitted with not one but two child seats, the motorcycles long ago sold or stolen, and our responsibilities commensurately graver than they've ever previously been. I have worked very late the previous night and didn't get home until three in the morning. I was awoken by the littler one, Leone, at seven-thirty, a mere four hours after I had put my head down on the pillow. I've had coffee but no breakfast, and now we are in trouble. Code Red. Michele—who eats indiscriminately and in his good-natured Italian way thinks everything is "nice" and "good"—tries to get me to pull over and park and go to one of the pretentious restaurants on Smith Street, that minor-league stretch of Brooklyn that always disappoints—and I just can't. I would rather starve and kill my children—Medea-like—than eat the truffle oil omelette with chorizo "foam" and piquillo peppers at Soleil or Blue Bird or whatever those restaurants are called on that stretch. And that's where we find ourselves, at that particular impasse—Michele trying to get me fed and me putting my foot down, with two whining children in the backseat. I am shouting shit into the backseat of the wagon that I'm not proud of and that would make it hard for anyone, anyone, to be attracted to me if they heard me shouting at them, when suddenly Michele tells me to pull over at the bus stop and turn on the hazards.

"What?" I say.

"Go," he says, pointing. We are in front of a pork store on Fifth Avenue.

As soon as I get in the door I can smell that it's a good one. It's a knockout. The smell of cured Italian meats and scamorza and dried oregano hits me as soon as I enter, and immediately I feel warm fluid resume its course through my spine and my veins and I realize I am in fact made of blood, warm blood, and I can't believe how perfect Michele can be. He has a way, frequently, of letting a crisis build to its peak and then just casually dropping in front of you exactly what you want and need when you most want and need it. The meat cases are eight feet long and packed and there are three of them. I've thrown on the hazards, left the kids howling, and their dad coping in the backseat and run into this old-school place where big Italian-American guys in flannel shirts under their long white coats make huge sandwiches with mortadella, soppressatta, prosciutto, salami, capicola, and the works of marinated peppers, mozzarella, and pitted, chopped olives. They use good olive oil and good semolina rolls. I'm watching the guy slice the meat to order. I've got my eye peeled out of one corner for a traffic cop and out of the other for the meat slicer man to *get on with it already* with his artisanal, neighborly Italian manner. He's taking the customers one at a time, making light neighborhood conversation. I smile, keeping quite still while in my mind an unkind monologue runs, until at last, at last, the guy hands over three meat-packed sandwiches that weigh so much my bood sugar creeps back to normal just from happily holding them. I'm back in the car in a heartbeat. Hazards flashing. And doling out sandwiches. I pass the mozzarella and prosciutto one into the backseat, while I start wolfing my mortadella. Michele asks if I got anything to drink and I'm chagrined; I feel like an ass. I didn't even think about something to drink.

"Should I go?" he asks.

I say, "Whatever, a water or something," as he hoists himself out of the backseat, climbs over the car seat with Leone sleeping in it—how did he manage that?—and stumbles out the car door. He spills out onto the sidewalk and disappears into a corner store for a few minutes. I don't even pay attention. I am shoving meat sandwich into my face and giving scraps to Marco as fast as I can.

Michele returns. He climbs, awkwardly, back into his spot in the backseat between the two car seats. The B63 bus pulls up alongside us, forced away from the curb and the bus stop by my double-parking. The bus spits out its hydraulic steam, lowers, and the passengers walk around the back of the Volvo and make it onto the bus. Michele presses into my hand an ice-cold beer in a can. And we sit there for a full leisurely, inappropriate twenty-five minutes, hazards blinking, forcing the bus and its patrons to accommodate us, while we eat meat sandwiches and drink beers at four o'clock in the afternoon. While the elderly and infirm struggle to get on the bus, I've never been happier. Leone is asleep, his fatigue finally trumping his fear of death, Marco is buried quietly in his own bits of sandwich, and Michele and I, with no silverware and only our open paper wrappers on our laps, sit double-parked with the hazards blinking in a public bus stop, grinning while eating Italian sandwiches and drinking beer, and I would swear to all that I've never met a better guy than this one that I've been cursing and loathing for the past bloody hour, and the past five years.

20

WE WERE IN THE CAR SERVICE MINIVAN, MICHELE AND I AND our two kids, and I was sitting in the broken seat, trying to balance without tipping back as we headed to the airport. Somehow we had survived another winter and were headed out for our one shared pleasure, the annual vacation in Italy. The driver had the radio on blaring mariachi as well as his dispatch radio making loud, static, ocean storm noises. He hung a Honduran flag from his rearview mirror along with a "strawberry" pine tree air freshener that poisoned the fresh July afternoon air blowing in the open windows.

In my handbag, I had our expensive tickets to Italy. Five thousand dollars' worth of tickets now that each kid is too big to fly free and requires his own seat.

We were riding to the airport in happy isolation; a kid in each lap, the Honduran driver going too fast for me. I was feeling close to Michele. The bags all packed with fresh and clean clothes neatly folded. Full bottles of toiletries neatly arranged in Ziploc bags. Swimsuits bundled in with sweatshirts and cotton T-shirts. Three weeks of vacation now ours! Our driver blew through Bed-Stuy, Bushwick, Brownsville, then East New York. People sat on their stoops, hung heavily from windows of tenement buildings, cooked little makeshift barbeques on their fire escapes. I thought of how far from this we would soon be, stomping through the olive tree orchard with the naked kids in nothing but sandals, and eating Michele's mother's delicious boiled zucchini, her buttery olive oil, her harsh but addictive homemade vinegar.

Michele and I can and do spend the entire year isolated from and unknown to each other, but as soon as we get in that car on the way to the airport, we smile at each other with a kind of bond, and we are unified—however briefly—by a nostalgia for the moment about to come. July in Italy.

"Happy?" I ask. He smiles as if guilty of something but only says, "Heh," a kind of grunt with raised eyebrows, which I now know means "abbastanza," *good enough,* the highest degree of happiness he can allow himself to experience. Italians are suspicious of American exuberance.

We ride a bit more in silence. The kids are babbling some crap between them, Leone particularly excited about all the trees as we pass the Jackie Robinson Parkway. "Tseees! Tsees! Tsees!" he points and yells. The sun is turning red and heavily slanted. Our evening flight to three full weeks of Italian vacation as near as night. Michele says, "I was theeenking . . ." and then pauses.

I don't look at him but I am fully attentive, expectant. It never ever ends how I wish it would, how I fantasize it will, but I nonetheless always imagine the rest of these started sentences. Ever since I understood that I was actually married, I have hoped for it to be everything I think a real marriage should be, an intimacy of the highest order. In the few moments between the beginning and end of the sentence, "I was theeenking . . ." I have readied myself, unnecessarily, for luminous pearls of his inner life, some word from his heart, some revelation of what he thinks about or fears or loves or agonizes over, which never arrives. Nonetheless, hope dies hard, and I still become alert in that brief pause in the Honduran minivan, and I imagine the sentence ending with him, finally saying "I was theeenking about hosting a dinner party this year in Leuca." But as we hit the Belt Parkway, he finishes instead with this:"Theee newa iPhonea ees only two hundred ninety-nine dollarrrrz!"

In all of the years we have spent together, all of the eight-hour car rides, the hours waiting together at airports, in transatlantic flight, in hospital rooms, the long silent hours at night when the kids are asleep and we are stuck in the same room together, all of the winter beaches we have sat on looking out at the oceans, he has never, incredibly, incomprehensibly, said anything important to me.

When he said he was thinking about the new iPhone, in spite of having a rather new iPhone right now this very moment already in his pocket, I dissolved irrevocably. I lost the first fifteen days of my vacation with that iPhone comment. I lost my vacation to a seething, hot black rage that crawled up the back of my neck and covered my head and nose and mouth until I was suffocated by it and could barely breathe and certainly could not speak or make eye contact. It's true; I tend to run a little hot.

And that is how I lost fifteen of my sorely needed, hard-earned vacation days.

And how I robbed him of his.

I became speechless and impenetrable for fifteen days. He couldn't reach me, and I couldn't be reached, and that ended our vacation before it even got off the ground. You never know when this kind of internal defeat is going to overcome you.

Once I saw an older woman fall down on the subway as the train lurched out of the station, and she landed on her ass. We all jumped to her aid, distressed to see this older, tired, heavy woman brought down by the careless, jerky transit driver. But she ignored us and our efforts to recover her as quickly as possible to an invulnerable, collected, and standing position. She waved away our eager grapplings to get her up out of this humiliating and embarrassing position. She remained flat on her ass on the dirty floor of the train, looking deeply exhausted, and she sat that way, fully present in her defeat, until we came to a halt at the next stop and she quietly and methodically lifted herself back up and took a seat on the bench.

And I swam in it, too, on this particular day unable to any longer pretend that our bags of neatly packed fresh clean clothes and swim-suits were a symbol of anything greater, of any kind of fresh start and clean slate. I relished my defeat. I said to myself: I am no match for you, anger and fatigue and loneliness. I am able to do only what I am able to do and I cannot nurse the infants, mother the toddlers, last two whole years without deep sleep, work one of the surgeon general's most stressful jobs, live in an unhappy marriage, carry the bulk of the finances, and suffer the idea of a new technology toy for you, Hus-band, and so today, today, is the day I have run out of American can-do spirit and today, I am not making or faking July in Italy with my Italian husband.

Our ritual meal of Wok Express fast-food Chinese at the airport before we will not see anything approximating Asian food—even such as this bullshit chicken broccoli on a Styrofoam plate—for twenty-one days was shared perfunctorily and, worst of all, politely. We shared the beer on the rocks with icy routine, while harnessing the two squirming high-strung kids.

Beer on ice, before nine p.m., is something for us. It's almost a conversation for us. Beer on ice, for example, does not happen, like, at three o'clock on a Tuesday between lunch and dinner service at the restaurant with only an hour to get the kiddy dinner rolling and the tubby ready, before heading back to work. When Michele shows up with two beers and two glasses of ice it says, suggestively, that We Have Time. Time to sit for a minute. Time to sleep off the alcohol, should we feel it. Time to lie down with each other. And we drank the beer on ice, in Terminal C, as usual, as we had every year before our flight. But it was not with a grinning, quiet excitement shimmering with sexual promise, freedom, youth, all the things that a couple of beers makes us remember.

"Beer?" he asks, proffering one as usual because he has not yet caught on that I have dropped out.

"Yes, please. Thank you."

When I am polite with Michele is when we are at our deadliest. When he is nothing more to me than a one-off customer at my restau-rant where my professional courtesy is required. When I don't even have the warmth and friendliness I can easily conjure for a beloved regular at the restaurant. When I am "Yes, please," and "No, thank you" is when we are dead in the water.

I've grown ambivalent about this annual trip to Italy as it is. Perhaps this is in direct proportion to questions I have about my continued stamina for the marriage itself. As early summer arrives and everyone's casual conversation turns to vacation—the hairdresser, the meat man, the exterminator—all ask: "Are you going to get away this summer? Any plans?"

And I answer matter-of-factly now, without animation, "Yup. I am going to Italy for the month of July. We go every year. My husband is Italian and we go every year to his home and his family in Italy."

And the meat man, the hairdresser, the exterminator light up as if plugged in. Eyes widen with delight and envy. Huge smiles. They burst as I did the very first time I went.

Italy! Oh my God! That's fantastic! Three weeks in Italy!

While I still share much of this delight, after the first few years it's no longer an unmitigated joy. I want to have seen much of the world before I bite the dust. I want to know more of Italy than the apartment in Rome and the crumbling old house in Puglia. I want to be with friends or people I can really talk to on my twenty-one days of vacation. To take the same one vacation every year, with someone I don't get along that well with, while much of the rest of the world remains unexplored and unknown by us, makes me a little less joyful than the exterminator. That we also only go from the house to the same beach or to the same swimming pool every day while we're in Puglia, makes me less electrified than the meat man. I like to be anchored by routine, not shackled by it. What I love about Italians is exactly what I also don't love: the incredible fastening down of routine, tradition, the nearly pathological preservation of habit. I love that they haven't torn down the ruins to make a highway, that the pasta is still made the same way, that certain foods are eaten only in certain places in certain preparations—Trippa Milanese is always Milanese and Trippa alla Romana is always alla Romana—this is so reliable and rich and fascinating. This is how countries older than ours become so rich in tradition. Repetition. Centuries of repetition. But it's that very repetition that makes my heart sing a little wanly when I think of my one vacation a year. Shouldn't we be on a houseboat on the Mekong River delta this year? Eating raw octopus head in Tokyo? Strolling the boulevards of Buenos Aires? Bicycling the coast of Portugal?

It's exactly the same when I tell people that I am married to an Italian.

"An Italian! Oh, from Italy? An Italian Italian!" and they are agog.

"Does he cook with you at the restaurant?"

And I laugh. "No, he's a doctor."

Well then they are just about levitating.

Even I am seduced by the idea of it. An Italian doctor! Three weeks in Italy!

The images I conjure when I hear myself or anyone say *three-week vacation in Italy* are probably the same as theirs: I imagine hiking the trails of the Cinque Terre, cooled by the clean fresh wind from the crystal sea, stopping for fish and wine—so local that you've been tripping over the vines all afternoon on your hike—from that very hillside.

I imagine inhaling truffles in Piemonte.

Going to a wild boar festival in Umbria.

Sitting in Campo de Fiore sipping a perfect negroni—one solid ice cube, the glass poured only two-thirds full in the true aperitivo correctness.

Having a tight espresso in the late afternoon at St. Eustachio looking up at the antlered deer and cross atop the church.

I imagine my Italian husband in a deep orange summer cashmere sweater playing off his tan, his good wristwatch strapped to his left wrist with a dark leather strap, showing me, why not, some spontaneous and deeply felt affection and warmth.

But my actual Italian Italian is in an untucked T-shirt with the Apple computer logo and a pair of khaki shorts from The Gap hanging down mid-calf like frat boys wear. He's got three days of razor stubble, having decided not to shave but twice a week, since during the academic year when he is teaching he must scrape that Gillette twin blade over his face every damn morning. He is resisting, with his black eyes in a pained face, to take us down to show our kids the Fontana di Trevi because, he complains, it's so hot, and because we will have to take a public bus, and because there will be tourists. When the Puglia nighttime sky is lousy with stars, and I fantasize lying down on our backs on the terrace—the stone still hot from the day's long hours of sun—to let them rain down over us, I find Michele sitting on the terrace hunched in his chair, glowing in his wireless connection, and he's Google-mapping on his laptop computer the very constellations he could just, by tilting his head back and looking up, practically inhale. Alone on the terrace looking up at the stars I would not feel lonely. With him glued to the screen, I feel gutted, as I lay on my back by myself in awe of the sky. But it sounds better when I say, "Yes! The month of July in Italy with my Italian Italian husband!"

Because I like the watercolor image better than the reality, and because I can't stand to be the kind of difficult person—the one unimaginable hag on the planet who is capable of not totally enjoying a month in Italy and who could not be totally levitated by the idea of her doctor Italian Italian husband—I just sit in the hairdresser's chair and say: "Yup. Italy. We go every year. My husband is Italian."

With this ambivalence, our flight is announced and we head to the gate.

Michele's brother, Giovanni, meets us at Fiumicino airport at nine a.m. It is already hot and the punishing white light of day assaults our bleary eyes. Michele and I are exhausted from a long sardine-packed transatlantic flight with a fussy pair of kids who couldn't settle properly in spite of the Benadryl we popped them. We have hissed at each other, each criticizing the other's strategy for taming the two- and four-year-old beasts. We have never agreed about pacifying the kids. Michele, in his excitement to be home, bolts quickly ahead toward the line of Italian people waiting to meet their arriving relatives while I straggle and struggle along behind hauling the little one and trying to push the heavy cart with all of our luggage. One of the wheels is malfunctioning, making me slow and hobbled. Michele does not look back. He has Marco on his shoulders. I have Leone and a mountain of luggage. Giovanni emerges from the line, ducking under the barrier and runs to help me. Michele says to his brother: "She doesn't want help." And I can't imagine how I've been so misunderstood all of these years. Yes. I want help.

I kiss Giovanni lightly on both cheeks, left cheek first with the Italians, I've finally learned. He has let his hair grow out; salt-and-pepper gray almost to his shoulders, and his eyebrows seem equally as long and ungroomed. Michele greets him by teasing him unkindly about his haircut or lack of one and laughs high and long. Ando, their sister's teenage son, has also come to greet us and to help us, and this year he has become fully a man, with every ounce of testosterone he's been allotted in full surge. He has real shoulders, a deep voice, he even reeks of the cigarette he just finished. At seventeen, he has definitely had sex. Michele greets him also by insulting him about his poor grades at school and his failure to pass two of his subjects. Long high-pitched laughter. I live in close proximity to this man all year long and I am accustomed to this backhanded, reverse psychology, this way of actually saying: *I am so happy to see you. I am so glad to be home. My family and country mean so much to me.*

But I am always taken aback in the first few minutes of arriving into the fold of the Fuortes family that no one protests or bursts into tears. I would and do fall apart with such starvation for genuine affection and sincerity, for one crumb of the true contents of this man's heart and mind. Yet no one but me winces.

For the past few years, I drive the car into Rome from the airport. Michele is better at handling the kids in the back of the car and I am better at driving, or at least this is what we have learned to cheerfully and constructively say to each other. It is a Saturday morning and the autostrada is relatively empty. As are the streets of Rome. The city has clusters of tourists, like overripe grapes, at every crosswalk, but the plague of wasps—the Romans on their Vespas—feels thin and hardly mortifying. I shift, accelerate, switch lanes, and take the corners as if I lived here year round. We pass ruins of aqueduct, Colosseum, and then wind down the hill around the fountain and the statues. Some of the tourists already have sunburn on their sleeveless shoulders though it is not yet eleven in the morning. This is, seven years later with two kids, no nighttime tour through Rome on the back of a lover's motorcycle but even so, hands down, this is the most beautiful city on earth, even in broad daylight with a remote husband who's actually considering buying a new iPhone. I love Rome.

We pull up in front of the large gate to the apartment and park under the tree out of the intense sun. Every single year we do this. The neighborhood is quiet, sleepy, intensely residential, and lately, too too civilized for me. Not one soul smokes on a balcony, suns themselves on a terrace, or reads a paper on a front stoop. The shutters are all closed but for a few windows of a few scattered apartments all around the adjoining and neighboring buildings. There is no music emanating from any apartment. No blare of a television. There are no children.

Michele's sister Manuela and his mother greet us from the balcony overhead. They look just exactly the same as last year, and for a moment it seems as if the reports from Rome all winter about Alda's failing health and failing memory have been exaggerated. It seems as if they haven't moved from the very spot where we waved good-bye last summer at the end of our vacation. I feel genuinely happy to see them both. I really love them.

In our hug, Alda always says to me, "Come sei brava, Gabrielle. Proprio brava!" "Che coraggio!" And I always well up in this shower of her kindness. She is forever complimenting me on what courage and strength I have to haul the two kids across the ocean and deliver them to her doorstep. She herself has a magnificent fear of flying. Manuela, always maternal and sympathetic, says, "Stancissima sei." Then she repeats "You must be very tired" in English, which she speaks perfectly.

The apartment in Rome where we spend the first couple and last few days—the bookends—of our annual vacation, is the whole ground floor of a large good-looking building that has been separated into two apartments. Manuela lives with her son Ando in one half—a beautiful sparse but tasteful apartment of four rooms with a hallway so lined with books in English and Italian and French that they reach the ceiling. And Alda in the other half, with Giulio, an elegant, massive apartment with three bedrooms and two large living rooms that is so packed with family mementos and heirloom silver and sepia photographs and centuries-old heavy furniture and wardrobes stuffed with exquisite linens and lace table covers passed down from great-great-great-grand ancestors that your shoe heel doesn't even click on the marble floors. Echo is immediately absorbed. The tall French doors open onto a huge terrace and front yard where orange trees and concord grapes grow over a pergola. Orange blossom grows in cascades over the stone railings of the terrace, the fragrance hitting you right in the kisser as soon as you enter. I could fall down drunk from that fresh perfume and lulled by the bubble of the fountain every time we enter through that gate, which clicks heavily behind us as we all go inside.

Bud, the golden retriever, has dug holes all over the modest patch of front yard and there's shit in so many places that have not been cleaned up that I am thinking twice about whether or not I want the kids running around in there with no shoes and no pants, and they always seem to get buck naked within six minutes of arriving anywhere, so I will have to decide quickly. The yard is no longer as charming as it was when I was first here, sitting under the pergola of grapes with Michele, having wine, intoxicated by the scent of honeysuckle, oranges, uva fregola, and each other. We hug and kiss Manuela and Alda hello while Michele's youngest brother Giulio stands at the periphery of the group, waiting to greet us. He leans forward and offers his cheek to be kissed but not to actually be kissed. This I have also finally learned.

The dining room table is set exactly as always with fresh mozzarella, boiled small zucchini, prosciutto, and melon, cruets of her olive oil and red wine vinegar. There is a pot of pasta water boiling on the old propane stove in the kitchen where Manuela is readying to cook some spaghetti. Bud is running around from room to room and out onto the terrace then back in again, running in and around and over the children, barking with great excitement. Michele yells at Bud and Manuela yells at Michele and within minutes the two of them are fighting about how to discipline the dog. It is one of Michele's habits to conduct himself as if he is the head of the household in spite of his lack of contribution to it or participation in it year-round. The dog is not his, this house is not his, the daily chores of caring for Giulio as well as caring for Alda who is now eighty-four and starting to fail is not his, and yet within fifteen minutes of entering the house he is scolding the dog and giving Manuela instruction on how to live. This also, is the same as every year. Giovanni, meanwhile, has methodically carried every piece of our heavy luggage from the car up the marble steps and into the foyer of the apartment. He has thrown the ball to Bud a few times, had a small avuncular conversation with Ando, whom Manuela raises alone, and now is seated at the dining room table next to Alda, across from me and the kids, sorting out and portioning her many lunchtime pills.

Oddly, this is where my full isolation sets in: at the dinner table, surrounded by family and good food. Here in the very place and the very moment of the grail I've been seeking to recover since my own family evaporated, thirty years ago. Everyone is speaking Italian, which I don't really speak. My kids are dislocated and shy and so clingy it is impossible to sit at the table for longer than a moment before one or the other or both drag me away from the strange people, the language they don't quite recognize, the loud and animated quality of the room. Because Michele is deep into reunion with his family, I will be the one who gets up from the table, leaving my plate of food, to attend to the children. The image of the Italian family, dining al fresco around a large table, the children running around in the grape vines or the olive trees, is the most seductive image in the world—a moment that exists in Robert Mondavi vineyard publicity shots in glossy magazines. You are welcome for a plate of spaghetti and a glass of wine—but it is not yours, and it will never belong to you and you will never belong to it.

I spend a lot of time on the terrace with the kids while everyone is inside having lunch and conversation. I, too, have just been through a long and difficult plane ride, am also sleep deprived, have exerted myself strenuously in the few days just before leaving in order to ready the family for our vacation, and I, too, long for my vacation to start with a fat plate of Alda's zucchini and a glass of cold white wine from the Alto Adige and a boisterous catch-up session with my family around the table. That is my image of vacation in Italy. It is my image of being married to an Italian Italian. It is my fantasy of recovering that fireside night, snug in a sleeping bag surrounded by my brilliant siblings and speaking our own, made-up language. But I am reliably alone for the first few days babysitting on the terrace while my glass of wine warms on the dining room table where my seat remains empty. My hunger feeds my exhaustion. My exhaustion fuels my sadness. Five thousand dollars' worth of plane tickets to wind up alone on the terrace, feeling like the nanny.

Later in the afternoon, with the kids zombied out in front of Italian cartoons on the television, I get a chance to speak with Manuela in the kitchen.

"Michele has told me that you aren't coming with us to Leuca?" I ask, disappointed.

"I will stay here, if you don't mind," she says, always this polite with me. As if she were asking my permission to stay in Rome during the hot weeks of July while we go down to the house in Leuca with the whole family, including Alda, who has waited eagerly for our arrival so that we can head south together.

"Of course I don't mind but I will miss you. Can't I persuade you with the promise of mojitos?"

I know that Manuela likes my cooking and she has liked some of the little cocktails I make during the summer for aperitivo. When I have been able to get my hands on mint and limes—not easy in that small town in Puglia—I have made mojitos and she has loved them. She shows genuine delight at the idea but she must stay in Rome she says. "Ando must take summer classes and I must stay here to be with him."

"So would it be good if I cook for the family this year, is that okay?" I ask. I had tried to discuss this with Michele before we left New York. I had insisted that we could not possibly arrive as a family of four and expect his mother to cook for us as usual, even with the help of Rosaria. But I was afraid of cooking for his mother and especially tentative about cooking so much pasta, which the family requires, a skill at which I am not very accomplished. Michele understood and agreed but answered only with his vague grunt and had not come up with a plan. So I had decided, maybe even on the plane ride over, that I would just take on the responsibility. But still I needed to check with Manuela. To assume that I might, for a few measly weeks of the summer, take over the kitchen of an Italian family who has lived under the matriarchy of their beloved and revered Alda Fuortes de Nitto, "Mamma," for eighty-four years, seemed extremely delicate to me.

"But do you think it will be okay with Alda?" I ask Manuela. "I will need to rearrange some of the furniture in that kitchen."

"Yes, I think she will love it. She will want to do some but not all. She wants to cook but can't cook all of those meals. It's too much: breakfast, lunch, and dinner every day for the whole family and then again all over the next day. It's too much for her. She has stopped, even, cooking Sunday lunch."

"Okay, I understand. I will cook then. But what about Giulio?"

Manuela assures me that he will find the new things to eat exciting and interesting.

"Alda has stopped cooking Sunday lunch?" I repeat, having missed a few sentences of our conversation.

"When will you drive to Leuca?" Manuela asks.

"Wait! There's no more Sunday lunch?"

Manuela nods sadly. "It's too much for her now."

For seven years there has been Sunday lunch. For something more like sixty-five years there has been Sunday lunch, but I mean for me there has been Sunday lunch for seven years. In spite of my isolation, my sadness, my long horrible winters with Michele, I live for Sunday lunch. It's four-fifths of my fantasy life about vacation in Italy each year. Even though I know perfectly well that it is not my Sunday lunch, even though I know that I spend Sunday lunch on the terrace with the kids feeling lonely, even though I barely get a sip of the wine poured at Sunday lunch, I love Sunday lunch. I love the image of the whole family sitting down at the table and even the arguing and the yelling at the dog seems exquisite in Italian.

I say to Manuela, "I will cook Sunday lunch tomorrow. The family and all should come as usual. And on Monday morning we will all drive to the south. How does that sound?"

"Brava," Manuela says. "Va bene."

I cook, easily:

Sepia with green beans and fennel and broken vinaigrette.
Shell beans with onions and tomatoes and herbs.
Fried zucchini agrodolce with fresh mint and hot chili flakes.
Cauliflower with salami and parsley and bread crumbs.
Smoked eggplant with garlic and lemon and olive oil.

There is plenty at the market in Rome. It is my first day of cooking and I am full of ideas about what to cook and how to cook. I will use all of their customary ingredients and bend them just toward my style, so that everything will be familiar but new simultaneously. To pull off lunch for these twelve people or so feels surprisingly fine. I cook alone in Manuela's kitchen, undisturbed. She has only three pots and I use them all in heavy rotation. And luckily, my kids have slept through the morning on a jet-lag schedule, affording the quietude and privacy and distractionless morning to accomplish my task just in time. I am just stepping out of the shower as my kids wake up and everyone arrives for lunch at two.

These first encounters are still exciting. I love to set eyes on everyone again for the first time since last year. I don't know if anyone in the family knows me or likes me, but I like them. Without language, I am left hyper, acutely tuned in to tone and body language and I can never trust my observations fully. People smile and seem happy to see us. Anna and Carlo, Michele's younger brother and his wife, arrive with one of their daughters. Paolone arrives with Angela—everyone is here in the way that I love nostalgically. The big din of Italian people, sitting around the table together, drinking wine and eating delicious food—it looks like a page in a magazine—but I am again exhausted, and on the terrace with my two kids alone, trying to keep them out of the dog shit. Michele comes outside and offers to sit with the kids awhile but even when I go inside and take a place at the table, I feel a gulf between me and the impossibility of what I want, what I crave from this family of which I am, still, not a part.

Alda and Carlo and Manuela and Giulio ask me about every part of the meal, how I cooked each thing, what was in each dish:

"Ma la sepia, how did you make them so tender?"

And what was in the zucchini?

How did you think of putting the salami in with the cauliflower?

This is perfect starter conversation for me because I can, in fact, understand in Italian and answer in Italian. It is not difficult for me to say the names of ingredients in Italian.

Everyone says they loved the food and I watched Alda's face intently to see if she was being polite. She seemed genuinely happy with the meal and the ability to sit and enjoy her family without having to cook. And that is all I give a shit about.

Every year I vow to learn to speak this language. Every year I arrive and am completely tongue-tied and disoriented in the first few days. By the end of the first week I have fully recovered everything I learned the year before and I can piece sentences together. By week three I'm more liquid, ready to really learn to speak this language, and just then we pack our bags with dirty laundry and Salentino pottery and taralli biscuits and fly home.

In the morning, we pack the rental car and drive the eight hours south to the house in Puglia, without speaking except as it pertains to or involves the kids. Our first few days of vacation in Italy and I have not left the apartment in Rome once, and Michele and I are starting to spiral like dishwater from cordiality toward the sucking hole of hostility.

WE ARRIVE AT THE HOUSE. This small seaside town has, curiously, a collection of wild and improbable villas right on the main drag facing the sea, built in the 1800s. In the two hundred intervening years since these lavish villas were built, some with turrets and parapets and some, like ours, with rooms with no ceilings!—this place has become the

Italian Asbury Park. I feel like I'm at the Jersey Shore. A dozen kiosks sell sequined bathing suits and tie-dyed beach wraps. Italian teenagers in mirror sunglasses and thongs up their asses sit on the tide wall and don't look at each other. Smoking. A karaoke bar now resides exactly adjacent to the Villa Fuortes, and until two in the morning each night we are serenaded by drunk twenty-year-olds half-singing Celine Dion songs in thick Italian accents, their mouths forming words they don't know the meaning of into a microphone. There's a sliver of a children's amusement park at the far end of the boardwalk promenade with rides that go around and around for five euros a pop.

The villa still impresses.

But whatever money there was has all run out. No one comes by with dusty carts of tomatoes and melons. There are no men working in the mornings to whom we could bring cold beers. There are many dead branches fallen in the driveway and the gravel is all but washed away. There are so many leaves encroaching from the sides like a riverbed, with the driveway now narrowing like a trickling stream and not the wide boulevard it has been in the past. It needs to be raked. And raked. And bagged and hauled away. It could take most of a week. The high wall that fronts onto the Via Tommaso Fuortes—the road named for Michele's great-grandfather—has been vandalized over the winter and the delicate lattice of stonework, which they smashed with hammers evidently, has been hastily repaired with big unattractive cinderblocks, laid by an apprentice, it looks like.

Michele gets out of the car and spends a long time looking at the wall and shaking his head.

"Look at theees!"

The kids follow him already barefoot, leaving their Crocs scattered haphazardly up the unkempt driveway. Already they are digging in the leaves and the gravel where they will spend many hours in the next days contentedly eating, pissing, digging, and fighting.

Here we are.

In the morning I clean out The Cabinet. The Cabinet houses the mismatched espresso cups, the everyday Pyrex cookware, the coffee itself, bread crumbs, very, very old spices in very old jars—faded aromaless sage in a black pepper jar, and cloves in an oregano bottle—as well as pasta in bags and boxes. Usually on the third shelf toward the bottom there are a couple of platters of room temperature food, cooked, if lucky, that morning, but not uncommonly the day before, and even—I've seen it—the day before that. The fried peppers and eggplant and potatoes that rest there have never seen refrigeration, which is on one hand kind of unsettling but also helps me see how hyper we Americans are about refrigeration. In Alda's house, the refrigerators themselves hardly make fifty degrees and prepared food rests for days in the cabinet and also in the turned-off oven. Everyone in the family eats this stuff and hasn't died from it yet.

As the new, temporary-surrogate-junior-helper-self-appointed-matriarch, or whatever I am here, the first thing I want to do is to prepare the kitchen so that I can cook in it. For some reason, everyone is surprised and there is much commotion and animated consternation when I start pulling out all the mealy-moth-infested bags of pasta and rice and old biscotti, which I have been politely noticing but ignoring for the prior six years. Everyone seems truly surprised to find these bags teeming with live moths and brimming with the husks of their eggs. A veritable fabric of cobweblike filament infests all the jars and bags of meal, bread crumbs, polenta, and hard wheat flour. Moths fly into the room and up up up to the top of the twenty-foot vaulted ceilings of this villa's old kitchen. I have been aware of this infestation since my first visit here, where it amused me and charmed me. In my third and fourth years I was maybe less charmed and more skeeved out. But this year, well, I feel completely neutral and unemotional: This shit's gotta go. For my first act as surrogate matriarch understudy or nanny or housekeeper or useful guest—I'll never know what I am in this family—I am chucking the mealy-moth-infested crap that I have known to be living in this crazy cabinet since the day I arrived here seven years ago. I feel it is appropriately respectful to have waited this long though I admit it was a challenge for me not to have at this cabinet five years ago.

I put the espresso cups with the espresso cups, the saucers with the saucers, the platters with the platters.

On the next shelf I put the viable pastas in a group, the spices to-gether in a row, and leave one shelf empty to receive the fried peppers and fried potatoes and the fried "croquettes" that I know Rosaria will put there in the morning when she arrives. I keep an eye on Alda's face, seated at the kitchen table squinting at the newspaper, to see if she hates me already. Giovanni shuffles in and pulls open a drawer crammed so full of corks and bottle caps and bits of string that I start to sweat slightly just looking at the chaos of it. He stands there for eleven or twelve minutes picking through the caps with one finger looking for the cap to the olive oil jug before giving up and heaving the heavy drawer shut.

At last, we rearrange the kitchen. Giovanni pushes the tables around as I describe and we take it one piece by one piece. The small table to the corner. The tall, granite table to the center in front of the stove and sink. The refrigerator against the wall by the door. Giovanni shakes his head many times, insisting that a certain piece won't fit or can't be moved, but I am not deterred. And I love working with him; even his stubborn resistance feels collaborative and he never conde-scends to me. "Let's just try it," I say. "If it doesn't fit, we can move it all back."

Soon, everything sits exactly as I have envisioned it for years as it "should" be. There is space for me to work, to produce all these meals, and the family can now sit at the other kitchen table with the news-paper, the coffeepot, the lunch plates, the random screwdriver, suntan lotion, pistachios in the shell as well as a pile of empty shells, mosquito coil, and the debris that accumulates in this family.

Then I go to the market. On this, the first day back in Leuca, I am happy to see some of my old favorites again: the puntarelle, the Lec-cese green beans, the small dense zucchini, and the eggplant. I buy big bundles of all of them and lots of peaches and a watermelon. Alda eats fruit after each meal and I think my kids will eat the watermelon. The meat is dismal as usual but there is a fish stall with some good-looking stuff. I get an octopus. A branzino. A few pounds of head-on shrimp.

At the supermarket, I push the cart slowly up and down each and every aisle, filling it with all of the things I have come to know each person in the family will like. There is bottled iced tea for Michele, and Coca-Cola for Giulio, and fruit juices in cartons that Giovanni and Alda drink. I get some Italian versions of junk food for the kids—just to see what the Italian chips are like—and as I am at the checkout, paying for the cartload on my American Express, I feel potent and capable and maternal. I am taking care of and providing for my family.

The checkout girl swipes the card and for the long minute it takes to dial up to an international satellite that can verify its legitimacy—and by extension, my own—I fall into a moment's emotional slump. I *do* want to be here; I just want my vacation in Italy with my Italian Italian husband to feel like what it sounds like. I *want* to do the cooking. It is what grounds me, gives me pleasure, and is the best way for me to communicate with the Italian-speaking family and to make a contribution. But it can also make me feel like the hired help. While Michele babysits the kids at the pool for the day, dozing in and out of naps and reading the newspaper and having fluid conversations with people in his native tongue, I am nagged by an emptiness while I am neatening and organizing the drawers and shelves in all the cabinets, and it continues as I move up and down each aisle in the grocery store, and interferes still while I am chopping each onion at the newly created cooking island in front of the kitchen stove. By the time I check out at the grocery store and I've put this grocery bill on my personal card, sautéed the onions with the potatoes, and wiped down the counter, I feel precariously poised exactly between totally perfect, as if I am exactly where I should be, and totally fucked-up, as if I were bankrolling my own martyrdom. If he had ever once finished one of those started sentences as I had always yearned for them to be finished, we may have had a different vacation, a different ending. But at the time, all I could think was, *Dottore, you don't get a new iPhone if I don't get a dinner party.*

I prepare the octopus as Alda prepares it. With potatoes and onions and a few hot chilis. But when I put it in the serving dish, one of her large old Salentino pottery pieces, she doesn't recognize it.

"Gabrielle, che c'è dentro?" What's in there?

"*Polpo*, Alda. *E tua recette. Con cipolle, patatas, e peperoncini pauci. Polpo.*" It's octopus, Alda. It's your recipe. I learned it from you. With onions and potatoes and a few chilis. It's your octopus!

"*Con cipolle?*" she asks, her brow knit up tight. Her black eyes not comprehending.

"Si!" I say.

"*E che altro?*" she asks. And what else?

I repeat, as if saying it for the first time. "*Patatas.*" "*Cipolle.*" "*Peperoncini.*"

This is Italian I can actually speak. Menu Italian.

Leone comes running into the kitchen, nearly impaling his head on the corner of the newly situated heavy granite cooking island. Everyone is back from the pool.

"*E . . . E. . . . E*, Gabrielle?" she finally manages. "*Come e chiama questo piccolo?*" What is this little one's name?

"*Questo e* Leone," I say.

"Leone!" she cries, her face now flush and bright with recognition and relief. She remembers Leone.

"*Si!* Leone. *Ciao,* Leone! *Tesoro mio! Ciao, piccolo!*" Yes! Leone. Hi, Leone. My treasure. Hi, little one!

And then she asks me, "*Quanti figli ci sono?*" How many kids are there?

"*Due*, Alda. *Ci sono due.* Marco *e* Leone."

This is new this year, this kind of memory loss. She gets a storm across her face, her brow knit so tight I would like to press my thumbs into the creases and massage them away.

"*Due figli??*" she exclaims. "*Due??!!*"

"*Si, si,*" I reply. "Marco *e* Leone."

And she falls silent and brooding for a couple of minutes, sitting at the kitchen table with the telephone in front of her. I wash the puntarelle and tip the green beans standing at the sink with my back to her, affording her, I hope, the privacy in which to experience her frustration and befuddlement and disorientation. Leone runs back out to the driveway to pee in what's left of the gravel.

The stove needs to be replaced, but after rearranging the kitchen so that the heavy granite topped table is now a cooking island and the low kitchen table with all the crap on it is pushed against the wall so that people can convene and eat there without getting in the way of the cooking, I feel there is strong and immovable resistance from Giovanni. There is only so much change this family can stand. Throw away the mealy-moths and move the kitchen table and call it quits for this year because this is at the threshold of what they can handle. The Fuortes brothers are practically sweating with nerves. I realize I have already gotten away with as much as I can for this year and will let go of the new stove. But it does not make me comfortable. The grids that rest over the burners have corroded away these past fifty years—and where there used to be four solid prongs over each burner atop which your pot could sit securely, there are now little stumps and missing legs altogether so that sometimes you must balance the pot to boil water or fry French fries on two little prongs.

The pots themselves, aluminum pieces of crap—as dented and buckled and mangled as little car wrecks—wobble on a perfectly flat surface, let alone on the stump of a burner grid. One ten-quart pasta pot full of boiling water at every meal and I'm tense, ultra-edgy when my kids come blasting into the kitchen clutching my thighs, shrieking, hugging me right where I stand, between the stove and the island, in an apron with a paring knife in my hand. If that fucking water tips over, we are not close enough, for my comfort, to a pediatric burn ward in this little seaside town. And that is not how I want to spend my vacation.

But Giovanni says no. Or acts no. He never says no. He just physically Will. Not. Budge.

It's Alda who is invoked as the reason nothing can change or be different. And yet Alda is delighted with the new arrangement of the kitchen. To everyone who visits or telephones, she gushes and gives them a tour—physical or verbal—of the new layout.

"*Guarda com'è piu' grande!*" "*Guarda, ci sono due spacii—uno per mangiare e uno per cucinare!*" Look how it's bigger now! Look how we now have two separate spaces—one for eating and one for cooking!

She seems genuinely thrilled. When I wanted to have a big party

Michele said no, because Mamma would be overwhelmed and exhausted. When I wanted to build a fire out near the front garden to cook a lamb outdoors, Michele said no, Mamma won't like it. But it's Mamma who pulls up the first chair and watches as I build the fire on a tiny makeshift grill and as I put the three-pound *branzino* stuffed with lemons and fennel branches over the coals. It's Mamma who stays out until one in the morning at the big party at Sergio and Mercedes's house, worrying her sons who have stayed at home, and who then upon returning home sits at the kitchen table and raps it with her crutch gently, calling for *"Un goccetto!"* A little drop.

Giovanni, with his long wavy eyebrows like Spanish moss mingling with his long wavy hair, repeats in amazement and admiration at his mother, at Mamma. *"Un goccetto voi?!"* A drop you want? Alda beams back at him, spirits high.

In unison, Michele and Giovanni repeat, disbelieving, *"Un goccetto?!"*

"Perche non?" she asks. And Michele laughs genuine, happy laughter. He loves this woman with all of his heart and mind. There is nothing *abbastanza* about it. This is the woman he loves; this is the woman he hoped to find in me when he first looked into the restaurant and saw me at the stove.

In classic Italian style, the brothers fumble around the kitchen, saying it again several times, while shaking their heads and smiling. *Un goccetto. Un goccetto.* And Giovanni finally pulls from the refrigerator a bottle of wine.

It is Alda who is singing the song of this new kitchen layout. It is Alda who stays out late at the party. Giovanni pours us all two sips of Salentino rosé and we sit at the kitchen table for a few minutes before going to bed. This woman, this magnificent woman, is not the one who fears change.

TWO WEEKS LATER I am hunting through the local market, scanning each vendor's crates, desperate to discover something new to cook. My jaw tightens and I'm grinding my molars a bit at all this eggplant.

In Leuca, there is nothing but eggplant. *Local. Seasonal.* These are the words that turn everybody on these days. But twenty-one days of local eggplant season is torture.

I think when people get all dreamy about local and seasonal, they are thinking of California, where you can get anything any time of year. But they are not referring to Santa Maria de Leuca, a small sea-side town at the tip of the heel of the boot of Italy in the state of Puglia. And they are not imagining eating that way—local and seasonal—for twenty-one days straight. They know they can go get a platter of sushi at their local joint any night of the week. Maybe they are thinking of their week-long trip to Tuscany.

I am grateful for the burratta, to be sure. We have eaten so much of the creamy, fresh cheese, often still warm from the *caseificio,* and it is so sweet and tender that I have not tired of it in the least. In fact, I have finally understood that we will not be eating burratta in the U.S. anymore, because even the best that you can get at Agata and Valentina, "fresh off the airplane," is not it. You can't eat burratta in the States because it can't stay fresh long enough to make the journey. It is always a hair sour and just starting to harden and it turns watery and "off" no matter how "just flown in from Bari" the wholesaler at Murray's insists it is.

But still I craved some arugula to go with it. Some broccoli rabe, even.

To Alda I said, "Is there arugula, even, anywhere?"

But Alda shook her head and *tsk*ed—*"Non è stagione. Non è stagione."* Not the season.

In the shade of the tree in front of the old school that sits on the market square, I see my old man. My spirits lift to see my *vecchio,* the old bent-in-half farmer with his pants held up by twine, but even he has only a few eggplants, four lonely eggs, and some incredibly small dried white beans in a knotted plastic bag in the wagon of his *ape.* I buy the eggs and the beans. I am running out of eggplant ideas. I have roasted it with harissa and caraway. I have smoked it with garlic and lemon and parsley. I have fried it with egg and bread crumbs. I have quickly pickled it, sort of, with Alda's rough red wine vinegar and some green onions. The beans might be a nice jump-start to my imagination. But when I soak them later and start to skim off the dried skins which are floating to the top of the pot, I notice that there is a brown spot on each pea. I split one open with my fingernail and inside is a larval shell of a tiny worm. I split open another and it holds another larval shell. And on I go, splitting each tiny bean, until I realize that the whole kilo is bad with worms.

"*Imbroglione!*" Alda cries when I show her the beans and tell her from whom I bought them.

There is only a week left of my vacation and I am falling apart from maintaining my chill with Michele, who has, oddly, perhaps in being faced with his failing mother, started to call me Mamma as well. He has always had difficulty saying my name, he kind of chokes on it, stumbles on it—but this is new, this calling me Mamma. With a tremendous fervor, since the day of the birth of Marco, Michele has taken to fatherhood so completely, so thoroughly, that it has become his priority to the exclusion of all other relationships, including our romantic one. This new habit of calling me Mamma sips the very last lungful of air from our romance.

I'm also falling apart from nothing but eggplant at the market since we arrived, from trying to strike a balance between cooking what I'd like to eat and cooking what Alda would like to eat. Alda has started to give me instructions while I am cooking, and seems no longer quite so pleased to have all the cooking done for her so she is free to enjoy her family around the table.

I cook a pot of mussels to tender perfection and she says, "*E, Gabrielle, non credi sono crudi?*" Don't you think they're still a bit raw?

I don't, obviously. I think they are all open, tender and perfectly cooked, but I say, "Should I cook them a little longer?"

"Five minutes," she says.

After each five-minute interval, she suggests another until I have cooked the mussels to rubbery bits, fifteen-minutes later, and she is satisfied with the results.

It's the last straw that my beloved *vecchio* sold me shitty wormy beans. Giovanni digs around in the heavy drawer once more, still searching, fifteen days later, for the right cap for the olive oil jug. To me, he seems insane. This repeated futile search for a thing that doesn't exist in a drawer full of promising crap is my definition of insanity. But of course, that is just the mechanism of hope itself. And it's not lost on me that I've been doing the exact same thing, in a way, digging around in that drawer looking for something that doesn't exist. It's promising and seductive, that huge Italian family, sitting around the dinner table, surrounded by the olive trees. But it's not my family and I am not their family, and no amount of birthing sons, and cooking dinner and raking the leaves or planting the gardens or paying for the plane tickets is going to change that. If I don't come back in eleven months, I will not be missed, and no one will write me or call me to acknowledge my absence. Which is not an accusation, just a small truth about clan and bloodline. To Giovanni, I seem insane. I spend a quick fifteen minutes before starting to cook each day, tidying up the cyclone debris of scattered toys and toy parts and single shoes and old dried bits of half-eaten toast that my kids have scattered about in each room. He laughs at me as I am bent over picking up little pieces of a miniature Italian soccer team.

"Why do you bother?" He smiles. "Fifteen minutes after they get back from the pool, it will be exactly like this again."

I stand up.

"Yeah, Giovanni. That's right. But I also brushed my teeth this morning even though I know perfectly well that I will have to brush them again tonight."

Michele is getting ready for a day at the pool with the kids, loading up his insulated bag with iced tea and frozen water and prosciutto for lunch while I am sitting here with wormy beans, a craving for arugula, radishes, scallions, well-marbled beef, cilantro, avocados, and other more spiritual impossibilities, and somehow, I don't even remember how, our fifteen-day frost heaves. In a flash we are yelling at each other in the kitchen, our first real conversation with each other since the taxicab to the airport—if you can count that as a conversation—and we're having it in my preferred, if vulgar, style, at full pitch, with his mother and two brothers sitting at the kitchen table. In English—our only form of privacy, if language can be considered that way—he yells, "Why didn't you just say so?"

Then he lectures, as if educating me: "Eeet's so eeeezy," he says. "Eeet's so eeezy to just say: Eennuffa with theeee new iPhone. We could have avoided this fifteen-day war!"

And in that moment I find it impossible to explain to him that it's not about the iPhone. *Eeeeezy* for somebody, but *impossibile* for me.

ALDA WANTS TO SEE THE SEA. The rest is a pity to her—the badly repaired front wall, the fallen dead branches, the dry dead garden, the leaves crowding out the driveway, the electricity that fails, the doorknobs that fall off, the burners on the stove worn away to nothing—but the rest is not as imperative as sitting on the front terrace overlooking the sea and actually being able to see the sea. The oleander trees in front have grown so tall over so many years, that, while beautiful, they nonetheless suffocate the house and obscure the incredible wide-open vista of the sea. I, like Alda, have been wanting to sit on that terrace and see the sea since we've been coming here. It's silly. You can stand on the terrace and look out at the sea, but as soon as you sit down with your negroni, you look straight ahead into a thicket of branches and pink-and-white flowers. Like the mealymoths in the cabinet, I've been quietly noting the fact that Michele has a villa, an actual giant villa by the actual sea in Italy Italy, from which you cannot see the sea because the oleander trees have grown over so thickly and tall. You feel stupid, sitting on the old splintered patio furniture, looking straight ahead into an encroaching jungle of soft branches, beyond which we can hear, smell, and feel the sea, the gentle breeze tinkling the mast cables and rings of all the boats in the marina, but we can never see the sea when we sit on the terrace.

Unexpectedly, I find myself offended by this. This casual nonchalance at the demise of great wealth. This effortless letting go of the last of what's left. Giovanni's quiet and easy submission to the force of entropy. Michele's willingness to let me go. The trees fall, the walls crumble, the doorknobs fall off; *easy come, easy go.* The way I'm wired, with my Protestant dishwasher's mentality, I bristle at the passivity, the way they just roll over and let defeat pat them on the head.

If I had this incredible asset, this wealth just handed to me, I would take obsessive scrupulous care of it. I would mend the fence myself. Prune back the trees. Oil the locks. Take a second job. Set aside forty dollars a week for a garden rake and seed packets and some soil. The property sags and crumbles each year, subject to weather and vandals, and no one puts up a fight. Michele warns me it would be offensive to his mother, who is legally and bodily the owner until she passes, to display any proprietary care for the place. The art and furniture and "objets" have been robbed and burgled so thoroughly over the years that the villa feels empty enough to rent. But Michele walks around barefooted, checking his email on wifi, leaving a juice glass or an espresso cup wherever he forgets it, as if the domestic staff were still about to show up. He seems to not have realized yet that there is no man coming to cut down the branches and rake the driveway. There is no Swiss au pair coming to take care of the kids. The aristocracy is over.

But Donna Alda wants to sit on the terrace and admire the sea from her chair. Besides the fact that I happen to totally agree with her, I also have felt an urgent need to make sure she has what she wants. I am possibly overconscious that this may be her last summer. She mentions it herself, with humor and matter-of-fact-ness, but I am really taking it to heart. I also can't shake this feeling that it may also be my last summer here—it seems likely that we will start to speak of divorce when we return to New York—and I want at least some of what I want. If I will never be close to, if I will never be truly known by this man, if we will never have the parties, the five kids, the fire that burns outside all night long, then the self-bankrolled martyr wants at least a negroni on the terrace while looking out at the sea, even if she has to make it herself. With only four days left of our vacation in the south, before we will have to pack up and head back to Rome, and then back to our lives lived separately in New York, I take the car and drive alone to Tricase, about twenty minutes away, and find the store that has clippers and saws and shovels and rakes. I buy a brand-new pair of sharp pruning scissors and a long-handled branch cutter, and while I am there I pick up packets of seeds for arugula and parsley and lettuce, knowing that I will never see them grow in our last four days, but reasoning that it will be good to show Marco and Leone how to plant and care for something daily. So I get them anyway.

For the next four afternoons in a row, when I am finished cooking and while Alda is taking her nap, I climb the trees, sometimes barefoot, with the scissors and the clippers. I trim at least six trees, bracing myself in their crotches in the hot summer sun, cursing and grimacing, trying to hold on with one hand and work the clippers with the other. I am twenty-five feet in the air, and can see the sea and all of the life on the promenade. I try to notice where each branch forms so as not to cut the very one I am standing on and plummet to the ground below, but sometimes it's so thick and tangled that I cut with a little niggling doubt hovering over me, between my head and the hot sun. When two hands are required I try to use another branch or my own body as leverage, but much of the time I am forced to simply wedge my foot into the tangle of branches below and then just reach all the way out with both hands on the clippers, hoping for the best.

Giovanni, in disbelief and I think maybe irritation, looks up from where he is reading on the terrace to discover what all the rustling is in the trees. Regarding my labor, he pauses, sitting still in his chair a moment, letting it sink in that this fucking girl has just climbed the tree and is now pruning it back. *Ma Donna,* I bet he mutters. He drops his book in his lap and sits there one more moment, relishing, I feel certain, his last few seconds of idleness. And then he patiently lifts himself from the chair and descends the stairs into the garden until I hear him below me, under the trees, dragging away the branches and sawing them into smaller manageable bundles. I can't see him but I hear him. It is exhilarating to be so high up, at the very tops of the trees, and to be able to look out at the sea and back at the house completely unobstructed. To have my bare feet wedged into the crotches of tree branches—like they haven't been for thirty years—makes me feel instantly, kinesthetically, very young again, as if the soles of my feet had memories of their own. Below, Giovanni quietly and deliberately cleans up every branch that falls to the ground. I hear him sawing below. In his undeclared way, he stays nearby to make sure that when the crazy American bird falls out of the tree, someone will be there to pick her up.

I laugh out loud from the treetop.

"Hey, Giovanni, what book are you *not* reading because of me?"

"Eehhh," he calls back, and I can hear the smile in his voice.

It is his vacation as well, but he has been religiously counting out all the pills Alda must take and gently putting them next to her plate at each meal. He has fixed the electricity, fetched the big glass canisters of olive oil, and made sure there is propane in the stove when I noticed the flames running low. Giovanni seems to truly like the food I've been cooking and jokes at the table one evening, about a week and a half into our vacation, with anchovy butter all over his lips and chin, a pile of shrimp shells and tails on his plate, "This can't possibly continue for three weeks!"

On our last day, when Alda comes out onto the terrace after her nap, I can see her clearly from my treetop. She looks confused. Before her lies the sea. "Sit down!" I yell, waving. "Sit!"

I tell Giovanni to go sit with her on the porch to see if she can see the sea.

"*Dimi si che besognio tagliare piu*," I say, butchering the Italian. *Tell me if I need to cut more.* But the job is finished. I have accomplished a full view. You can sit on the terrace and look out at the sea. Everything feels different. I feel unclenched, thawed-out, and hopeful. I have defied the entropy. I descend from the trees and walk up to the terrace to look out. Michele returns home and even manages to compliment my work, modestly.

"*Brava, Mamma,*" he grunts with an acceding tone, but touches me warmly on the back.

Alda is glued to her chair and won't move. I take a seat next to her, equally unable to move. The view is riveting, as if a whole new room in the house suddenly appeared that no one had known about before. The kids run in and out. Michele goes inside to make them some pasta and I don't budge. Giovanni neatly stacks the last of the fallen branches. The wide-open expanse of sea lies before us, reflecting us. Alda gazes out at the boats coming into the marina for the night, anchoring, and the lights come on along the promenade as the teenagers start to convene in little packs and the sun starts to set. Michele calls from inside the house, "Mamma?"

And in unison, we answer.

"*Si?*"

Author's Note

I have changed the names of some people in this book and on two occasions have made the names up when I couldn't remember them. I have airbrushed a couple of people right out of scenes where they should have existed because they had nothing to do with, and would have distracted from, the larger story. I have compressed, contracted, and subtly rearranged time in several instances, effectively reducing two or three or four consecutive years into one. And I have conflated several recurring, similar events into one for clarity, drive, and momentum. Otherwise, this book is a true account of my experiences as I remember them.

Acknowledgments

I would like to thank Kimberly Witherspoon, the hands-down best agent in the business, who's had my back in a way I've never known before, who is as tough as she is warm, and for whom I would do anything, anytime, anywhere.

I would like to thank David Young who singlehandedly and effortlessly improved my writing—and my whole life—just by rolling his giant glowing glass marbles of wisdom down the hill and letting me pocket them.

I would like to thank Pamela Cannon, equal parts gentle mensch and prodding editor, as well as Jennifer Hershey and the rest of the team for creating the exact environment for me at Random House in which I thrive.

I would like to thank the many hardworking crews who have cooked and served and cleaned at Prune during the five interminable years of my engagement with this book, who held Prune in one delicious piece when I was locked in the office, typing madly before and after and often during my shift.

And finally I would like to thank my bestie Heidi Dorow, who pushed me, pulled me, bullied me, and cheered me to the finish.

Blood, Bones
& Butter

Gabrielle Hamilton

A READER'S GUIDE

FINALLY, I STOPPED GOING.

In most ways, the sweet and dewy appeal of that annual month in Italy had burned dry. That moody, electric, highly charged month when we used to wander around Rome by ourselves at night, eat long Sunday lunches around the table with the whole family, and sit on the terrace at sunset for a negroni with his mother—a month once eagerly awaited and shimmering like a promise throughout all the other eleven months of the year—became one dreaded and made leaden by the scepter of all that eggplant, the unvarying heavy orrecchiette pasta, the lacerating arguments not only preceded by but then also followed by weeks-long silences. A vacation month like that—with four good days out of thirty-one possible—became a deadly prospect.

But there shone, bright as ever, Alda. Hardly anyone is as lucky as I am. All the women I know feel oppressed by, judged by, or in competition with their mothers-in-law. Not me. I bask in her.

Even now at eighty-six years old, she still stands at the kitchen table and works the dough. She still keeps the tablecloths crisp and ironed. She still makes the baked eggplant in two batches, one large pan for everybody and one small pan left to the side for Giovanni, who doesn't like mozzarella. And still, she determinedly boils all the vegetables into sweet submission and then douses them, once cooled, in her own olive oil. She continues to drink wine with her meals and coffee in the mornings and still begrudges that they won't let her drive anymore. Married to Michele or not, I still adore her.

And I'd lost her.

I choked on it at the airport that first summer of our all-but-the-signed-paperwork divorce, gulping down the sobs as my little guys walked through the security checkpoint toward Italian summer vacation with the man who was now "their father" and no longer "my husband." It is not that my relationship with Alda is so intimate. It's not that we get together in the kitchen and start prattling on, subject after subject, deepening our regard for each other through lengthy conversation while we prepare the meals. But still, in that house, in Alda's house, in Alda herself, the promise of family as I had always wanted and imagined it, lives strong. The shutters are still open wide and the Sunday lunch starts at two p.m. She still loves that you've arrived with an extra stray friend, she still insists that you sit in the comfortable chair, she still scolds her children for not offering you a third round of tortelloni. When your glass is empty she taps whichever one of her sons who is closest on the elbow and points at the wine bottle. Still. She hasn't quit. To simply sit with her at the kitchen table cleaning puntarelle and tipping the green beans is a quiet bath in her affection that I had hoped to take for as long as she draws breath.

Would I ever see her again? Had I lost all of them? Had I lost that whole mob of loud, argumentative, chattering, gesticulating, well-educated people with Alda at the center, cooking salt-and-pepper pork cutlets in her battered aluminum pans on the stovetop while the artichokes roast in the ancient propane oven below? Had I lost this woman who sun dries her own tomato paste by laying it out in trays on the woven cane patio furniture under the blazing sun? It's a plausibility that I remained so uncomfortably married for so long just to keep her. Just to stay tethered to the making of the tomato sauce each year with Rosaria, the housekeeper, as Alda looks on, advising. Just to continue those predawn excursions to the local *caseificio* to help with the making of the day's burratta and mozzarella and giuncata and to live out for years to come the long hot mornings raking and bagging the leaves with stout, toothless Antonio, the groundskeeper, while Alda chills the beers and has them brought out to the yard on a tray. Just to keep my place at the kitchen table for the midday meals serenaded by the angry hum of Vespas swarming down in the street below, with Alda peeling the fresh figs from her own trees for dessert before her afternoon nap. Just to be part of her family. Would there be not even one more sunset negroni on the terrace, with Alda holding my hand for an affectionate moment?

Had I lost all of that for good?

Evidently I had. It'd been too many months and no one had called. No one had emailed to lament my absence. I knew they wouldn't. That's not their way. The family has a gorgeous way of inviting you to the table for the *spaghetti al burro* and to drink the salice salentino—but that is a summer postcard. For the long twelve month stretch of daily life, particularly our mercurial and fraught kind—it's best to keep ten yards back. I had birthed sons, paid for the annual summer vacations, cooked meals, dug the gardens, raked the leaves, sawed the dead branches, and still, I remained—for the ten years of my relationship with Michele—a visitor. A guest. Probably most people would be endeared by that—how charming and lovely to always be treated so nicely, to have your in-laws fix you a cup of coffee in the afternoon, and to make sure you have clean, dry towels even though you are perfectly capable of pulling some from the laundry room cabinet yourself—but I was irked by it. Sitting alone on my fire escape in the humid slick of New York City summer, while my naked boys were across an ocean, digging in the gravel of the villa's driveway without me, I thought: Ten years of everything—food, babies, money, work, sickness and health—and still . . . just a guest? A freelancer?

That first summer ended and I thought, *I've lost them.*

Fall came and I thought, *How is that possible?*

And then my November birthday rolled around and I thought, *No. F'ing. Way.*

I bought a plane ticket to Rome. I registered for an intensive immersion language class. I found a place that rented Vespas by the week. Then I hesitantly called Manuela and was received—as soon as she recognized my voice, before I'd even said I was coming—with great boisterous and genuine enthusiasm. *"Vieni! Vieni da noi! Stai con noi!!"*

I called Michele and asked if he would manage our kids with the help of a babysitter for a week. He emailed all of his friends in Rome to let them know I was coming; he arranged the technology so that I could actually see our kids in live time on the computer when we spoke each day; and I suspect, though I can't be sure, that he instructed his family to stop being so nice to me and to treat me *as casually as family.*

Nonetheless, Giovanni was kindly waiting for me at Fiumicino airport. Family or not, he insisted on meeting me at the airport and helping me with my luggage; that is just how he's wired.

And in half an hour there we were, zooming around the graceful snaking curves of the Corso d'Italia which winds down hospitably, past nearly every beautiful and ancient thing that you might need to see in Rome if you only had ten minutes. The route to the apartment from the airport brings us along certain remaining parts of the aqueduct and then down the long serpentine hill past the Piazza Venezia and the Fontana dei Dioscuri and the Palazzo del Quirinale and every single time it accelerates my heartbeat.

We arrive at the apartment just in time for Sunday lunch and I don't care if we won't ever say much more to each other than "Ciao!" and "Ciao!"—it is just so damned good to see Alda and to kiss and hug her again. She is clear-eyed, smiling, standing firmly with her cane, and apparently recuperated from her year of precarious health. I recognize and fall into the rhythm of Sunday lunch as if this were any other week, any other year. The buzzer buzzes. The gate is clicked open electronically and more family arrives. Bud barks and jumps incessantly. The brothers yell at the dog. The sister yells at the brothers and then lunch begins! Carlo has brought the wines for lunch. They are from Bulzoni—the fifth generation wine store in Rome which used to be—not more than a generation ago—a *vini e olio* place: you came with your empty glass canisters and filled them from massive canteens with wine or olive oil from their own land.

Sunday lunch without Michele, with just me sitting at the table, keeping up with the conversation, passing the platters of ravioli and tortellini and boiled puntarelle around, trying to gauge surreptitiously if I even belong here, if I have a place here, feels exactly the same. The only thing different is that everyone is in sweaters and long pants and no one is tan and the terrace garden, instead of being grassy and filled with potted geraniums and a few leafy trees, is now in full crop of all of the fruits that I had never known existed there, just outside the tall green shutters. Tangerines bursting and laden on the branches. Brazilian Feijeje. Little crimson fruits—corbezzoli—that look like nothing you know, eaten like cherries. We pick them all and set them out for dessert. The only fruit I had ever seen in the ten years prior were the Concord grapes that dangled in tantalizing bunches from the pergola, but that is because I had never seen a November in Rome. In ten years, I had seen only ten Julys. It was unnatural. I was led to think that everyone was always tan, always at leisure, always beating back the heat with a fan in hand. But November found a whole harvest of fruit in the front garden, and the family clad in dark-colored wool.

The following morning, not more than twenty blocks from the apartment, I latched onto the phrase "sono persa"—*I am lost*—and I repeated it possibly two hundred times in that single week, as I made my own way to language class on a rented Vespa and around the city and back to the family home each day. My in-laws seemed to ache to take me efficiently to where I needed to go, to escort and accompany me so that I would not get so lost, but I insisted on not being treated like a guest, and in truth, it was extraordinary, uproarious lostness. If there are seven hills in Rome, I am certain I came over the crest of every single one of them, at least twice, and was breathless every time to see the dome of St. Peter's against the streaked dusk sky. I became a member of the zooming mass of Romans on their Vespas—at evening rush hour—and felt an unspeakable exhilaration to have joined them. As I had never seen in the summer, I was spellbound to discover the massive flocks of small black starlings that swoop and arc—like music—from steeple to steeple. And then to finally land—as if I knew exactly where I was going—at the end of a tiny silent cobblestone street, too narrow for even a Fiat, right exactly in front of the caffè at Sant'Eustachio was a triumph so tremendous that I laughed out loud, unclipped my helmet, and exclaimed to no one, "Check me out, people!"

But I still had not quite spoken with Alda in the way that I'd wanted. Even though I now had a sense of orientation in the city, a certain confidence on the scooter, and a grip on the language, we barely spoke. By the end of the week, Manuela and I were chatting away in Italian as never before, both during and long-after mealtimes, while Alda and I remained just the same affectionate admirers. But I wanted to say something to her and I think I wanted her to say something to me. I don't even know what, but something. Maybe even just: Hey, marriage doesn't work out always. But let's stay in touch?

Then I cooked dinner at home one night. It was small, as these things go; just the immediate family and a couple of guests. I made uncomplicated food—roasted quail, boiled puntarelle, romanesco dressed in brown butter, shaved raw fennel, green cabbage with parmesan—that would be tasty, that I could produce in an hour, and that would let me just sit down and be at the table for my last evening. When Giovanni arrived from work, I made negronis for all of us, and while it was too cold to be able to sit out on the terrace like we did in the summers, it still felt nostalgic and festive to clink glasses while standing around the kitchen table under the glare of the overhead lightbulb while I finished the last of my dinner prep. As we ate, no fewer than three energetic conversations overlapped one another chaotically and there was such a good humor and easy-going mood at the table that I quietly let go of my pressing need to be declared as a member of the family and just felt glad enough to have had this week, as a well-cared-for and very welcomed guest. That heavy agenda I'd brought—and been carrying around for years—effortlessly slipped from my body and disappeared, like a dinner napkin, under the table. I sat next to Alda at the meal and smiled at her and put my hand on her back for a moment, finally needing nothing more. Giovanni appreciatively ate from all of the platters on the table and as he was enthusiastically sucking the very last meat from the quail bones, I teased off-handedly, "I wasn't sure I'd be welcome anymore!" I had meant it as a joke, but suddenly Alda's face flashed dark, fiercely offended, and truly insulted. Sharply, she said my name curt and loud—"Gabrielle!"—as if she were scolding me, as if I were her child, as she had never spoken to me before. And I could not have been happier.

Reading Group Questions
and Topics for Discussion

1. What does food mean to the author? How did your particular attitude toward food develop?

2. What challenges do writers and chefs share? Are they unique to those professions?

3. What saved the author from a life of substance abuse and crime?

4. Gabrielle Hamilton's mother-in-law is a central figure in her book. Why did she become so important for her? Do you have someone equally important in your own life?

5. Being invited by Misty Callies to prep for a large dinner party and, later, to work at her restaurant were milestones for Gabrielle Hamilton. Why were these experiences significant for her?

6. Gabrielle Hamilton writes about her ambivalence in wedding her husband. Why do you think she married him? Have you ever felt similarly about your own relationships?

7. Getting one's needs met is a recurring theme. How do you think Gabrielle Hamilton feels about this and how has it influenced her journey?

8. Is *Blood, Bones & Butter* a funny book?

9. Many have commented on the "honesty" of the book, suggesting that such candor and intimacy are uncommon. Are readers mostly responding to the way Gabrielle Hamilton writes about her own family or does that "honesty" manifest elsewhere? What is her point or objective in being so forthcoming? Do you think you would be so upfront in your own memoir?

10. Did you like/not like the ending and why?

GABRIELLE HAMILTON is the chef/owner of Prune restaurant in New York's East Village. The author received an MFA in fiction writing from the University of Michigan, and her work has appeared in *The New Yorker*, *The New York Times*, *GQ*, *Bon Appetit*, *Saveur*, and *Food & Wine*. She has also authored the 8-week Chef column in *The New York Times*, and her work has been anthologized in six volumes of *Best Food Writing*. She has appeared on *The Martha Stewart Show* and the Food Network, among other television. She lives in Manhattan with her two sons.

Chat.
Comment.
Connect.

Visit our online book club community at
www.randomhousereaderscircle.com

Chat
Meet fellow book lovers and discuss what you're reading.

Comment
Post reviews of books, ask—and answer—thought-provoking
questions, or give and receive book club ideas.

Connect
Find an author on tour, visit our author blog, or invite one of
our 150 available authors to chat with your group on the phone.

Explore
Also visit our site for discussion questions, excerpts, author
interviews, videos, free books, news on the latest releases,
and more.

Books are better with buddies.
www.RandomHouseReadersCircle.com